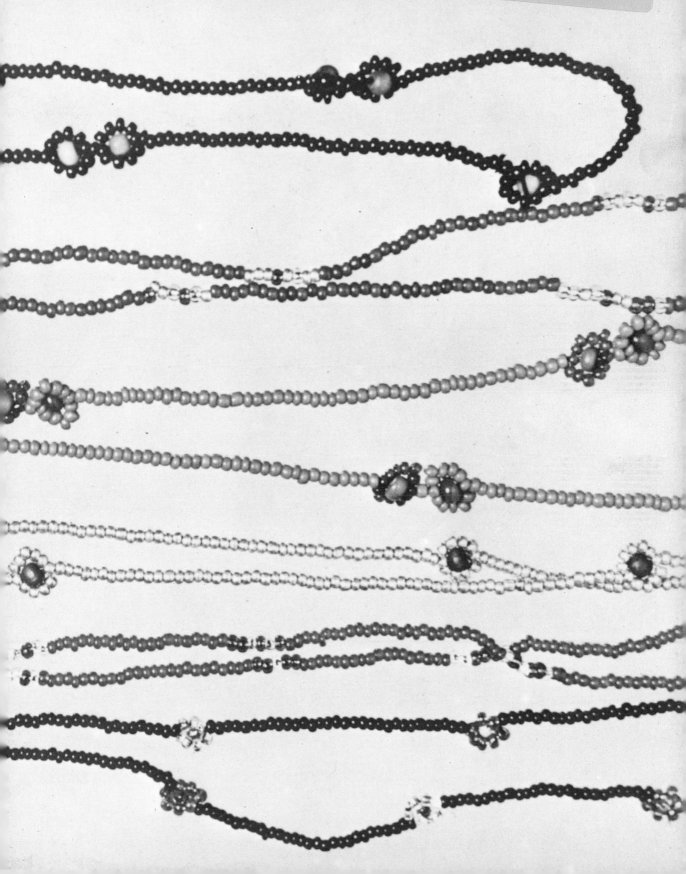

14

1976
£15·00

beadwork:
the technique of stringing, threading and weaving

beadwork:
the technique of stringing, threading and weaving

Ann E Gill

B T Batsford Limited, London

© Ann E Gill 1976
First published 1976

All rights reserved. No part of this publication
may be reproduced, in any form or by any means, without
permission from the Publishers

ISBN 0 7134 3236 5

Designed by Kathryn S A Booth

Filmset by Servis Filmsetting Ltd, Manchester
Printed by The Anchor Press, Tiptree, Essex

for the publishers B T Batsford Ltd
4 Fitzhardinge Street, London W1H 0AH

contents

Many of my students, past and present, young and old, have contributed to the growth of this book. Not only by their enthusiastic involvement with beads, but also with the loan of examples of their work to illustrate the text. Little did they realize how often they acted as guinea pigs so that I might test a pattern or an idea. For all these things I am deeply grateful.

My husband has lived with, slept with – and all but eaten – beads for many months and I can offer no hope of respite for the future. I can, however, offer my thanks for his tolerance, understanding and infinite help. Regrettably, his attempts to organize me have failed miserably; he has, however, learned a great deal about beads.

My thanks also to my parents who have given me unfailing encouragement and, perhaps sometimes unwittingly, have catered to my obsession.

Very special thanks go to Keith Pattison who took the photographs. Tiny beads are not easy subjects and I think he sometimes imagined that his work might never end. The results of his patience and care are justification enough.

I must thank also those people who, at various times, struggled to decipher my writing in order that the manuscript might become not only presentable but also legible.

Without these people, and the many others whose only involvement was a genuine interest and curiosity about the project, this book would still be only a bright idea.

As a child I had a bead box. Many pleasant hours were filled, comparing and exchanging beads with my friends. Once I found, in the lining of an ancient handbag destined for a jumble sale, a string of glorious shiny, blue-glass beads. I wonder, did it all really start then?

Ann E. Gill
Stockton-on-Tees, County Cleveland, England
1976

introduction

What is there about beads that so charms and fascinates both those who wear them and those who work with them? Is it their simplicity, their variety or the fact that throughout the ages they have adorned mankind, rich and poor alike, in life and in death. Perhaps more than any other single object they have been of significance to man as well as being attractive and decorative. They have clothed man's nakedness as decorative symbols of wealth and status, or formed the only adornment – perhaps a defiant gesture against the harshness and difficulties of life for the very poor. Beads have been used to buy land, food, cattle and – other men. They have identified those of special title or rank, served to differentiate friend from enemy and marked the specially favoured from ordinary people. But whatever special significance or distinctive rôle they have had within any single society or nation, there is one feature of their long and varied history which appears universal and constant; they have been, and they are, enjoyed.

Beads have travelled between and across continents in the holds of ships, around the necks of men and women or among their possessions, providing a common link between races and nations, between an old world and a new.

Children, regardless of their race, colour or creed when playing with beads display an unconscious and innocent delight in shapes, colours and sizes. The appeal of beads is as universal as their use and form; they are ageless and timeless.

There are countless variations of shape, size and colour, even of materials. Plain beads, striped beads, painted beads. Beads of clay, glass, bone, wood, metal, precious and semi-precious stones, shell, ivory and even beads of plaited grass. Inventive and curious man has used seeds, nuts, berries, feathers and, in some cases, the legs and wings of colourful insects. The criterion appears to be: if it can be shaped and if it can be pierced then it can become a bead. There are numerous ways of using and wearing beads, perhaps as many ways as there are beads themselves.

The powers which have been attributed to beads and the superstitions and legends which surround them are intriguing. In many parts of the globe they are still used as good-luck charms, as amulets with powers of healing and as charms against evil. The charm may depend on the material from which the beads are made: amber and coral, for instance, are regarded as healers. Sometimes the shape and form of the bead have magical properties: eye beads, in particular, are believed to protect the wearer from the evil eye – because the 'eyes' look in several directions the wearer is afforded protection on all sides. The Turkish eye beads shown

1 Turkish eye beads, three eyes mounted in gold with turquoise

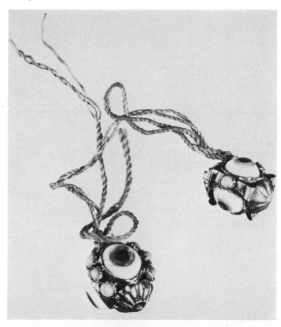

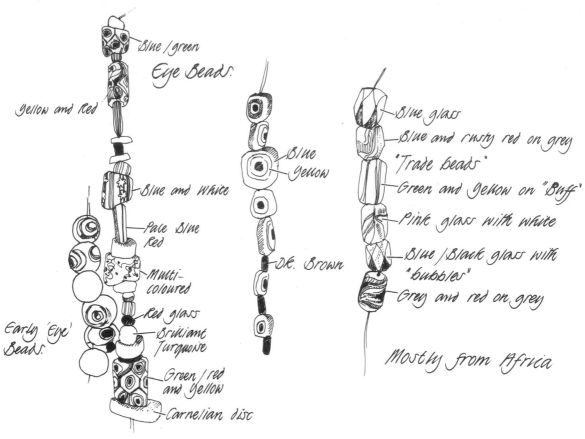

Eye Beads.

Blue /green

Yellow and Red

Blue and white

Pale Blue
Red

Multi-
coloured

Early 'Eye'
Beads.

Red glass

Brilliant
Turquoise

Green / red
and Yellow

Carnelian disc

Blue
Yellow

Dk. Brown

Blue glass

Blue and rusty red on grey
"Trade beads"

Green and Yellow on "Buff"

Pink glass with white

Blue / Black glass with
"bubbles"

Grey and red on grey

Mostly from Africa

2 Eye beads from Africa made of glass and wood

in illustration 1 are mounted in gold with eyes looking three ways. Should the owner be careless enough to lose his protection he will not feel safe until he has either found it or purchased a replacement. The eye bead exists in many parts of the world, the Middle East and Africa providing a vast array of colourful examples (see illustration 2).

I am surrounded by beads, working with them, wearing and collecting them, and am constantly finding new ways to use them. The background and history of a particular craft and the techniques related to it are always useful to the modern practitioner, and the knowledge of those who have developed them and used them, and the uses to which the work has been put, can be an inspiration and incentive no matter how primitive the original techniques might have been. It is partly for this reason that each section of the book begins with a brief history. Hopefully, it will lead to a deeper appreciation of the craft and perhaps encourage further research.

There is enormous personal satisfaction in making and producing articles which are uniquely one's own. This is not only the satisfaction of making a specific item, it extends to the giving of very personal and therefore special gifts, and to the pride felt when you can say that *you* made it.

Some years ago I saw some beautiful examples of Victorian and Edwardian beadwork in a museum and at the same time I became interested in American-Indian beadwork. Thus began my involvement but nowhere could I find out how the work was produced. Mary Seyd in her book *Introducing Beads* points out that there is little literature to help an enthusiastic but inexperienced beginner. Much information exists about making beads, about their composition, their mythological and magical properties and about their place in various societies but there is surprisingly little written about the techniques of beadwork. The recent revival of interest in old crafts has done much to alleviate this situation, but a gap still exists.

My initial experiments, which took place without guide or teacher, convinced me that there is a need for this kind of book, dealing not simply with the techniques and the development of them but also with the problems encountered. It is not enough to describe how to start and finish a piece of work nor is it enough to give patterns to be followed, for between the start and the finish of the work a whole host of problems can arise, due more to lack of experience and the very nature of beads than to any fault of the worker. I hope to deal with these, thus making your first efforts far less frustrating than were my own.

You are not bound to begin with Section One. Each technique makes different demands and requires the acquisition of a new skill, and so you may begin with any section. However, each technique owes something to the others – each one may be used with another, and in combination they are enhanced – so there is a logical and satisfying progression. None of the techniques is difficult. Some require little more than patience and, of course, the spark of interest which encouraged you to pick up this book in the first place while others call for the skill to manipulate needle and thread, plus patience and, perhaps, a love of beads.

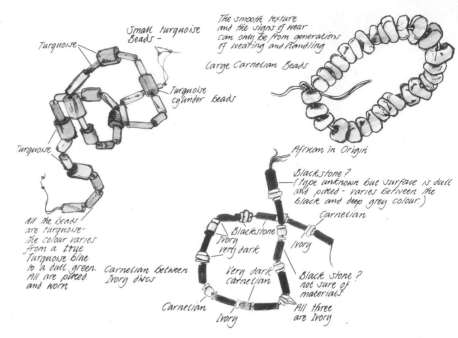

Turquoise

Small turquoise Beads—

The smooth texture and the signs of wear can only be from generations of wearing and handling

Turquoise cylinder beads

Large Carnelian Beads

Turquoise

African in Origin

Blackstone? (type unknown but surface is dull and pitted - varies between the black and deep grey colour.)

Carnelian

Blackstone

Ivory very dark

Ivory

All the beads are turquoise the colour varies from a true Turquoise blue to a dull green. All are pitted and worn

Carnelian between Ivory discs

Very dark Carnelian

Black stone? not sure of material

Carnelian

Ivory

All three are Ivory

3 Very old discoidal carnelian beads from Africa

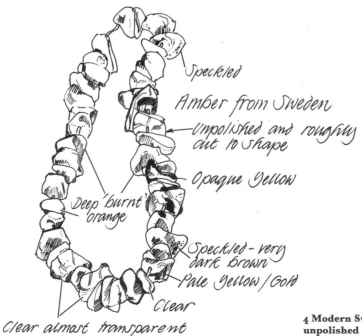

Speckled

Amber from Sweden

Unpolished and roughly cut to shape

Opaque Yellow

Deep 'burnt' orange

Speckled - very dark brown

Pale Yellow/Gold

Clear

Clear almost transparent

4 Modern Swedish amber, uncut and unpolished

part one
section one strings from
pearls to melon seeds

The finest string of pearls gives no more pleasure to its owner than does the necklace of melon seeds, dried and strung by a child, and indeed the latter may have far greater meaning. Beads strung together, or as single units, have been used and worn for centuries, passing from generation to generation, gathering over the years a store of memories and, in some cultures, being venerated for their very age. The string of large carnelian beads from Africa in illustration 3 is of unknown age. The beads are worn and smooth, some of them bear very tangible marks which can only have resulted from many generations of wearing and touching, but they are beautiful with age and for the simplicity of their shape. The other two examples in the drawings are also old but, for me, they do not possess that intangible quality which speaks of *care*. The amber beads in illustration 4, are modern, brought from Sweden some years ago. These beads demonstrate well the use of natural materials; some are almost untouched by the maker apart from having been pierced for threading onto a string. Many of the necklaces follow a widely-used pattern in that they are graduated towards the centre of the string. Perhaps it is their discoidal shape which lends itself to this treatment.

Ancient man adorned himself with a variety of beads. Some were certainly worn for purely decorative purposes but others had a greater significance: they gave him security, protected him from evil, cured his ills, assured him luck in his hunting, afforded him safety when he fought and guarded him when he slept. Beads of certain shapes and of particular materials were imbued with greater magical properties than their size might warrant. Mary Seyd in *Introducing Beads* has provided a fascinating and comprehensive history to the bead and I can do no better than to recommend it for further, more detailed, historical information.

One of the most widely used strings of beads in the modern world is the rosary, which can be made from plain beads, carved beads, precious and semi-precious beads. Whatever the beads are made from the rosary has one purpose; it is an aid to memory, a counter. Each bead is a prayer; as the fingers touch the memory is prompted. Other mnemonics exist. The Moslems use a string of 99 beads to tell the attributes of Allah (see the Iraqi prayer and worry beads in illustration 5). Throughout the Middle East a string of 33 beads is also used for this same function and also as worry beads. The large amber beads in the illustration have been used for this. They are slipped through the fingers in nervous play, a perpetual movement which becomes as much part of the user as his hands.

It is impossible to write about strings of beads without a mention of the beads of Africa. The peoples of that vast continent are renowned for their beads and beadwork; men, women, children, the old and the young alike, consider them part of their everyday dress. The use of natural materials is superb; shells, seeds, wood and stone are often strung together without more workmanship than the piercing of a hole. Other materials are shaped, drilled and arranged with attention to size, shape and colour. See the Nubian necklace in illustration 6.

Old beads are treasured and cherished. Some are so old that their origins are lost in time and legend, true historical fact being replaced by a more exciting mythology. These are the true native beads, expressing the African's sympathy and affinity with his environment. Other beads reached Africa via the traders from Europe, who found in that huge and unexplored continent a rich store of minerals, animals and, sadly, men. The peoples of Africa *do* have a true affinity with beads and have used with sensitivity and care not only their own natural resources, but

5 Worry and prayer beads from Iraq. The worry beads (33 beads) are in amber. The prayer beads are of an unidentifiable material. (Courtesy of Mr and Mrs J E Bradfield)

glass, clay and ceramics from other lands. The Ugandan necklace and bracelet in illustration 7 shows this well. Native African beads can serve as a useful model when you begin to experiment with strings and as a source of inspiration for colours and design.

It is worth considering this first section as an introduction to using and handling beads. The later sections call for some skill in actually manipulating the tools, and threading strings of beads will make you familiar with most of these. As well as the materials given below, a collection of odd beads is useful; these can serve as fasteners or as added interest in an otherwise plain necklace. Beads of unusual shapes, colours and materials often suggest new ways of using more ordinary beads.

Materials for strings

Beads. You will require Rocaille beads which are made of glass and are available in various sizes. They are stocked by several craft shops and large stores some of whom will supply almost any quantity by post. A list of suppliers appears on p. 182. You will need sizes 10, 7 and 4, the larger the number the smaller the bead. All the beads used in this section come from one supplier and so the sizing is given according to their catalogue. Where possible, however, similar beads and their sizes are also stated.

You will also require wooden beads, matt and shiny, in sizes 4mm, 6mm and 8mm; these are used for fastenings and in some of the patterns given below. Small square wooden beads, wooden discs and long and short ovals are also used. Bugle beads, whilst limited in usefulness in later sections are suitable for some of the patterns in Section One. Odd beads from old or broken necklaces can also be used.

Needles. Unless otherwise stated, special beading needles are required for beadwork techniques. Many of the beads have very tiny holes through which an ordinary sewing needle cannot pass. Beading needles are very long and fine with an

6 Very old necklace of semi-precious stones and glass

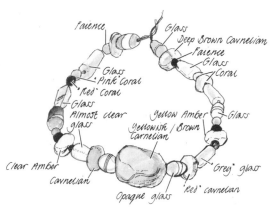

7 Zulu threaded collar, and Ugandan bead bracelet and necklace. (Courtesy Horniman Museum)

eye not very much thicker than the point. They are made in several sizes, size 9 being used in most of the patterns, size 10 where it is necessary to pass the needle several times through one bead and size 12, which are extremely fine and flexible, for some of the techniques. These are all available from the bead stockists listed or from some large haberdashery counters.

Threads. These should be strong enough to carry the weight of the beads. The thread used throughout this book is Gütermann Polytwist (M1003), a strong but soft thread with none of the stiffness found in ordinary buttonhole twist. If the Polytwist is unobtainable then double strands of

Gütermann Polyester sewing thread or Drima synthetic thread are used. Some of the patterns require you to use monofilament nylon line – in other words, fishing line. This is easily obtained from anglers' suppliers and you should use $3\frac{1}{2}$–4lb test (breaking strain). This line is so fine and smooth that a double strand is always used.

In addition to the main tools of the craft there are some useful items which help considerably, particularly if you are inexperienced.

Beeswax. Long lengths of thread tangle very easily, but if the thread is drawn once or twice through a piece of beeswax this will not happen (do not wax monafilament nylon). The wax will last for a long time and is available from most chemists.

Small sharp scissors. Nail scissors with curved blades are the most suitable for the beadworker. It is all too easy to snip through the thread when finishing off a piece of work, and the curved blades allow you to cut off the thread close to the work without this risk.

Fasteners. It is unnecessary to use bought fasteners unless you really wish to. Beadwork fasteners are far more appropriate to the nature of the work and the technique for constructing these is included with the pattern instructions. If, however, you wish to use commercial fasteners, ring bolds and split rings, screw fasteners, and push in hooks are available from most craft shops. Hooks and eyes are useful if the fastening must be concealed, and so are a selection of small buttons for making button and loop fasteners. Press studs also have a limited use.

Containers for Beads. The smallest quantity of size 10 and 7 beads are supplied in plastic containers with clear lids. Larger amounts arrive in plastic bags which are unsuitable to work from directly and so the beads should be transferred to other containers such as typewriter-ribbon boxes with transparent plastic lids. If you have nothing else suitable, put the beads into a shallow dish or a saucer while you work and replace them in the bag when you finish. A shallow container allows you to slide the needle in and pick up several beads at a time. Looking for the hole in the bead is time-wasting but you will soon acquire the knack of picking up the right number of beads on the needle.

Suggestions and some general hints

1 Work on a table, at a comfortable height and in a good light. See that you can reach all your materials easily.
2 Keep unnecessary clutter out of the way and open only the boxes of beads you wish to use.
3 Use a pincushion for spare needles or keep them in a box or packet. They are so fine that they are easily lost.
4 If any beads get spilt on carpeting, pick them up by drawing a large spoon across the area.
5 Have sufficient quantities of beads in the colours you wish to use. Beads from haberdashery counters may be difficult to match for colour and size at a later time.
6 If you have young children, they will enjoy watching you work and will also join in.

Most of the patterns and techniques are suitable for a child although the more complex threading patterns and the counted patterns for the strings may not suit those under the age of seven or eight. A very young child may find it difficult to handle the fine needle and very long thread, but will have fun threading wooden beads which have holes large enough for a sewing or darning needle to pass through.

7 Where possible, thread should match the colour of the beads. For multicoloured work use nylon or black thread.

Using the beads

Practise first by threading a long string of beads in a single colour. From this you will learn something of your materials and how to handle the needle, thread and beads; you may be surprised that it takes longer at first than you imagined. Use thread rather than nylon as it is much more flexible for a long string of beads and a long necklace should hang gracefully; monofilament nylon is rather stiff when tied tightly.

Diagram 1   Slip knot for strings, shown with single thread

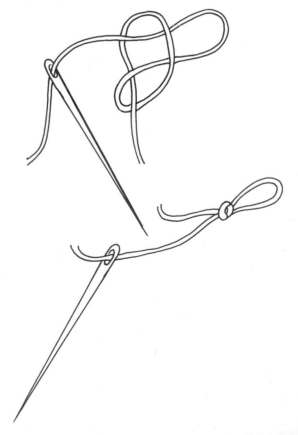

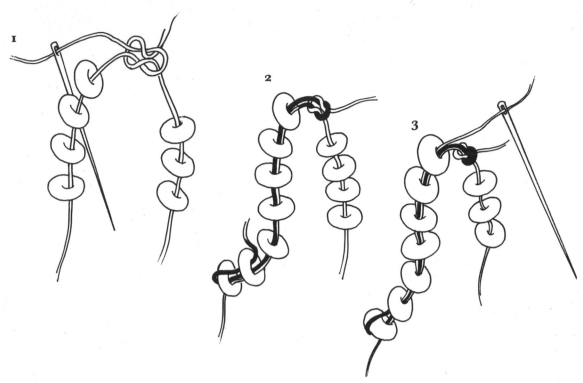

Diagram 2   Joining a string

Diagram 2A   Slip knot over threads to secure
working thread
1 Scoop up all thread with needle and pass through
loop made by working thread
2 Pull tight

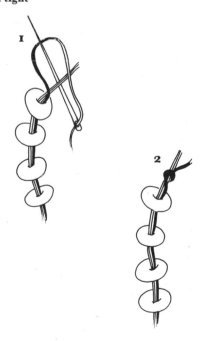

Begin the work by making a slip knot in the thread 10–15cm (4–6in) from the end of the thread. This is easily closed or pulled free when you need to join the two ends of the string (see diagram 1), by simply pulling the main thread. When you wish to join the work make sure that several inches of thread remain free, otherwise you will not be able to complete the join.

The join

1. Without removing the needle from the end of the working thread, release the slip knot and tie the two free ends of the string together as shown. Do not pull the ends together too tightly otherwise the string will pucker and great strain will be put on both beads and thread.

2. Take the needle with thread back into the work, through 25mm (1in) or so of beads, as shown. Pass back over one bead (if thread and beads match in colour this will hardly show), pass back to the knot, make a slip knot here (see diagram 2A) and unthread the needle, but do not cut off the thread.

3. Thread the needle on to the 'tail' (the length of thread beyond the first knot) and repeat the

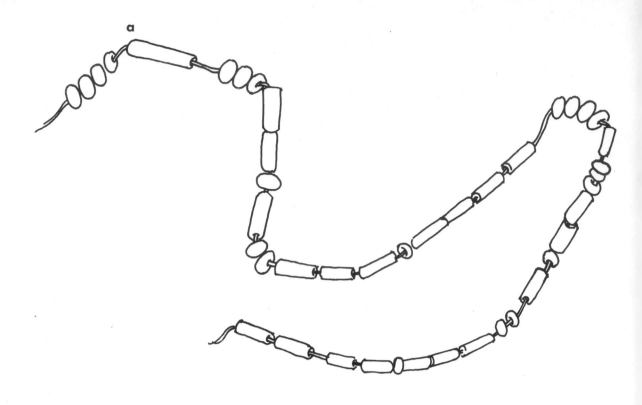

fastening off process, then tie the two ends firmly together and cut off the remaining ends of thread. Run the completed string through your fingers several times to ease the beads on the thread; this will also tighten the fastening. If you have drawn the work up too tightly you will be able to feel this simply by the way the beads resist the movement of your fingers.

Use this method to fasten off all long strings of beads, unless an alternative method is stated. If you wish to wind the string several times around your neck so that it fits closely, choker fashion, then a fastening of some kind should be used.

For further practice, try threading a long string using two or three colours or even more: a different working pattern results when you must dip into several containers of beads. At first the sequence of beads could be random but a counted sequence – even if it is only red, white and blue, using two of each all along the string – will help you acquire the knack of picking up just the right number of beads on the needle at one time. You might also begin to note colour combinations for use in future work.

These suggestions apply to size 10 Rocaille beads but you could just as effectively use size 7. A useful practice piece is based on the Egyptian

Diagram 3 Mummy Beads
a Bugle and Rocaille beads make a 'dot-dash' pattern, based on the so-called 'Mummy Beads' which were found in some Egyptian tombs
b The same pattern sequence using large wooden beads in place of bugle beads

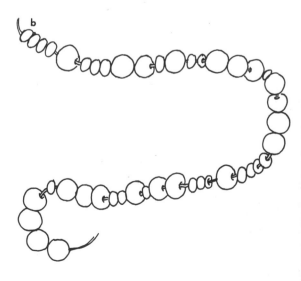

Mummy beads in diagram 3. These beads are so called because similar strings were found around the necks of the mummies in the tombs of the ancient Egyptian kings. The Dot and Dash pattern may be random or, as in the pattern below, formal and counted.

Dot and dash. Diagram 3

Materials:
Long bugle beads.
Size 10 beads.
Either use one colour for all, or different colours for each different kind of bead.
A single Polytwist thread approximately 90cm (36in) to match the beads.
Size 9 needle.
Beeswax.
Key:
b-bugle beads
r-Rocaille beads
Pattern:
Run thread through beeswax.
Tie slip knot in end leaving 15–20cm (4–6in) thread in tail.
The pattern sequence of beads is as follows, or you may simply refer to the diagram.
Pick up 4r, 1b, 3r, 2b, 1r, 1b, 2r, 3b, 1r, 4b. This is repeated until the necklace reaches whatever length you desire. Finish the string by fastening off the thread in the same way as the first experiment.

Larger beads, or simply beads of different colours, or size 10 and 7 beads could be used to work the same pattern, and several necklaces using different beads would illustrate well the difference that size, colour and shape make to a very simple pattern. Mixing the sizes, especially with Rocaille beads which can be matched to each other, will also result in a different appearance. The wooden beads which are used throughout the book are available in several sizes and colours; the colours are extremely vivid and beautiful and fortunately all sizes are available in the same colours. A string of these all the same colour but in several sizes makes a very attractive necklace. Remember, though, that you will need a large number of wooden beads in order to make a long string. A more economical way to use them is to combine them with the Rocaille beads. Several colours in size 4mm, strung at intervals on a plain black string, is most striking.

Use either 4mm or 6mm beads in this way. Eight mm are so much larger than the tiny glass beads that they look rather clumsy and detract from the effect of combined sizes and materials. As with most creative activities, elements of balance and harmony are important in beadwork.

Experiment with large beads among small; groups of 4mm wooden beads in several colours; on plain strings of Rocaille beads; random spacing of size 10, 7 and 4 Rocaille beads; and then very formal (counted) spacing of the same beads. All this will help to develop your understanding of the nature of the materials you are using. The opaque Rocaille beads have a smooth and shiny finish, the lustre beads a metallic surface, the wooden beads a matt or highly-polished surface. When these are used together there is not only a contrast of size and materials, but the added interest of different surfaces and textures.

This may be taken further still. Transparent-glass beads are available in size 10 and 7, and it is also possible to buy beads of similar size which have a silvered lining, giving them a sparkle. Bugle beads are available in several lengths, with a tubular or hexagonal body and in a vast array of colours. Pearlized beads in many shapes and sizes are another possible addition to the list, as are 'drop' beads and those with faceted or cut surfaces.

African peoples have long used the products of nature in their beadwork. Many kinds of seeds, nuts and berries are available to them, several of which only require a hole in order to be strung. Our culture is not so rich in these natural resources, but it is possible to compromise and produce unusual and attractive strings using very simple materials. Melon seeds are readily available during the summer, and easily dried and coloured. They combine especially well with small glass beads and there are several ways in which they can be pierced in order to obtain different effects. If this is done whilst the seeds are still soft and damp it is easier, and since they dry on the thread they can be stored until you wish to use them. Whole threaded strings can be dipped into dye, lifted out, dried and the required amount removed for use, the rest are left on the string until needed. An unusual and very simple method of dying the seeds is readily available in the home. Beautiful shades of brown and gold result from dipping the seeds for varying lengths of time into hot, strong black coffee and tea (a shaded necklace is interesting to make). Experiment with other seeds, orange and lemon pips, dried pulses, sunflower seeds – all these are potential beads. Half the pleasure in producing

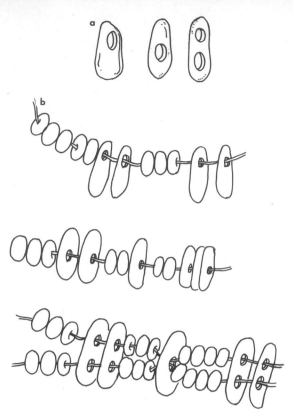

Diagram 4 **a The placing of holes in melon seeds
b Different effects achieved when melon seeds are
strung with small beads**

living – in fact anything and everything which has a hole and might be strung and which may at some time add interest to my work. They are stored on a piece of cord and hang among other beads in my workroom (see illustration 9).

Care must be taken when using old or unusual beads because those of semi-precious materials do not always combine well with glass or wood, and it is a pity to mar their beauty with ill-chosen companions. Faceted Venetian-glass beads in delicate colours, hollow spheres with delicate traceries of coloured glass decorating them, crystals and tubular glass beads – all have a special and unique character. Far better to use them as single examples on a plain string than to mix them in haphazard fashion with modern beads (see illustration 10).

Jet was once so popular that many old carved necklaces are still in existence, although it is now avidly collected and therefore expensive. Jet has special qualities, like those of amber and coral, and whilst these substances combine and complement each other, modern beads add nothing to them. It is for this reason that I have included on p. 37 a short section on rethreading and repairing old beads (see illustration 11).

The term 'strings' covers numerous techniques. The long single string is simple to make and fun to wear, but limited in scope and design. Shorter strings which follow the revived fashion for choker necklaces offer a wider area for experimental work. Short strings of beads must be constructed with care and imagination if they are to be effective. The short string of beads must have a fastener, and if a long string is to be worn as a choker, then this too should have some means of fastening.

The fastener consists of a beaded loop and a large wooden bead which slips through the loop. The fastenings are made as part of the string itself since separate attachments are less secure and far more difficult to construct.

Full choker. Illustrations 12 and 13

Materials:
Size 10 and 4 (approximately 166) Rocaille beads, all the same colour.

your own, natural, beads is in experimenting. To pierce the seeds in ways which will give different effects see diagram 4. Those pierced at one end will form drops which appear to hang from the string of beads (illustration 8). Shells are difficult to pierce and require special tools, but it is worthwhile looking for those with a natural hole. Sometimes this is produced naturally by the action of the sea on weak parts of the shell, long after the creature to which it belonged has died. Some shells have a small neat hole which has been bored by another sea creature; these are ideal ready-made beads, and several shells of the same kind used with carefully-chosen manufactured beads make an unusual piece of jewellery.

Making a collection of small natural objects which have a ready-made hole is as much a part of my beadwork as the beads I buy. For some of them I will never have a use, others will some day find their way into a special project. I collect pebbles, pieces of water-worn wood bleached and smoothed by the action of water, shells, nuts, seeds, bits of bone – mostly unrecognizable as ever having been part of anything

9 'Found' beads of shell, wood and stone ▶

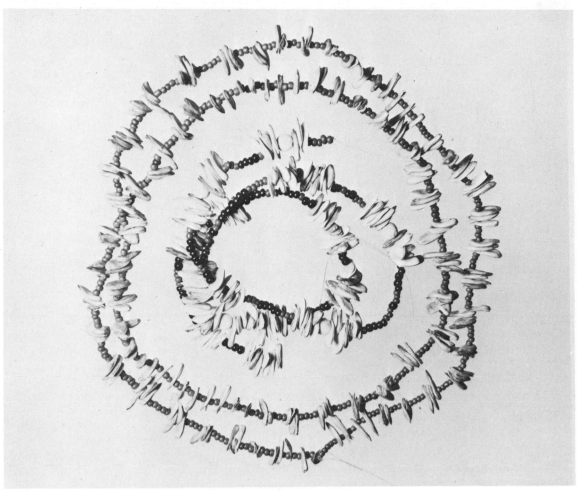

8 Melon seeds and Rocaille beads

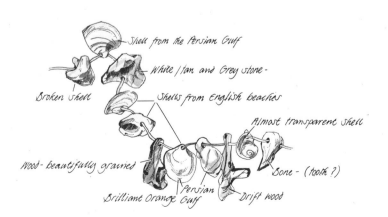

Shell from the Persian Gulf

White / tan and Grey stone –

Broken shell

Shells from English beaches

Almost transparent shell

Wood – beautifully grained

Bone – (tooth?)

Brilliant Orange

Persian Gulf

Drift wood

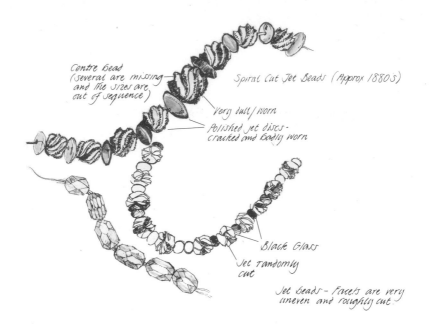

Centre bead
(several are missing
and the sizes are
out of sequence)

Spiral Cut Jet Beads (Approx 1880's)

Very dull/worn

Polished jet discs-
cracked and badly worn

Black Glass

Jet randomly
cut

Jet beads - Facets are very
uneven and roughly cut.

11 Carved and polished jet beads, dating approximately from the 1880s

10 Venetian glass beads consisting of hollow spheres with a delicate 'dribbled' pattern. (Courtesy of Carol Lister)

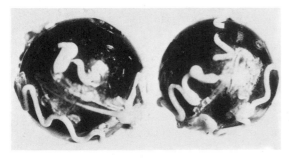

Twelve matt and 18 shiny black Rotelle beads.
One 6mm black wooden bead.
Black Polytwist thread (approximately 1m (36in)).
Size 9 beading needle.
Beeswax.
Key:
  B–10's
  BL–4's
  RB–Rotelle shiny
  RM–Rotelle matt

The Rotelle beads have very large holes because their main use is in macramé work where thicker threads must pass through them. They are useful in beadwork, but to avoid them sliding over the smaller beads they should be flanked on either side by size 4 beads.

This choker does not fit tightly around the neck, but lies instead around the base of the throat. It is approximately 34cm long, and will fit most people using the quantities of beads given here. To be sure, however, measure your neck and check the choker against this measurement as the work progresses, increasing or decreasing

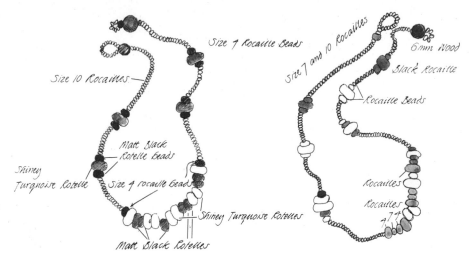

Size 7 Rocaille Beads

Size 10 Rocailles

Size 7 and 10 Rocailles

6mm Wood

Black Rocaille

Rocaille Beads

Matt Black
Rotelle Beads

Shiney
Turquoise Rotelle

Size 4 rocaille beads

Rocailles

Rocailles
7 7

Shiney Turquoise Rotelles

Matt Black Rotelles

12 Chokers based on African bead jewellery, using Rotelle and Rocaille beads

13 Chokers using various beads

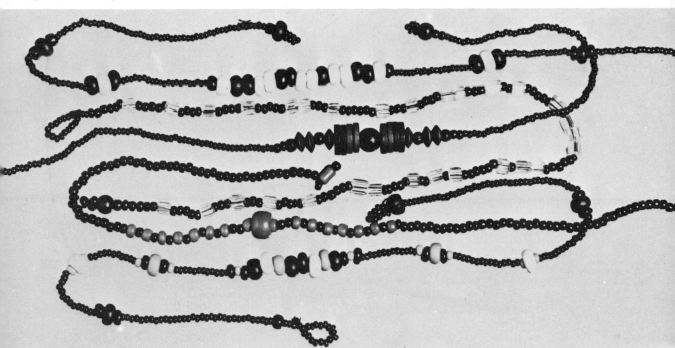

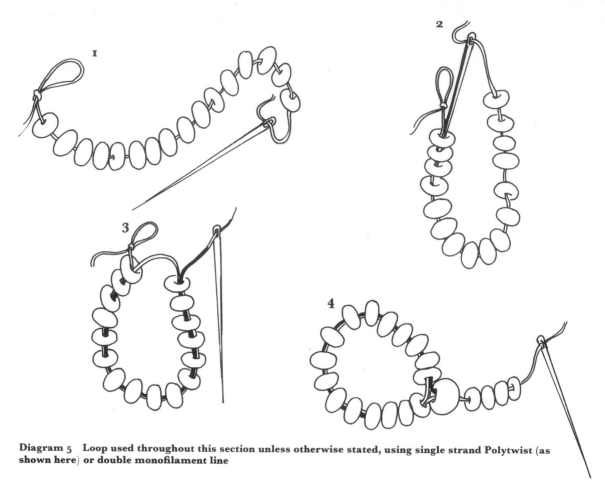

Diagram 5   **Loop used throughout this section unless otherwise stated, using single strand Polytwist (as shown here) or double monofilament line**

the size 10 beads according to your findings. Illustrations 12 and 13 show a selection of similar chokers.

The fastening loop. Diagram 5

This is constructed first. The numbers in the text correspond to the numbered sections of the diagrams in each example.

Run thread through beeswax.

Tie slip knot in thread 20–15cm from end (4–6in).

1   Pick up and thread 16 size 10 beads.

2/3   Pass the needle and thread through the 16 beads a second time and pull up to form the loop.

4   Release the slip knot and tie the free end of the thread and the working end together firmly – test this to make sure that it will not pull free. Take the thread around the loop again for extra strength. Cut off tail end of thread and pick up one size 4 bead. Slide down to cover knot. The loop is now complete.

Pattern:

1   Make the loop as described and shown in the diagrams.

2   Pick up and thread
    40B,   1BL, 1RB, 1RM, 1BL,
    16B,   1BL, 1RB, 1RM, 1RB, 1BL,
    18B,   1BL, 1RB, 2RM, 2RB, 1BL, 2RB,
    2RM, 1RB, 1BL

The pattern is now worked in reverse from 18B. Remember to check that the choker will be long enough to fit your neck.

Fastening: Method 1. Diagram 6

A 6mm wooden bead fits through the 16 bead loop.

Thread 1BL then follow the diagrams for working the fastener.

Treat the bead below the 6mm bead in diagram 6 as 1BL.

1   Pick up the 6mm bead and five size 10 beads.

2   Pass the needle and thread back down through

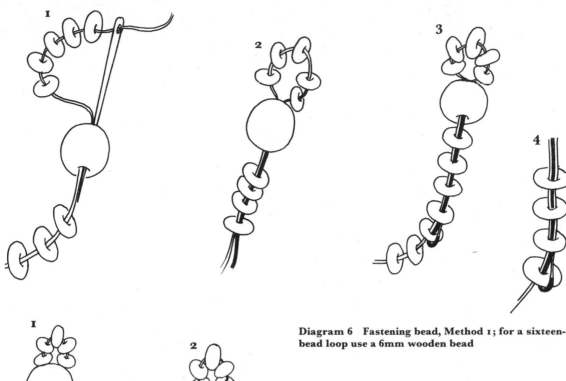

Diagram 6   Fastening bead, Method 1; for a sixteen-bead loop use a 6mm wooden bead

Diagram 7   Using a slip knot to secure the thread; at this stage make two knots below the bead, pass into fastener, make slip knot and trim thread

the 6mm bead making a small loop of five beads.

3 Take the needle and thread down through several beads and pass it back over one bead and back into the beads. Bring it out below the 6mm bead.

4 Make a slip knot over all the threads and pull tight. See diagram 7.

For extra security pass in to the 6mm bead and make a slip knot beneath the first bead in the five-bead loop. Cut off excess thread.

Ease the work through your fingers as you did with the long strings, to tighten the securing knots and ease the thread a little.

Illustration 12 includes two similar chokers. Rotelle beads in several colours were used in these, both the matt and shiny finishes being included.

The method of construction just given may be used to make many chokers; a variety of beads are possible and you might like to consider using some of your odd beads in this way. All the beads could be large ones of different colours, spaced by small beads in one colour; an alternative is to concentrate the pattern and colour in the centre of the work, particularly useful if you have only a small number of special beads. In your collection of odd, old or unusual beads there may be one which is outstanding; this could be used in the centre of a plain choker-length string where it would not be overpowered by other beads. The beads used in the chokers in illustration 14 are hand-painted wooden beads. These were purchased in their plain, unvarnished wood state and painted with a fine sable brush and Designers' Gouache colours.

14 Hand-painted wooden beads, loose and made up

When dry they were given a coat of clear quick-drying varnish. Each bead is unique; on a plain black choker they speak for themselves.

It is easier to paint the beads if they are held on a stick of some kind – a slim garden cane or dowel is ideal. In this way it is possible to turn the bead and so work all over the surface without fear of smudging the paint. Stand the beads on the dowel in a jar, or stick them into plasticine or a block of styrofoam whilst they are drying. The beads are varnished while still on the sticks and replaced in the holder until the varnish is completely dry. Plain wooden beads make a wonderful canvas for abstract designs, flowers, spots, stripes or just blobs of colour.

Many craft and ethnic goods shops stock beautiful and colourful cylindrical glass beads. These are often eye or trade beads from Africa, and they make unusual additions to your working materials. The beads are very heavy and are best used in work which fits closely around the base of the throat. Eight mm shiny wooden beads combine very well with these beads.

The round wooden beads are produced in a wide range of colours, sizes and shapes – discs, small square, small 'lice', elliptical, many-sided and beads with a pronounced wood grain. Such a range allows the beadworker to experiment and develop the simple string even further. The chokers in illustration 15 make use of several

15 Chokers using several sizes and shapes of wooden beads with graduated centre patterns

16 Double strings – choker style

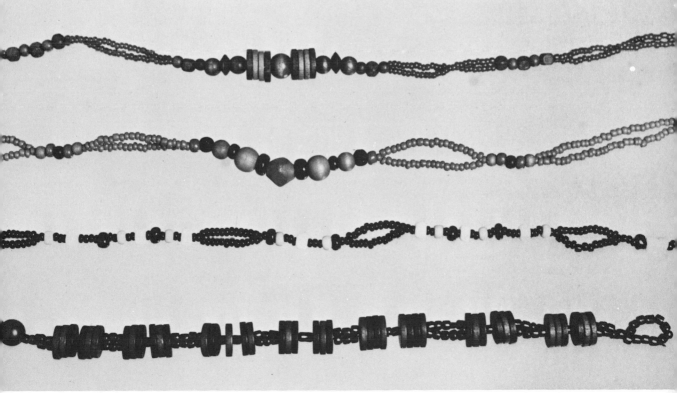

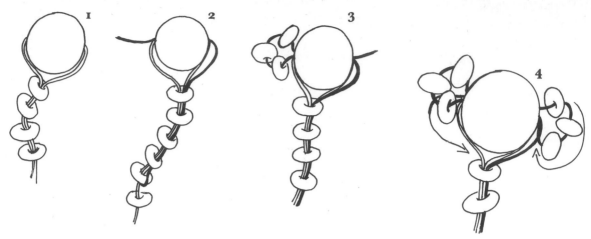

Diagram 8 Fastening bead, Method 2: to be used when the 6mm bead is too small for the loop or when bracelets need extra securing. The 'ears' catch the loop and hold the bead in place

shapes and sizes of wooden beads, the graduated sizes of the round beads falling into naturally harmonious patterns when skilfully used. These chokers were all constructed to make a long tapered shape: the wooden discs draw the design together and make it much more solid in appearance.

Chokers using several sizes and shapes of wooden beads. Illustration 15

Materials:

    Size 10 or 7 orange Rocaille beads
    Size 4mm and 6mm dark-brown wooden beads
    Discs of the same colour
    Small 'lice'
    Size 4mm orange wooden beads
    Size 8mm orange beads with a shiny finish
    Size 10mm dark-brown beads with shiny finish
    One 12mm light-brown bead with shiny finish
    Orange Polytwist thread
    Size 9 beading needle
    Beeswax

Key:

    O – orange 10's
    Os – shiny orange wood
    Or – orange 4mm
    B – brown 4mm
    Br – brown 6mm
    L – small lice
    D – disc bead
    LB – 10 mm shiny brown wood
    C – centre bead in brown shiny wood

You may change the colours to suit whatever beads you have to hand, but follow the sequence of sizes in the pattern and remember to check the length and adjust it accordingly.

Pattern:

Thread needle and run the thread through beeswax.
Make slip knot.
Make the fastening loop.

1 Pick up and thread 75O.
2 Pick up and thread 1B, 1Or, 1Br, 1L, 1Os, 1D, 1LB, 2D, C. Repeat from 2D to 1B, and thread 75O. Make the fastener using a dark-brown 6mm bead.

    Many similar chokers can be constructed along these lines, and 4mm wooden beads could be used for the whole length of the plain part of the choker. Matching bracelets are easy to make using the same method; to do this reduce the number of Rocaille beads at each end of the work. Remember to measure your wrist first.

    Diagram 8 shows an alternative way of securing the fastening bead.

    Fastenings on bracelets must be strong to cope with the greater wear sustained and so method 2 should be used.

Fastening: method 2

1 Pick up and thread the large bead as for method 1 but take the needle back into the work as shown, easing the wooden bead onto its side as you do so. Tighten the thread.
2 Take the needle and thread over one bead. Pass back up into the row of beads and up to the large bead. Pass needle through this.

3 Pick up three Rocaille beads and take the needle and thread back through the 6mm bead. Pull tight.

4 Thread three Rocaille beads and return the needle to the other side. See diagram 8.

5 Take the needle and thread down into the work and make a slip knot. Tighten and pass into the work again. Repeat and then cut off excess thread.

This method gives the large bead 'ears'. When slipped through a loop these catch against it and secure the article. Fastenings like this can be seen in several illustrations.

So far all the examples have been relatively simple strings which depend for their charm on the variety of beads. Before moving on, however, it is worth considering how the string can be further developed. Must only one thread be used? One string of beads?

Inspiration is derived from many sources, it can begin for instance with the Ugandan necklace in illustration 7. This has many strings of beads which pass through larger beads at intervals. So many threads and needles are very difficult for even the most adept beadworker to handle, but two or three strings work just as effectively. Wooden beads, large glass and ceramic beads are necessary parts of such work. The holes are sufficiently large to take several threads and as you will have found, they blend well with the tiny beads. Many colours may be used in direct imitation of the illustrated work, but initially it is less confusing to stick to two or three. In the examples the choker style is used again, but the multiple string works just as well as a long necklace or as a bracelet.

Double string choker

Materials:
    Size 10 dark-blue Rocaille beads
    Size 4mm, 6mm and 8mm purple and turquoise wooden beads
    One 12mm purple wooden bead for the centre
    Two size 9 or, if the Rocaille beads have very tiny holes, two size 10 needles
    Dark-blue Polytwist thread
    Beeswax
Key:
    B – Rocaille beads
    P – purple 4mm
    Pu – purple 6mm
    Pp – purple 8mm
    T – turquoise 4mm

    Tu – turquoise 6mm
    Tr – turquoise 8mm
    Td – turquoise wooden discs
    Pd – purple disc
To make the loop:

Wax a length of thread, remembering that you will need twice the usual length for a choker with two strings of beads. Thread a needle at each end of one long thread leaving a long loop between the needles – have an equal amount of thread on each side.

The fastening loop is made differently for this technique, and is in fact far simpler (see diagram 9).

1 Pick up 16 size 10 beads with one needle and draw them down to the centre of the thread.

2 Pick up one 4mm purple bead with both needles and draw it down the thread until it meets the size 10's. The loop is now completed.

Pattern for the choker:
Make the loop.

1 Pick up and thread 20B on each needle.

2 With both needles together pick up and thread 2B. If the holes are too small for the two needles to pass through together take them through one at a time, taking care that you do not pass through the thread.

3 With both needles pick up 1P, 2T, 1P, 2B.

4 Separate the needles and pick up 15B on each one.

5 With both needles pick up 2B, 1T, 1P, 1Tu, 1P, 1T, 2B.

6 On each needle thread 10B.

7 With both needles pick up and thread 2B, 1T, 1Pu, 1Tu, 1Pp, 1Pd, 1Td, one 12mm purple bead – this is the centre front of the work. The pattern is now repeated in reverse from 1Td to the first of the Rocaille beads.

Attaching and securing the bead fastener on the double-string choker is quite different to the method used for a single string (see diagram 9).

Completing the choker fastening. Diagram 10

1 Pick up one 4mm P with both needles, and one 6mm purple or turquoise wooden bead. On one needle pick up 3B, and pass the second needle through them in the opposite direction.

2 Pass both needles down into the 6mm bead and then on down the work, taking each needle into a separate string. Return the threads by passing over one bead in the string and into the remainder, bringing the needles and thread out of the work below the 6mm bead and

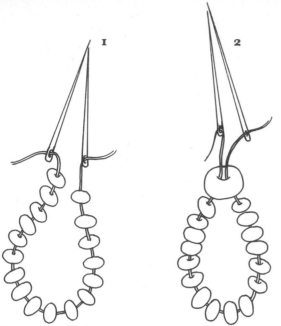

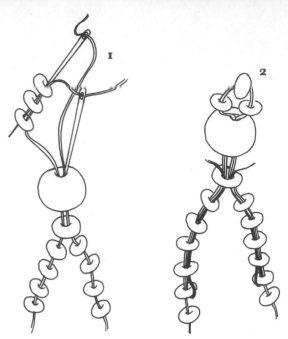

Diagram 9   Loop for double strings, passing both needles through as one

Diagram 10   Fastening bead for double strings. Make slip knots to secure the threads

making a separate slip knot with each needle.

Pull tight and cut off the excess threads.

This method is used to fasten all the multiple-string work in this section. Several examples of the technique appear in illustration 16.

The technique is equally suitable for bracelets, where the number of beads used in the two threads is much reduced or increased so that they pass together through only a centre pattern, or through single beads only (see illustration 17). Long necklaces are made in the same way, but look best if the threads pass through only one large bead at intervals rather than several. These may be joined as for long single strings, or a fastener can be attached.

Long or short oval beads, small square beads, many-sided beads and small 'lice' beads, are all suitable for use as connecting beads when a multiple string is to be passed through them. It is difficult to pass many threads through the tiny beads and should it be necessary a larger glass bead of the same colour and shape should be used – a size 7 or 4 Rocaille bead, or a Rotelle bead.

How the string develops is now a matter of personal taste and skill. All the strings described and illustrated are comparatively easy and take only a little time to make.

Attractive and 'different' strings are made by manipulating the beads on the thread. Some of the patterns for these strings serve as an introduction to the next section since they use a variation of the threading patterns.

If at first it seems that you have just begun to make progress only to return to square one, do not worry – you will make better and faster progress if you begin with the simple patterns than if you now jump to more complicated techniques.

The simplest of the variations is the flower string and this also has variations of its own. The first example is a very simple one (see illustration 18). The flower motif hangs from the string rather than being *in* it.

Flower string 1. Diagram 11a

Materials:
    Size 10 green and yellow Rocaille beads
    Size 9 needle
    Green Polytwist thread – 1·5m
    Beeswax
Key:
    Y – yellow
    G – green
The necklace does not have a fastener.
Pattern:
Wax thread and make a slip knot.

18 Flower strings 1, 2 and 3 ▶

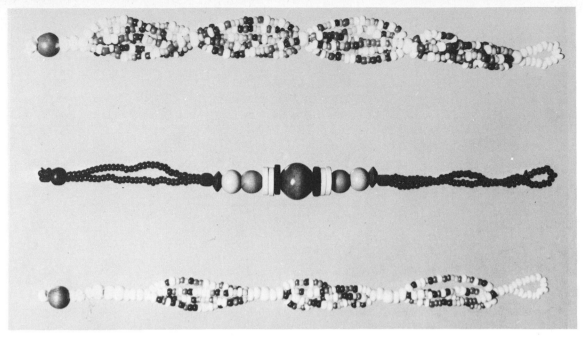

17 Two multi-string and one double-string bracelets

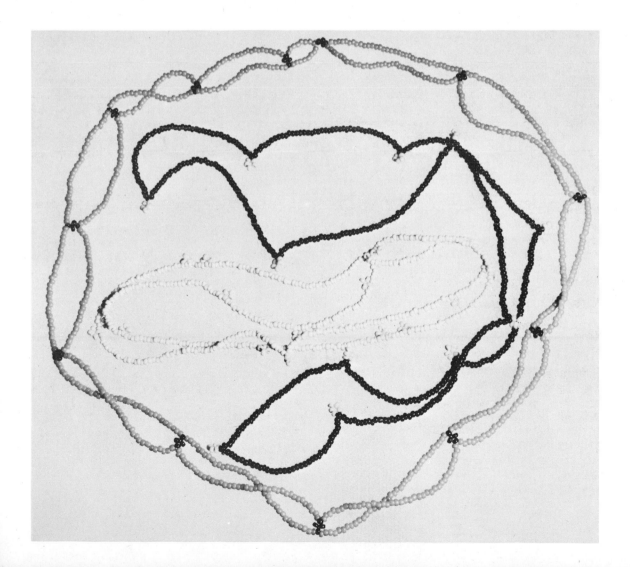

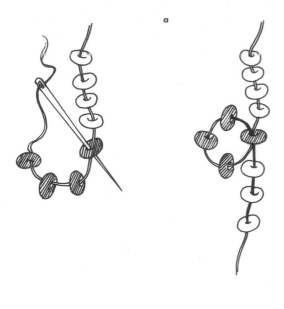
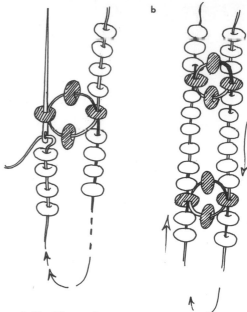

Diagram 11   a Three-bead hanging flower   **b Double version**

1 Pick up 30G, 4Y. Pass needle down through first Y bead as shown.
2 Thread 30G, 4Y. Pass needle down through first Y bead.
Repeat until string is long enough.
Finish as for single strings.

   The number of beads in the strung section may be varied so that the contrasting flower beads are in groups, or simply closer together. Different colours may be used for each flower or a different colour for each of the petals. Three beads only could be threaded and a main-colour bead used as bead 1 so that three beads are suspended from a solid string of colour.

Flower string 2. Diagram 11b

The second flower string is a simple variation of the first. Thread needle with a long thread and make a slip knot. Work a string as in pattern 1. Do not join this, but make sure you have finished the string with 30 beads (diagram 11a). Pick up another 30 main-colour beads and take needle through the bottom bead of the flower (see diagram). Repeat this all along the string until the beginning of the first string is reached again. Join the work. This double-flower string can be varied in the same manner as the first, by altering the sequence and number of the flowers and

colours of the beads in the flower and petals. Both the patterns may be worked as chokers when the fastening methods described previously are used.

   A similar string uses more beads in the flower petals. These are either all one colour or are suspended from a bead on the main string (see diagram 12).

Flower string 3. Diagram 12

Materials:
   Size 10 black and yellow beads
   Black thread
   Size 9 needle
   Beeswax
Key:
   b – black
   y – yellow
Pattern:
The first bead in the flower is part of the main string.
Wax thread and tie slip knot in the end.
1 Pick up and thread 31b, 5y and pass the needle down through bead 31.
2 Repeat this along the string until you have sufficient length. Finish and cut excess thread. (See illustration 18).

Variations

As for the first flower string, several colours may be used for the petals.

All six petals beads can be in a contrast colour. Flowers can be close together in groups, or in several colours.

This string can be made into a double string in the same way as Flower string 1.

The patterns above are the simplest of all the 'manipulated' strings, demanding only that you remember to pass the needle *down* through the first bead of the pattern sequence for a second time.

Other decorative flower strings have a flower motif which is actually part of the string. These are adaptations of the threading patterns in Section Two. There is a variety of ways in which these patterns can be used and once you have mastered the basic technique you will no doubt begin to invent new ways for yourself. Beads bought in small quantities from haberdashery counters are often larger than the size 10 beads used for the following patterns, so you may find that you need to experiment with the number of beads used to form the petals because the size of the beads used may alter the shape of the flower and throw the balance of the motif off centre. Unless it is otherwise stated, the beads used in the patterns are size 10.

Flower string 4. Diagram 13

Materials:
    Size 10 beads in two colours, one for the petals and one for the main string
    Size 9 needle

Diagram 12   Five-bead hanging flower

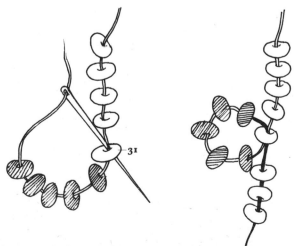

Single-strand Polytwist thread to match the main colour
    Beeswax
Key:
    m – main colour
    c – contrast or petal beads
Pattern:
Wax the thread and make a slip knot.
1 Pick up and thread 8m, 5c, 1m. Pass the needle up through the first c bead. Pull tight and hold the work firmly between finger and thumb.
2 Pick up 3c. Pass needle down through bead 5 (c) (see diagram).
3 Pull tightly to complete the flower motif. Pick up 40m, 5c, 1m and repeat the movement in stage 1.
    Repeat stage 2.
    Do this in the same sequence until you have enough length to make a long necklace. End with 12m then join as for long strings. This method ensures that the flowers along the string are an equal distance apart.

You could make a number of flower strings to be worn together, perhaps with flowers of different colours on strings of one colour. There are many permutations of colour with the petals, whole flowers, centres and strings.

The flowers may also be worked in groups along the string. When you do this, remember to use a main-colour bead between each of the flowers to give the string continuity (see diagram 14).

Illustration 19 shows several versions of the flower string. Other variations using a larger bead in the centre of the flower, a size 4 Rocaille bead, or a 4mm wooden bead, are also shown.

Using a larger centre bead means that the number of petal beads must be increased. If too many are used the flower will be loose, and if there are too few the centre bead will be forced out of the surround. The petals should fit around the centre bead closely, and there should be an equal number on either side of it.

Pattern 5: Flower string with large centre bead. Diagram 15

Materials:
    Size 10 beads in red and yellow
    Size 4 dark-blue Rocaille beads
    Red Polytwist thread
    Size 9 needle
    Beeswax

Key:
   r – red
   b – blue
   y – yellow
Pattern:
Wax thread and make a slip knot in the end.

1 Pick up 20r, 6y, 1b and pass needle up through first y bead. Pull tight and hold work firmly between finger and thumb to prevent the beads slipping.

2 Pick up 4y and pass needle down through bead 6. Pull tight. Hold work until several of the beads in stage 3 have been threaded.

3 Pick up 40r, 6y, 1b and repeat from stage 1. To complete the string, pick up 20r and join in the same manner as a long string.

These flowers look effective if they are grouped along the string. (See illustration 19 and diagram 16). Remember to include a bead in the main colour between the flowers if you do this. The petals may, of course, be the same colour as the main string of beads, or each flower a different colour with a centre bead to match the main colour. The variations are almost endless and you will enjoy experimenting for yourself.

Pattern 6: Flower string with wooden bead centres. Diagram 16

Following diagram 16 use black size 10 beads and a different colour for each centre. Two necklaces, one with single flowers and one with groups, are pretty.

To work a plain-colour string with only the centres in contrast you must remember to count the beads as you thread them. The spacing of the flowers need not be exact but there should be six petal beads picked up for the first side and four for the second.

Example:

To work a necklace with a black surround you would pick up the beads as follows:

1 Forty-six black, one 4mm wood. Pass up through bead 41. Pick up four black and pass down through bead 46. You will soon learn which bead to pass through a second time in the second part of the pattern in order to complete the flower.

Wooden and glass beads mix well, as has already been demonstrated. An attractive and different kind of choker can be made by using the flower

Diagram 13   Flower string 4

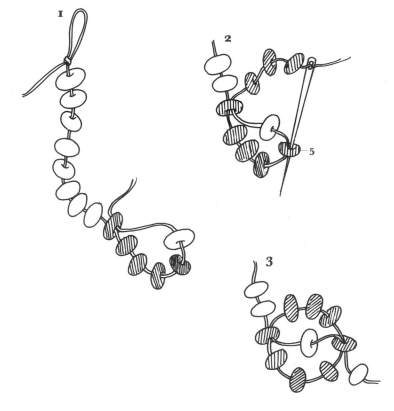

Diagram 14   Series of flowers

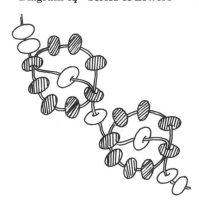

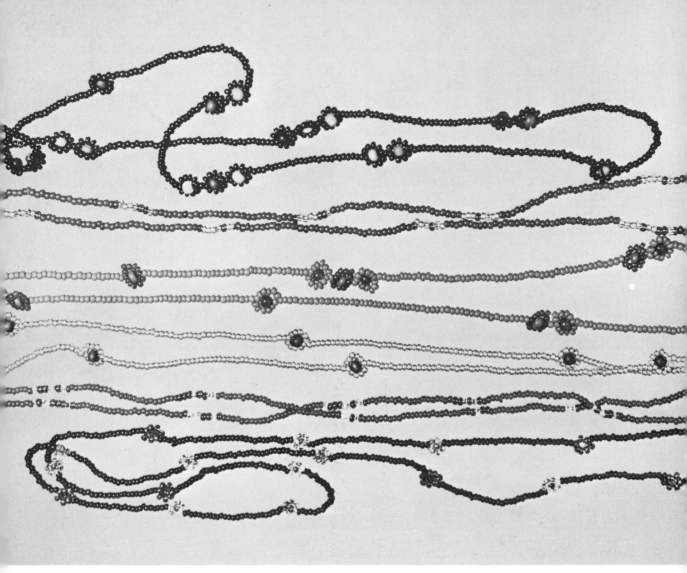

19 Flower strings 4 and 5

motif in the centre of the string, and larger wooden beads for the centres of the flowers.

For these patterns I use nothing larger than a size 8mm wooden bead since there are problems in keeping the petals around the middle of the bead when a larger size is used. Black size 10 beads are used for string and petals in the following pattern.

Flower centre choker. Illustration 20

Materials:
    Size 10 beads in black (approximately 210)
    4mm wooden beads (12)
    Five 6mm wooden beads (one is for fastener)

One 8mm bead for the centre (brown or orange)
Black Polytwist thread
Size 9 needle
Beeswax

Key:
    B – black
    O – 4mm orange
    Bb – 4mm brown
    Qr – 6mm orange
    Br – 6mm brown

Pattern:
Make sure to check your neck measurement and adjust the number of size 10 beads in the string accordingly.
Thread the needle with waxed thread.

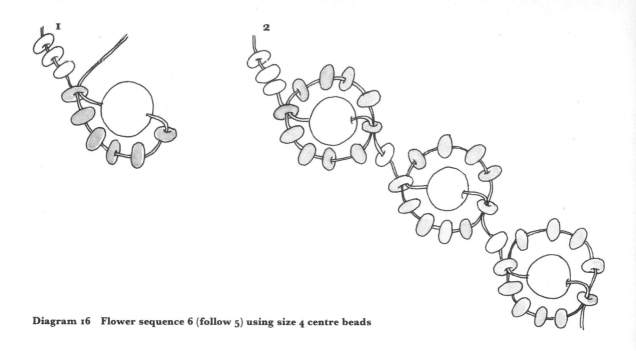

Diagram 16 Flower sequence 6 (follow 5) using size 4 centre beads

Make the fastening loop as for the previous chokers.

1 Pick up and thread 50B, 1O, 3B, 1Bb, 1O.
2 Pick up and thread 20B, 1Bb, 2B, 1Or, 2B, 1Bb.
3 Check the length of the choker against your neck at this point and adjust the number of beads in stage 3 accordingly. The choker should be just a little over half the measurement required to fit around the base of the throat. If not, add some black beads; if it is just right proceed with stage 4. If too long, remove stage 2 pattern and reduce from 20B to an appropriate number.
4 The centre pattern – follow diagram 17. Pick up and thread 1Or, 9B, 1 8mm. Pass needle up through the first of the 9B. Pull tight and hold firmly to prevent the beads slipping.
5 Pick up 9B and pass the needle and thread down through bead 9 of the last series. Pull tight to form the flower. Pick up 1Or and repeat from stage 3 to 1.

The choker should now be the correct length to fit your neck.

The fastener should be made in the same manner as those worked for the chokers described earlier, but if you do not have a suitable 6mm bead, an alternative method of making a fastener is shown in diagram 8. Wooden 4mm beads or size 4 Rocaille beads should be used for this.

The flower used as a centrepiece may of course be multiplied so that several appear at intervals along the choker. Size 7 beads are equally suitable for this pattern, but remember to experiment first to find out how many beads are needed to work the petals around the centre bead. It is not necessary to use an 8mm bead in the centre, the 6mm, or even the 4mm, are just as effective as long as you remember to adjust the number of petal beads accordingly.

The centre flower may be placed between several of the wooden discs. For this choker, thread and needle are the same as for pattern 6. The smaller wooden beads are not used until the centre pattern is worked.

Flower centre with wooden discs

Materials:
  Size 10 beads in black (approximately 240)
  Four olive discs
  Four purple discs
  2.4mm olive; 2.4mm purple; 2.6mm olive;
  1.8mm purple; 1.6mm black.

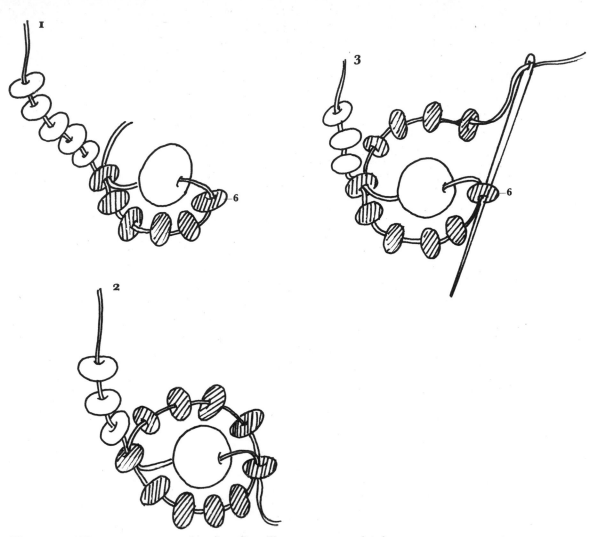

Diagram 15   Flower sequence 5, using size 4 Rocaille or 4mm centre beads

Diagram 17   Flower choker 5, showing the working for stages 4 and 5 for centre pattern

Stage 4   **Stage 5**

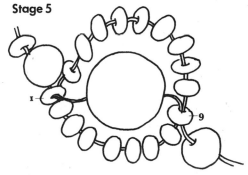

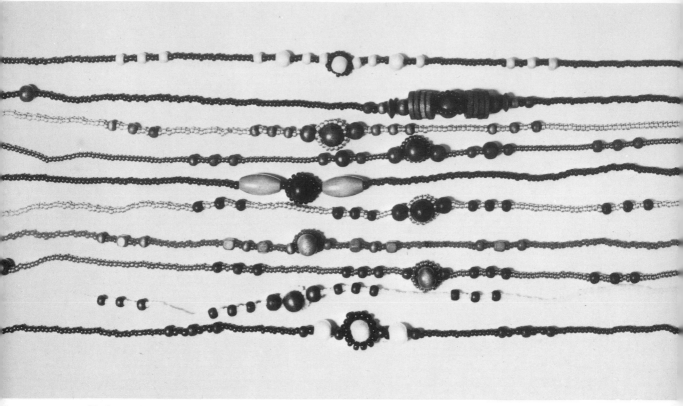

20 Chokers with flower centres

Pattern:
Wax the thread, make a slip knot and work the loop using 16 size 10 beads.

1. Pick up 90 size 10 beads in black, then one olive 4mm, two purple discs and two olive discs.
2. Pick up and thread nine size 10 and one purple 8mm. Pass needle up through first of the nine size 10 beads. Pull tight. Pick up nine size 10.
3. Pass needle down through bead 9 of the first series of 9b and pull tight to form the flower.
4. Repeat from discs in reverse until the choker is complete. Make fastener and trim thread.

Once again, there are endless variations of the choker: lice may be used in place of discs; long ovals may be placed on either side of the flower (see illustration 20); or several different-sized wooden beads spaced by size 10's may be used. Experiment for yourself and see what other variations are possible.

Finally, in this section about strings of beads here is a pattern which uses all wooden beads to make a flower centre.

Choker with wooden flower centre. Diagram 18

Materials:
  Size 10 yellow Rocaille beads
  4mm deep yellow beads
  6mm yellow bead
  Yellow Polytwist thread
  Size 9 needle
  Beeswax
Key:
  Y – Size 10 yellow
  Dy – 4mm deep yellow
Pattern:
Wax the thread and make the loop with 16 yellow beads.

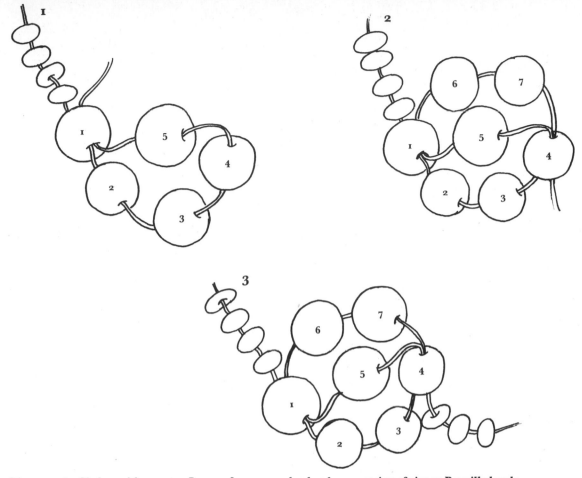

Diagram 18 Choker with a centre flower of 4mm wooden beads on a string of size 10 Rocaille beads

1 Pick and thread 50Y, 1Dy, 3Y, 1Dy, 3Y, 1Dy, 20Y, 1Dy, 2Y, 1Dy, 2Y, 1Dy, 2Y, 1Dy, 2Y, 1Dy, 2Y (a series of 5).

2 4Y, 5Dy. Follow diagram 18, stages 1–3. Pass the needle back up through bead 1 of the series of 5 Dy. Pull tight.

Pick up 2Dy, and pass down through bead 4. Pull tight to form the wooden flower.

Repeat the pattern in reverse back to the beginning and attach the fastening bead.

All the strings and chokers use Rocaille beads; the range of colours for these and for the wooden beads allows for almost endless combinations. Also available from some of the suppliers listed at the end of the book are 0/2 beads. These are approximately the same size as the 10's and some of the colours are the same. This wide choice of colours allows you to experiment widely with the combinations.

Shiny wooden beads are very useful for this kind of work, the sizes being approximately the same although the general shape is more ovoid than round. However, they correspond to 4mm, 8mm, and so on, and the same number of small beads is used to make petals if they are used as flower centres. Many-sided beads may be used in the centre of the flowers, but you should experiment to find out the number of beads used for the petals. Wood-grained beads may also be used successfully for this purpose. Pearlized beads from old necklaces are a very useful addition to your bead box. They are often 6mm or 8mm size and so can be used in the same way as the wooden beads. Try anything and everything so that your work will develop and become uniquely your own.

Strings: repairs, renovations and rejuvenations

I am often asked if I can repair or even redesign

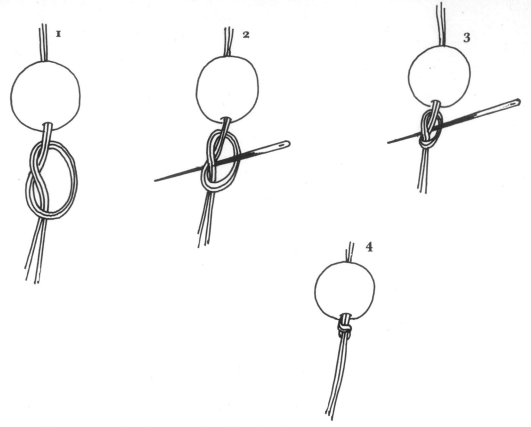

Diagram 19   Knots between beads (rethreading). Two threads are shown, several more may be used

broken strings of beads. Mending is a relatively simple matter if they are small glass beads which the owner wants rethreading on a string; an easy matter too to redesign these and to replace with beads from my own stock. However, these necklaces are often very old and even valuable. Restringing, repairing and redesigning these is quite a different matter. A special technique is required. It is not sufficient to thread them, make a fastener and return them.

Many old necklaces, specifically real or cultured pearls, have a knot between each bead. This is not a decorative device, nor is it simply to prevent the beautiful surfaces rubbing together and becoming marred, nor merely to give extra length to the necklace. Certainly all these things are achieved, but the purpose of the knot is much more practical. If the string should break, only one, or at most two, of the precious beads will be lost. The knots keep the rest of the beads securely in place. Necklaces strung like this are more flexible and are in fact less likely to break than those on a simple strand of thread.

Perfecting the tying of the knot between each bead takes practice, and you should also make

sure that you have sufficient thread to complete the work since it is not possible to join a new one. You may find, on taking old necklaces apart prior to rethreading them, that several very fine threads were used for the original. I usually use two strands of Polytwist for beads with small holes and up to six strands for those with larger holes – the latter will usually allow a large-eyed darning or embroidery needle plus several strands of thread to pass through them. All threads are drawn through beeswax first to strengthen them and prevent tangles. Strong, fine linen crotchet thread is also suitable for rethreading. Monofilament nylon line is not a suitable thread for this work. It is inflexible when used in several strands; does not tie into a suitable knot; and develops a pronounced curl along its length with too much pulling.

Completely new necklaces may be created with this technique from a few odd, but pretty, beads but before experimenting the art of actually tying the knots should be perfected. The thread which is sold specifically for restringing pearls may be used, but if you are making a very long string you will probably find that you do not have sufficient length. An alternative, therefore, if you must use this thread, is to separate the beads with small matching (Rocaille-type) beads and not draw the thread up too tightly.

The knot between the beads diagram 19, illustration 21

Thread the needle with a double strand of waxed thread. Either make a slip knot in the end or tie on a bead to prevent the first bead slipping off the thread. You will also require another needle: a blunt tapestry needle or a large darner is ideal. Make sure the beads you are using do not have a very big hole, otherwise they will slip over the knots.

1 Thread the first bead and make a loose knot in the manner shown.

2 Slip the spare needle into the knot as in the diagram, and ease knot up to the bead.
3 Tighten the knot *around the needle*, and slide the needle out.
4 Complete the tightening of the knot and thread the next bead.

The first knot is the simplest at this stage since the bead will tend to sit against it. The second one is made in the same way and you should make sure that the second bead is pushed up against the first knot when you tighten the second. A double knot is sometimes used between the beads and if the beads have large holes requiring several threads, this double knot may be the most suitable (see diagram 20).

Practise both knots before you begin any major rethreading work, and also try to calculate from these practice pieces just how much thread

21 Knots between beads – single and double

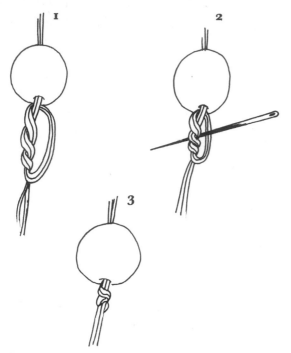

Diagram 20 Double knot

you will require. If the beads you wish to rethread have a fastener which is in good condition, then reuse it. Valuable beads and those which are very old may have special fasteners so check that they are working properly. Note how they were originally attached to the thread so that when you rethread the beads you can attach the fastener in the same way. If the fastener is broken or weak, use a commercial fastener rather than a bead and loop. Ring bolts, split rings, screw-type fasteners and hooks with a locking device may all be purchased from craft shops quite inexpensively. On a long string, which slips over the head, secure the join with a blob of clear nail varnish or glue.

Many old strands of beads are graduated towards the centre and to work out the threading sequence from a mass of loose beads is often impossible, so you should do this before starting. To do this if the beads were originally strung without knots: lay them on a strip of masking tape or Sellotape; cut through thread below fastener at each end and gently ease it out leaving the beads in sequence stuck on to the tape. If there are some missing you will then be able to reorder them or perhaps remove those without a corresponding size. If there are knots between the beads on the original thread then each bead

should be removed in turn and placed either in line on a flat surface in front of you, or once again placed on sticky tape. Do not treat pearls in this way as you may damage the surface; they should be placed on a flat surface and the beads picked up one by one as you work. Multiple strands of beads, with each string slightly longer than the preceding one, should be dealt with in the same manner. A special type of fastener may be required for these.

As an added bonus to this restringing you have yet another way of making strings of beads. Some of your odd, unusual or simply old beads could be rethreaded with knots between them, perhaps making them into a string of a usable length. You could experiment as follows.

Where there are insufficient beads to make a necklace even with the knots to extend the length, the thread can become part of the overall design. Brightly-coloured threads mixed together are suitable for some beads: thicker threads such as macramé cord, coloured twine, embroidery threads, Polytwist, ordinary string, fine cord, leather thongs or suede are all suitable provided the beads have holes large enough to take them. Each bead is secured between two knots and a length of the thread is left between them. This should either match or contrast with the beads. Illustration 22 shows various ways of using the thread as part of the design.

First, cut a piece of card or stiff paper to correspond with the length of the space you wish to have between the beads. Use this as a gauge when working (you could make two dots on paper and use it in the same way). If the spacing is to be random this does not apply. A slip knot is not necessary unless you wish to join the threads to make a long string. Make a knot in the same manner as those between the beads, and thread the first bead. Make another knot to hold this in place.

Cord which will not go through a needle eye should be dipped into glue such as PVA and allowed to dry. As it dries, roll the end between your fingers to make a point. When dry, the glue will have stiffened the end sufficiently for it to go through the beads without fraying. The ends of the work may be attached to a fastener, thicker cords simply knotted together at the back of the neck, or the work may be finished as follows.

There should be approximately 15cm (6in) in the tail. If the beads are spaced 3cm apart make a knot this distance from the first bead you threaded. Thread a bead and make the

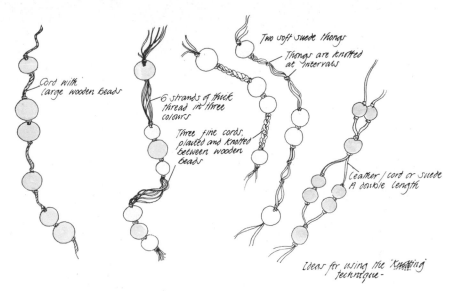

Cord with large wooden beads

6 strands of thick thread in three colours

Three fine cords, plaited and knotted between wooden beads

Two soft suede thongs

Thongs are knotted at intervals

Leather / cord or suede A double length

Ideas for using the Knotting technique –

22 Using the knotting technique in several ways

holding knot by tying the working thread and the tail together close to the bead. Use a double knot and pull it tight. The threads are cut and a dab of colourless glue used to secure the knot (see diagram 20A).

Having mastered the techniques of knotting between the beads and of securing the beads in order to show connecting lengths of thread, there are many ways in which you can experiment. Long and short spacing may be used to make several strings to be worn together, the size of the beads could differ, and when finished the spaces on one string could correspond with the beads on another. Try several rows of beads in complementary (decreasing) sizes.

It is sometimes impossible to use the knotting technique between beads, perhaps because the holes or the beads themselves are too small. If you decide to use small Rocaille beads between them do consider whether or not they are suitable additions. Beads with delicate surfaces may be damaged by the friction of the glass beads however smooth the surface of these may seem. Amber, coral and jet, like pearls, do not gain anything from the addition of these foreigners. This being so, they are better simply restrung on a strong thread, if the knotting technique is impossible.

Diagram 20A   Joining a long knotted string with a knot

a

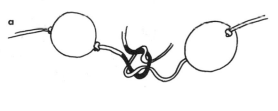

b

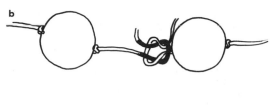

c

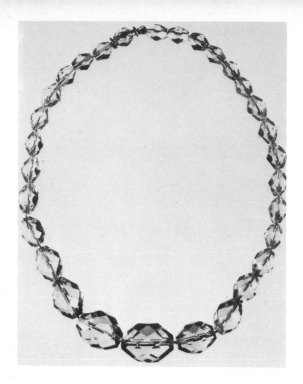

23b Victorian glass beads used in a modern
necklace and bracelet

23a **Venetian blue glass necklace—simply restrung
in its original form**

In illustration 23b you can see old glass beads threaded with Rocaille beads. These, though 'only glass', still require sensitive treatment. Illustration 24 shows semi-precious stone beads and silver though not strictly a string nor really rethreaded these are a good example of using a small number of beads which would not otherwise make a necklace.

Turquoise beads also require careful handling. This semi-precious mineral is very porous and any contact with grease or oil will stain and darken the surface beyond repair. Polished stone beads such as those in illustration 25 – agates, carnelian, azurite, malachite, moss agate, bloodstone – are very heavy and so a very strong thread should be used for them. The string of stone beads with the pendant heart have between each bead large 'turks head' knots which are a mixture of red threads and fine gold wire. It is impossible to find the join in this string of beads.

Finally, a short note on making your own beads. There is simply not enough space here to deal with the many materials and ways in which you can fashion beads of your own. Seeds, shells, and other natural materials have already been suggested, but there remains a wealth of material which may be carved, moulded, fired and polished. Clay is perhaps the most obvious material and illustration 26 shows some simple but effective sizes and shapes. These beads are unglazed but are still an attractive and unusual decoration.

In *Introducing Beads* Mary Seyd discusses and describes in some detail the making of beads using paper, clay, wood and many junk objects. There is a wealth of suggestions together with clear and detailed instructions. These will serve you far better than any brief outline I can give.

24 Necklace by Trevor Neagle using silver and semi-precious stone beads

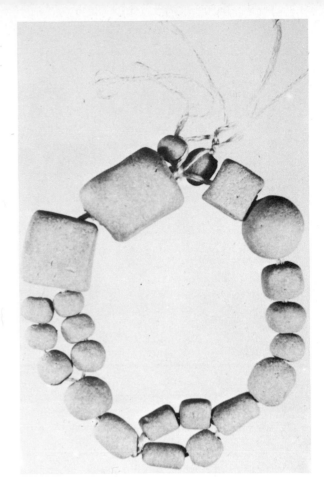

25a Saudi Arabian polished stone beads with 'Turks' head knots of red and gold between each bead

26 Unglazed stoneware clay beads by Soo Tasker

25b American Indian polished stone beads

section two threading
one needle, one thread

This technique, with variations, has been used at one time or another in just about every part of the globe. North American Indians especially have always used beads of some kind, and the introduction of glass beads from Europe supplemented the shells and seeds which were once used, thus encouraging the development of much more intricate patterns some of which are included in the following section.

The materials in this section are modern, but a great many of the designs and patterns are very old. I have called this section Threading, but in some parts of the world it is known as stripwork and the Victorians and Edwardians called items made by the first two methods chains.

African natives and the people of New Guinea make intricate collars by the threading technique; they use brilliant colours and fringe their work with thousands of beads. The colours and the type of bead used owe more to the influence of the Europeans than to the natives themselves, but they nonetheless have much to offer in the way of inspiration. In England this particular kind of beadwork enjoyed a vogue during the nineteenth century when Victorian ladies worked beads into purses, mats, pincushions, lamp fringes and a dozen other articles. Several examples of beaded purses are seen in illustration 27. Some of these are worked on to a net backing using a technique known as tamboure work. A further example of nineteenth century beadwork is the mat (illustration 28) worked by the alternate bead method, which is yet another technique. It long ago lost its fringed edge but remains a fair example of late Victorian beadwork; it is clumsy however when compared with the Samoan beadwork mat in illustration 29 with its thousands of tiny beads and very complicated pattern.

I used strings as an introduction to working with beads, hoping to give you a sound knowledge of the materials, their possibilities and their limitations. I have attempted to keep the following descriptions of techniques as simple as possible.

In all the diagrams the beads are shown widely spaced. This is simply to make them easier to follow and, in practice, the beads should be drawn closely together so that as little thread as possible is visible. It is inevitable that some thread will show between the beads owing to the nature of the threading technique so it is wise to match thread to beads if you can and, if not, to use monofilament nylon if the pattern is suitable. For multicoloured work use black or white depending on whether light or dark beads dominate. To keep the tension of the work even the beads should be rolled between the fingers of the left hand whilst pulling gently on the thread with the right. Many beautiful, useful and some purely decorative articles from the simplest rings to complicated collars can be made by the threading techniques. None of them is so complex however that they are impossible to master with a little time and patience.

Beads, containers, and thread are the same as in Section One, although you may find it necessary to use a finer needle with much greater frequency than before because the needle sometimes has to pass several times through the same bead. A size 10 needle is adequate for this, but it is wise to have a supply of size 12's.

There are a few simple rules, some new and some worth repeating.

1 Always use more thread than you think you will need. Joining, though possible and inevitable with larger articles, is a nuisance and weakens the work if done carelessly.

2 Keep the tension of the work even and if you use monofilament nylon be careful not to pull too tightly otherwise the work will pucker and be very stiff. The thread should be pulled just enough to bring the beads together while rolling them between the fingers of the other hand.

44

27 Victorian and Edwardian beaded bags. The bag
on the right is worked by tamboure technique

28 Victorian mat showing alternate bead
technique

29 Samoan mat, contrasting in style and technique
to the Victorian mat

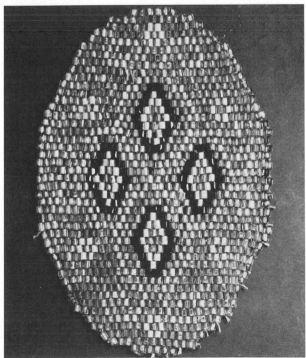

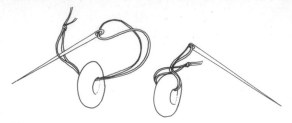

Diagram 21   Securing the first bead when double thread is used

3 Use a double thread of nylon, unless otherwise stated, and a single thread of Polytwist. Where the beads have very small holes a single strand of nylon should be used.

4 If you use thread, draw it through beeswax a couple of times to smooth it and prevent it tangling as you work. This also helps to preserve the thread.

5 A fastening loop is often used in the following section. If this is not to be the case the first bead is always attached in the following way, if you are using a double thread (otherwise a slip knot is used). To secure the first bead (see diagram 21), tie a knot in the end of the double thread, pick up one bead and slide it down almost to the knot, pass the needle between the two threads under the knot as shown, and pull tight.

6 For clarity, the diagrams for the working techniques show a single thread only.

7 In all cases each part of the instructions is numbered to correspond with those of the diagrams.

8 The work should be held between finger and thumb to keep the beads in place while the pattern is being worked.

9 Beads, unless it is stated in the materials required section for each pattern, are of uniform size and shape. The thread is Gütermann Polytwist and the monofilament nylon (fishing line) used is 4lb test (breaking strain).

Pattern A: the basic flower pattern

You have already used a flower as a single unit in the previous section. The first pattern in this section is a linked flower which forms a continuous strip or chain of flowers when complete. Once you are familiar with holding the work you will see that as the thread is pulled tight the beads fall into place and form the flower. Once you have worked two or three flowers you will be able to see quite easily through which bead the needle must pass a second time. You will find it simpler, however, if you continue to follow the

diagrams for the first few patterns and variations.

The easiest item for you to begin with is a ring. This will also teach you how to join the flowers together without breaking the sequence of the pattern.

Pattern A. Ring with nine flowers

Materials:
  Size 10 black Rocaille beads (approximately 72)
  Size 10 yellow Rocaille beads (approximately 9)
  Monofilament nylon (approximately 70cm 28in))
  Size 9 needle
Key:
  m – main-colour bead – black
  c – yellow
Finger sizes differ greatly so adjust to fit finger or make as example for practice.
Pattern:
Use the nylon double, tie a knot, and secure the first bead as shown in diagram 21.

1 Count the bead already threaded as 1. Pick up 4m making 5m and 1c. Pass the needle up through bead 1 as shown.

2 Pick up and thread 3m and pass the needle down through bead 5. Pull tight.

3 Pick up 2m and pass needle down through beads 9 and 5.

4 Pull tight and pass up through beads 10 and 11. Pull tight.

5 Pick up and thread 3m, 1c. Pass needle down through bead 10.

6 Pick up 3m and pass up through bead 14. Pull tight (two flowers). Repeat stage 3.

Continue in this way until there are nine flowers in all.

To join the work follow diagram 23. Joining is easier if you first bend the strip of flowers around your finger and hold them there.

The first two side-petal beads 1 and 2, and the last two Z and V are linked together to form the circle. Pass through these beads, several times if you can, and then work back into the pattern making a slip knot at intervals. For a slip knot, scoop up all the threads with the needle and pass through the resulting loop, pulling tight. This is, in effect, buttonhole stitch, exactly as worked in Section One.

The excess thread in the tail should be worked into the first flower before trimming.

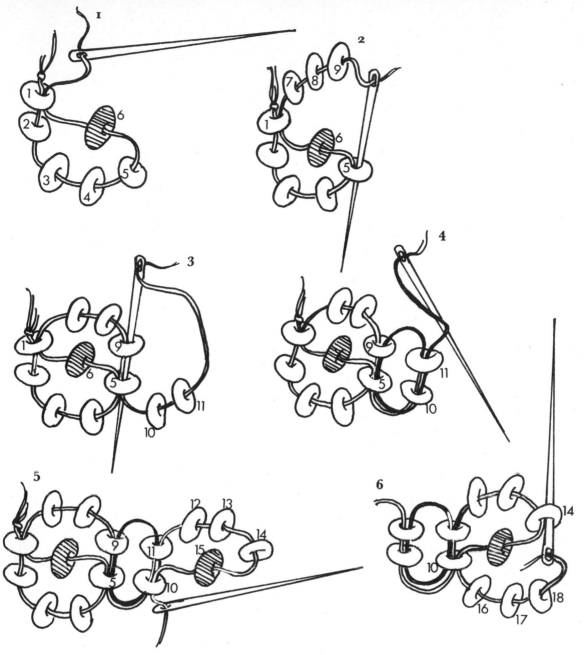

Diagram 22 Pattern A threading for basic pattern in two colours. Only one working thread is shown to avoid confusion

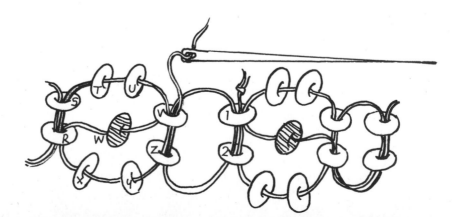

Diagram 23
Join for Pattern A

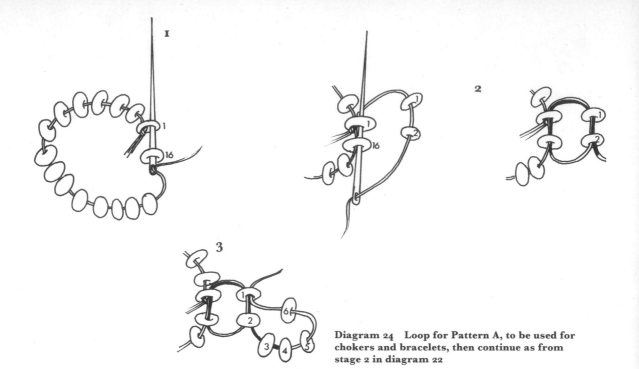

Diagram 24   Loop for Pattern A, to be used for chokers and bracelets, then continue as from stage 2 in diagram 22

The pattern is suitable for long necklaces and should be joined in the same manner as the ring. Shorter necklaces, however, require a fastener.

Pattern A. Making a two-colour choker with a loop and bead fastener

Materials:
    Size 10 red and gold lustre beads (approximately 340 beads, 45 of which are gold and the centre of the flowers)
    Monofilament nylon or Polytwist thread (approximately 1m)
    Size 9 needle
    One 6mm wooden bead for the fastener.
Key:
    r – red
    g – gold
    Do not use thread for rings, they need to be fairly rigid and so nylon is more suitable. Thread gives a softer more flexible finish and should be used for chokers.
Pattern:
The loop is made with 16 beads as described in Section One. The first flower is part of this loop (see diagram 24). You may work the second series of two beads, or use the two from the loop to make the first two side petals of the first flower.

To make the first flower (see diagram 24).

Diagram 25   Stem and bead for Pattern A, worked from the last complete flower. Use with loop for A

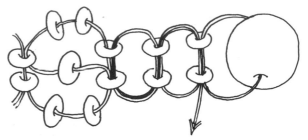

1 Pick up 2r. Pass needle up through beads 16 and 1 of the loop.
2 Pull tight and pass needle down through the beads picked up in stage 1. These beads now become beads 1 and 2 of the first flower.
3 Pick up 3r, 1g and pass needle up through bead 1. Pull tight. Work from stage 2 of diagram 22 and pick up 3r. Pass down through bead 5. Pull tight to complete first flower.

Attaching the 6mm bead fastener—see diagram 25

Complete the last flower.
1 Pick up 2r and pass the needle down as shown through the last two side-petal beads of the last flower. Pull tight.
2 Pick up 2r and repeat the movement so that a stem is formed. Pick up 6mm bead and pass down through last two beads picked up.

48

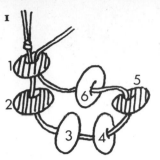

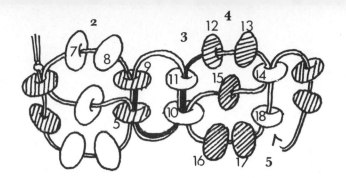

Diagram 26   Pattern A variation 1

Work back into the choker for several flowers. Make a slip knot and trim thread.

If you wish to make a very long flower necklace then it is not necessary to make either loop or fastening bead. Simply join the pattern as for the ring.

The following are variations of pattern A, which depend for their effect on the sequence in which different colours are picked up.

Pattern A. Variation 1. Making a nine-flower ring. Diagram 26

Materials:

  Size 10 beads in gunmetal and pearl (approximately 81 beads)
  Size 9 needle
  Monofilament nylon thread, used double

Key:

  g – gunmetal

  p – pearl

Pattern:

Secure first bead and treat as bead 1.

1 Pick up (including first bead) 2g, 2p, 1g, 1p and pass up through bead 1. Pull tight.
2 Pick up 2p, 1g and pass down through bead 5. Tighten.
3 Continue by picking up 2p, pass down through beads 9 and 5 and pull tightly. Pass up through beads 10 and 11.
4 Pick up 2g, 1p, 1g. Pass down through bead 10 and pull tight.
5 Pick up 2g, 1p. Pass the needle up through bead 14 and pull to tighten.

This is repeated along the work, alternating the pattern with each flower worked. When beads are worked in a sequence of colours like this you must make sure that the ring will join and make a pattern repeat, otherwise the continuity is lost. To join the ring above, two petal beads in g, and two in p, should meet.

30 Pattern A in three colours

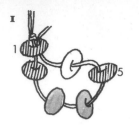

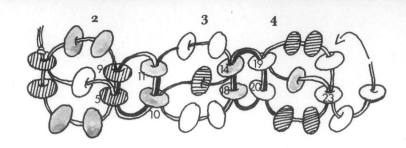

Diagram 27   Pattern A variation 2

Pattern A. Variation 2. Long three-colour necklace without fastener. Diagram 27

Materials:
   Size 10 beads in gold, black and red
   Monofilament nylon
   Size 9 needle
Key:
   r – red
   g – gold
   b – black
Pattern:
The first bead is black. Secure this and remember to count it as bead 1.

1 Pick up 2b, 2r, 1b, 1g. Pass needle up through bead 1. Pull tightly.
2 Pick up 2r, 1b. Pass needle down through bead 5. Pick up 2r and pass down through beads 9 and 5. Pull to tighten. Pass back up through beads 10 and 11.
3 Pick up 2g, 1r, 1b. Pass needle down through bead 10. Pick up 2g, 1r and pass needle up through bead 14. Tighten.
4 Pick up 2g. Pass back up through beads 18 and 14 and then back down through 19 and 20. Pick up 2b, 1g, 1r. Pass needle up through bead 19. Pick up 2b, 1g and pass down through bead 23. This completes the pattern/colour sequence. Repeat until the work is long enough to pass easily over your head and then join with the beads in the correct sequence.

The next pattern may be worked in many ways. The basic flower motif is used again, but each flower, alternate flowers, or perhaps a series of three/four, is worked in a different colour. Thus you make a 'daisy chain' of flowers. A ring, bracelet, necklace or choker would look pretty worked this way. Use as many colours as you wish, but keep the centres all one colour so that there is some link between the beads. If you choose simply to alternate the flowers, then the centres should also be alternated.

Pattern A. Variation 3. Diagram 28 Illustration 30

Materials:
   Size 10 Rocaille beads in two or many colours
   Monofilament nylon
   Size 9 needle
Key:
   m – main colour
   c – contrast or centre colour
Pattern:
Secure first bead and count as bead 1.

1 Pick up and thread 5m, 1c. Pass needle up through bead 1. Pull to tighten.
2 Pick up 3m and pass needle down through bead 5. Pull tight. Pick up 2c. Pass back down through beads 9 and 5.

Diagram 28   Pattern A variation 3

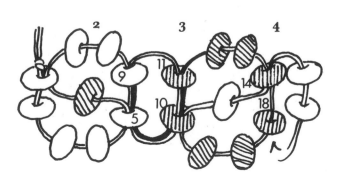

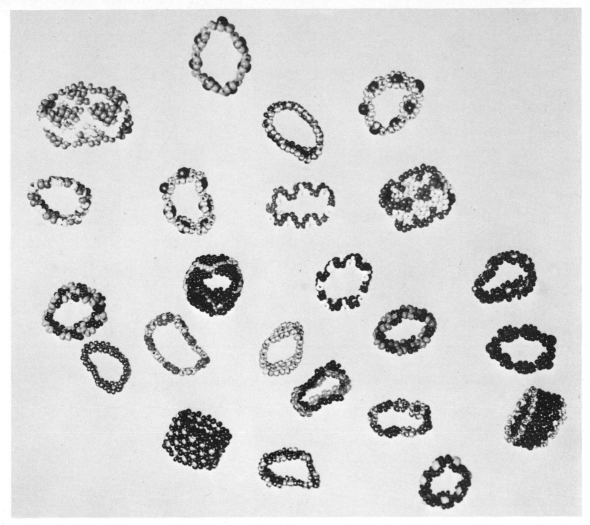

31 Rings in A, B and C patterns, including A and B with 4mm wooden beads, plain B, arrow B in two and three colours, zigzag B, two-colour A, striped B, zigzag C, striped C, and two-colour C

3 Pass back up through beads 10 and 11 and pull to tighten. Pick up 3c, 1m and pass needle down through bead 10.

4 Pick up 3c and pass up through bead 14. Pull to tighten.

This is the basic series, with each flower worked in one colour and the next flower in a different colour. Work until you have sufficient length and join as shown in diagram 23, or work the loop and bead fastener.

I have given only three of the variations possible and you will be able to find many more. Try working the pattern in only one colour because not only is this attractive but it will fix the pattern firmly in your mind, since you will have no contrast beads to guide you when you have to pass through a bead for a second time. To help you work out patterns for yourself try drawing the shapes of the beads in a similar manner to those in the diagrams, then with coloured pencils or pens fill in the ovals to find new designs. Diagram 28A shows a simple method of doing this. Some of the possible ways to use the flower pattern are shown in illustration 31.

Just as with the flowers you worked along the strings there are ways to use larger beads with this threading technique.

With some larger beads the number of petal beads must be increased, either so that you pass through three instead of two beads when the flowers are linked, or so that the outer petals are increased in number. A 4mm wooden bead or a size 4 Rocaille bead is a useful addition in the flower pattern.

The number of beads in the petals is increased so that while two remain at the sides there are now three at the top and the bottom of the flower (10 beads in all). The sequence in which

51

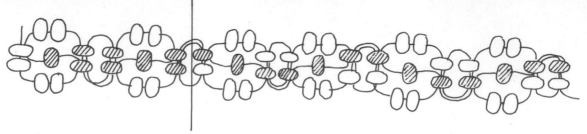

Diagram 28A   Use simplified diagrams to work out your own patterns. This diagram shows two variations

32 Pattern A choker with 4mm wooden beads, and bracelet with small wooden squares

these are picked up is now symmetrical (see diagram 29). Illustrations 32–3 provide some good examples.

Pattern A. Large centre bead. Diagram 29

Work a ring first so that you become familiar with using the increased number of beads.

Materials:
Eighty size 10 blue/grey lustre Rocaille beads
Eight 4mm purple wooden beads
Large centre bead 4mm or size 4 Rocaille
Monofilament nylon
Size 9 needle

Key:
g – blue/grey lustre
p – purple wood

Pattern:
Secure the first bead in the usual way. Count it as bead 1.

1 Pick up and thread 5g, 1p and pass needle up through bead 1.
2 Pick up 5g and pass needle down through bead 5. Pull to tighten.
3 Pick up 2g and pass needle down through beads 11 and 5 and back up through beads 12 and 13. Pull to tighten.

4 Pick up 4g, 1p. Pass needle down through bead 12. Pick up 4g. Pass needle up through bead 17. Tighten.
Continue to work the pattern in this way, and join as for the basic pattern A.

Chokers and bracelets are very pretty worked in this way, the wooden beads making them firmer and more substantial than those worked entirely with Rocaille beads. Polytwist thread will give a softer finish to chokers or longer necklaces, but if you prefer a more rigid bracelet use monofilament nylon.

Pattern A. Large centres. Bracelet 1. Illustrations 33 and 34

Materials:
Size 10 dark-blue Rocaille beads
Thirteen 4mm red wooden beads
Seven 6mm red wooden beads (one for the fastener)
Monofilament nylon
Size 9 needle

Key:
b – blue
r – red 4mm
rd – red 6mm

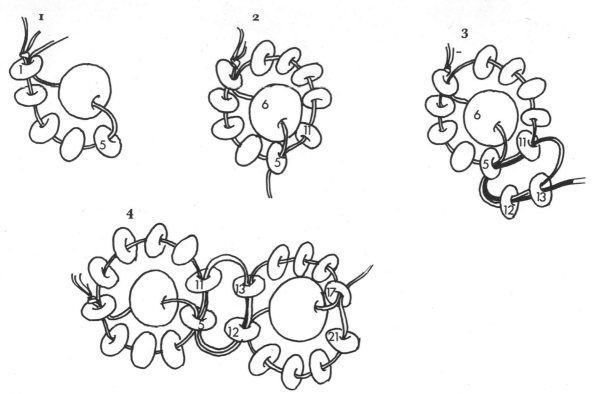

Diagram 29 Pattern A, using a 4mm wooden bead in the centre of the flowers and increasing the number of petal beads in each stage

Diagram 30 Loop for bracelet using sixteen size 10 beads

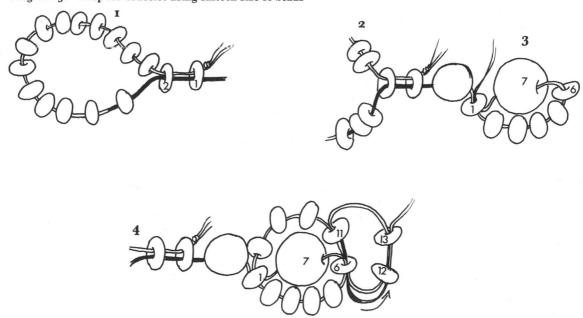

53

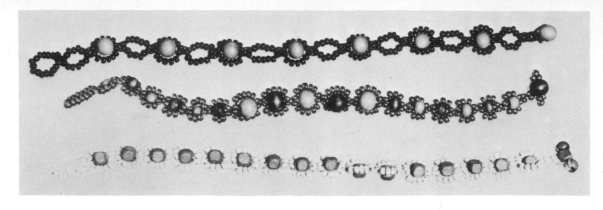

33 **Pattern A bracelets with several sizes of wooden beads and different approaches**

Ten beads make the petals for the flowers with 4mm centres, 14 beads for the 6mm.

The construction of the loop is slightly different.

The loop. Diagram 30

1 Pick up and thread 16b. Pass the needle down through beads 2 and 1.
2 Pick up 1r.
Pattern:
3 Pick up 6b, 1r. Pass needle up through first of six beads.
4 Pick up 4b and pass down through bead 6. Pick up 2b and pass back down beads 11 and up 6, up beads 12 and 13. Pull tight. Repeat three more times. After the first flower the petal sequence becomes 4 and 4 as for the ring.
5 Pick up 6b, 1rd. Pass needle down through bead 45. Pick up 6b and pass needle up through bead 52. Pull tight. Pick up 2b and pass needle up through beads 59 and 52 and down beads 60 and 61. Repeat this twice more then repeat the smaller sequence again five times. Repeat the three larger flowers, then four small and make fastener. Refer to illustration 34.

Alternate large and small wooden beads would also be attractive. Bracelet 3 in illustration 34 was worked with pearl-lustre Rocaille beads and turquoise wood-grained 6mm beads. The fastening loop was worked as shown in diagram 24 and the bead to fasten was given 'ears'. The bracelet in the centre is worked with size 7 Rocaille beads and the number of beads around the large beads

adjusted accordingly. Fourteen beads are required for the loop, three of these forming the join for the side petals of the first flower (see diagram 31).

Pattern A. Large flowers linked with ovals. Diagram 32. Illustration 34

Materials:
    Size 7 black Rocaille beads
    Size 8mm shiny purple wooden beads
    Long ovals in matt purple (wood)
    Monofilament nylon
    Size 9 needle
Key:
    b – black

Diagram 31   Loop beginning oval sequence

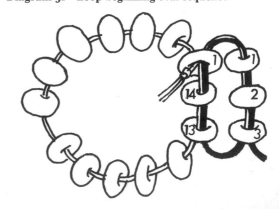

p – purple 8mm
o – purple ovals

Pattern:

Make loop according to diagram 31. First petals 1, 2 and 3 are shown with the loop.

1 Pick up 5b, 1p and pass needle up through bead 1 as diagram shows. Pick up 6b pass needle down through bead 8. Pull tight.

Continue to make flowers this way, picking up 5b, 1p, 6b until you have three flowers.

2 Work three connecting beads as if making a flower, but instead of 5b pick up 10 3b 10 and pass needle up through the first three b of the series through the oval and down the second three b; at this point work another flower. Repeat stage 2. Work three flowers and attach the fastening bead.

You can work several series of oval beads if you wish.

The pattern may be worked with a size 4 Rocaille bead in the centre of the flowers. The number of beads used for this can be varied, though the technique used for the 4mm beads is also suitable.

However, the Rocaille beads are not spherical like the wooden beads but much more ovoid in shape, and look best if there are three petal beads on each side (12 beads in all).

Pattern A. Size 4 Rocaille bead centres. Ring. Diagram 33

Materials:

Size 10 red Rocaille beads
Size 4 black Rocaille beads
Monofilament nylon
Size 9 needle

Key:

r – red
b – black

Pattern:

Secure first bead and count as bead 1.

1 Pick up and thread 7r, 1b and pass needle up through bead 1.

2 Pick up 5b and pass needle down through bead 7. Pull thread tight.

Diagram 32   Oval sequence using 8mm and size 7 beads

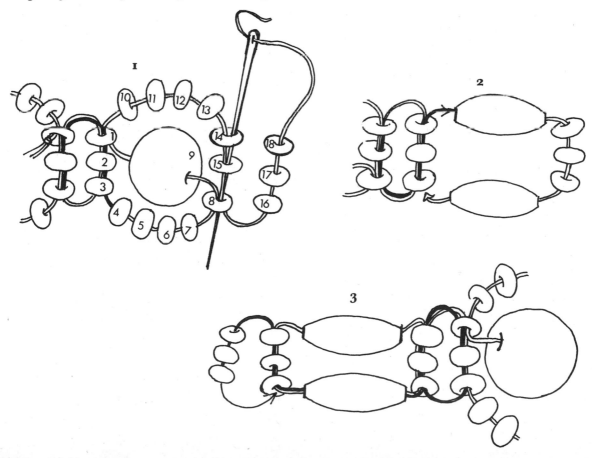

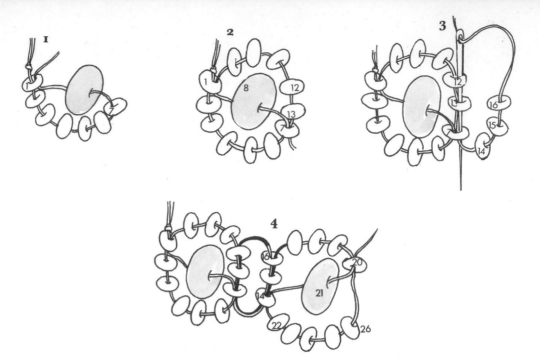

Diagram 33 Pattern A using size 4 Rocaille bead centres

3 Pick up 3b. Pass needle down through beads 12, 13, 7. Pull tight and pass needle up beads 14, 15, 16. Pull tight.

4 Pick up 5b, 1b and pass needle down through bead 14. Pull tight. Pick up 4r. Pass needle up through bead 20.

Repeat from stage 3. Join into ring and fasten off thread. The join is made exactly as for basic pattern A but two sets of three petals are linked.

This variation of pattern A is as versatile as the others. Many colours, different centres, and patterns very similar to those given for size 10 beads only, are all possible developments once the technique is mastered.

The chokers in illustration 35 are similar to those in Section One which used a single-centre flower. However, these use the threading method in that there are several flowers – some of different sizes linked together with connecting beads. Size 4mm, 6mm and 8mm are used, either to narrow then widen and narrow again the centre of the choker where the pattern is concentrated, or in a series of the same size.

Two of the illustrated chokers have beads from old 'pearl' necklaces in the centre of the flowers.

If you want to make one of these chokers you should make a string with the loop constructed in the appropriate manner (see Section One). Thread about 10–15cm of beads, check length, and then begin the threaded centre pattern by making one flower in the manner used in Section One (p. 35). The successive flowers are constructed using the techniques in this section.

Pattern A. Choker with centre pattern. Diagram 34

Materials:
 Size 10 black Rocaille beads
 4mm yellow wooden beads
 8mm yellow wooden bead
 6mm black wooden bead for fastener
 Black Polytwist thread
 Size 9 needle
 Beeswax

Key:
 b – black
 y – 4mm wooden beads
 yl – 8mm wooden bead

Pattern:
Make a fastening loop as described in Section One (p. 22) and thread 50b, adjusting neck measurement if more than 31cm (12½in).

1 Pick up 6b, 1y and pass needle up through first bead of series of six. Pick up 4b and pass needle down through beads 6 and 5 of first series. Pull tight.

2 Pick up 2b and pass needle down through beads 6 and 5 of flower. Pass needle up through beads 12 and 13. Pull tight and continue pattern using a series of four Rocaille, one

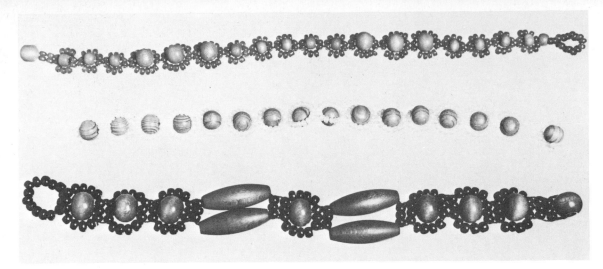

34 Pattern A – more fastenings and bracelet with ovals

35 Pattern A flower chokers using several techniques

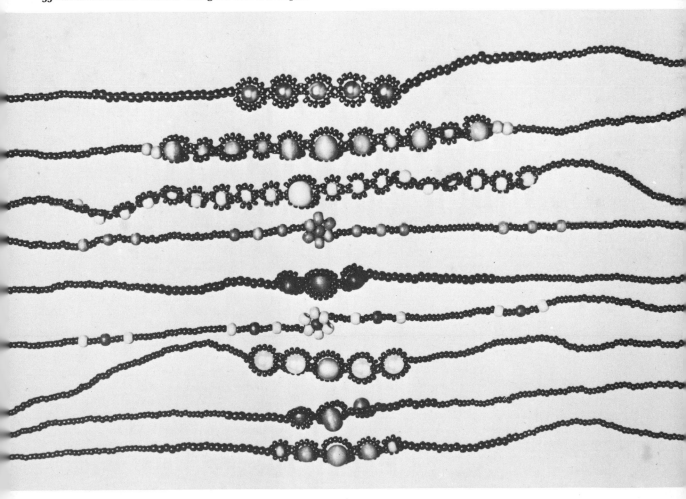

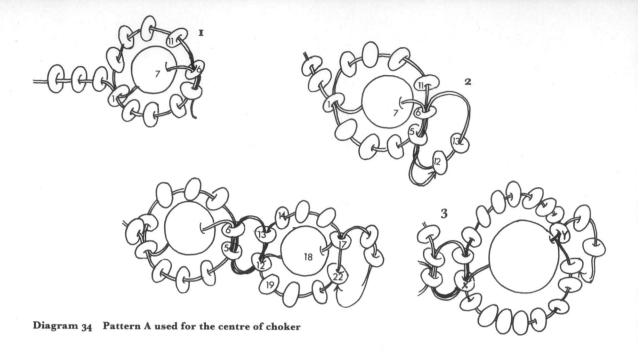

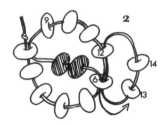

Diagram 34   Pattern A used for the centre of choker

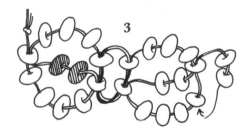

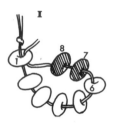

Diagram 35   Pattern A

4mm, four Rocaille, until you have nine flowers with 4mm centres.

3 Pick up 8b, 1yl and pass needle down through bead x as shown in diagram 34. Pull tight and pick up 8b. Pass up through bead marked y on diagram. Repeat nine small flowers. Then string 50b; attach 6mm bead to fasten and finish off the choker as for the chokers in Section One (p. 23).

The last pattern used only two sizes of wooden bead – you could try using several, or even just one. The chokers in illustration 36 may give you some ideas and inspire you to design more for yourself.

Some of the flowers in the inner necklace in illustration 36 have two beads in the centre (see diagram 35). The beads surrounding this centre must be increased just as they are increased for the larger bead centres. This is an attractive way of varying the centres of pattern A.

Pattern A. Choker with double centre. Diagrams 35 and 36

Materials:
    Size 10 Rocaille beads in two colours
    Monofilament nylon
    Size 9 needle
Key:
    m – main colour
    c – centre or contrast beads
Pattern:
Make a loop and join two m beads to act as beads 1 and 2 (see diagram 36).

1 Pick up 4m, 2c and pass needle up through bead 1. Pull tight and pick up 4m. Pass needle down through bead 6 as shown.
2 Pick up 2m and pass needle down through beads 12 and 6. Tighten and pass back up through beads 13 and 14.
3 Continue until the work is long enough to fit,

then attach 6mm fastening bead and finish the choker.

Vary this design in the same manner as the other pattern A variations, making rings, bracelets, chokers, long necklaces, and a variety of sequences and colours with the beads.

Making a double centre with the larger beads (4mm and size 4 Rocaille), is not very successful as the beads are simply too big.

All these variations, and plain pattern A, may be worked to any length you require, but it will be necessary at some point to join a new working thread as shown in diagram 37. The pattern is pattern A in its simplest form; the method is, however, used for all work. With the old thread left in the needle make sure that at least 15cm (6in) remains. Join the new thread several flowers back in the work. Make slip knots as you work towards the end of the old thread. When that point is reached work a few flowers with the new thread, pick up the old thread and work forwards making slip knots over the new thread. You may take the old thread back into

the work if you prefer, so that it is joined to itself and the new thread. Trim old thread and continue the work with the new one.

Very long strips of flowers make excellent braids when sewn to clothing and look most attractive; they also make unusual hatbands, hairbands and, in ring form, are suitable for scarves or rings. Not only are they pretty accessories but around the home they can give new life to lampshades and window blinds. You will think of many ways to use the techniques when you have mastered them all.

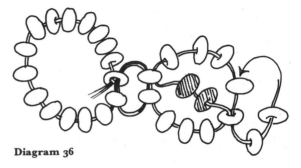

Diagram 36

Diagram 37   Joining a new thread. The example shows Pattern A, but the method applies to all patterns

1

2

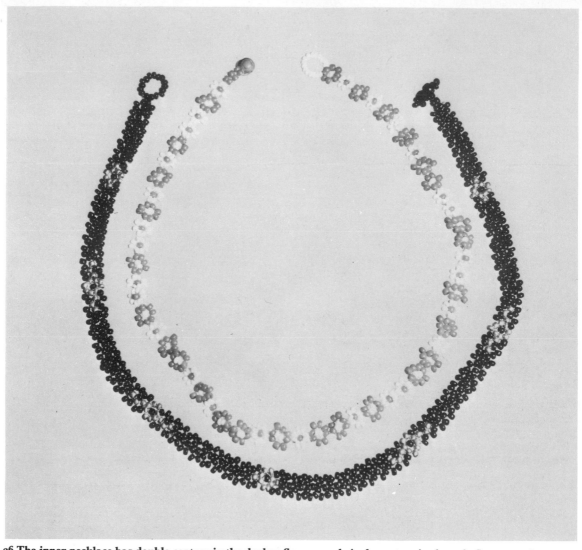

36 The inner necklace has double centres in the darker flowers and single centres in the pale flowers, using pattern A. The outer necklace has the 'flowers' variation of pattern B

37 Arrow pattern B using three, two, and three colours

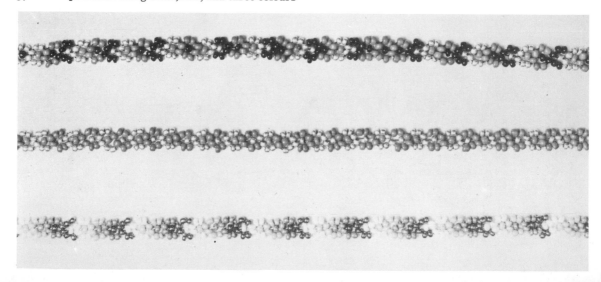

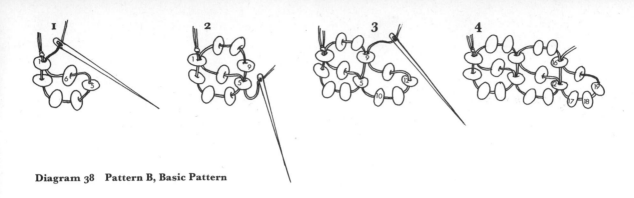

Diagram 38   Pattern B, Basic Pattern

Pattern B

This is similar to pattern A, but the connecting beads which in A make each flower a separate unit, are missing. Each flower is worked as part of the next. This makes the pattern even more versatile than the first. The necklaces in illustration 37 are all pattern B.

All materials used are the same as for pattern A.

Basic pattern B. Diagram 38

In order to become familiar with the pattern you should attempt this in one colour only. You should now be adept at handling the beads and holding the work and this experience will allow you to see which bead you must pass through for a second time. The following pattern is for a ring.

Materials:
    Eighty-four size 10 black Rocaille beads
    Monofilament nylon thread
    Size 9 needles
Pattern:
A greater number of flowers (approximately 11) are needed to fit your finger because there are no connecting beads as there are in A.

The first bead is attached in the usual way and counted as bead 1.

1 Pick up and thread six beads and pass the needle and thread up through the first bead. Pull the thread to tighten it.
2 Pick up three beads and pass the needle down through bead 5.
3 Pick up four beads, pass the needle up through bead 9 and pull thread to tighten.
4 Pick up three beads and pass needle down through bead 12. The pattern continues in this manner until the ring is long enough.
Remember the sequence is, pick up four, pick up three, each time.

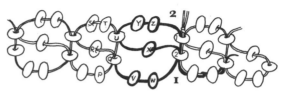

Diagram 39   Join, Pattern B

The join. Diagram 39

The join for this ring is quite different to the join for A.
Bend the ring around your finger as for A.
1 Pick up beads V and W. Pass needle up through bead 2.
2 Pick up bead X (centre bead). Pass needle up through bead U. Pick up beads Y and Z. Pass the needle down through beads 1 and 2. Pull the pattern together and work around the joining sequence again if it is possible.
Work the thread back into the pattern and make several slip knots as you do so. Cut off the ends of thread. If there is a tail of thread at the start work this, too, into the ring. The join is the same for all the variations of pattern B, only the sequence of the colours varies according to the design used.
Do not be alarmed if the pattern seems too small after eleven flowers – the join will increase the circumference and the pattern *does*, in any case, have a slight stretch. However, you will need to experiment with the numbers of flowers needed to fit your own fingers.

Pattern B. Using two colours. Diagram 38

Materials:
    Size 10 gold and brown Rocaille beads
    Monofilament thread
    Size 9 needle

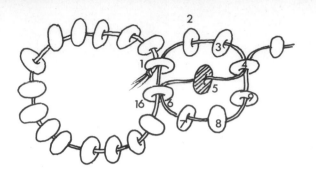

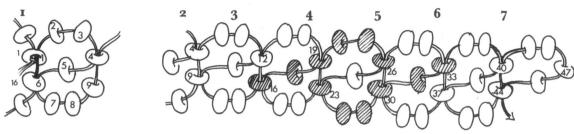

Diagram 40   Loop for Pattern B. The first flower can be made as part of the loop, or made as for Pattern A. Use for any of the chokers or bracelets, may also be used for A. Count beads 1 and 16 as beads 1 and 2.

Diagram 41   Pattern B, Variation 1

Key:
  g – gold
  b – brown
Pattern:
The contrast bead is the centre bead.
Attach first bead as usual, and count as bead 1 of pattern.
1 Pick up 5g, 1b and pass needle up through bead 1.
2 Pick up 3g. Pass needle down through bead 5 and pull tight.
3 Pick up 3g, 1b and pass needle up through bead 9. Pick up 3g and pass needle down through bead 12. Continue and join as before but use a brown bead for bead X.

The following choker has a series of flowers with 'leaves' spaced along its length. It is necessary to make a loop fastener before commencing the pattern (see diagram 40). The loop consists of 16 size 10 beads as for the majority of the chokers. Beads 1 and 16 of the loop form the beads 1 and 6 of the first flower.

Pattern B variation 1. Flowered choker. Diagram 41

Materials:
  Size 10 black and gold Rocaille beads
  One 6mm black wooden bead for fastener
  Monofilament nylon
  Size 9 needle

Key:
  g – gold
  b – black
Remember to measure the work against your neck at intervals as it progresses.
Pattern:
Make the loop as shown in diagram 40. Count beads 1 and 16 as beads 1 and 6.
1 Pick up 4b and pass needle down through bead 6.
2 Pick up 3b and pass up through bead 4. Tighten thread.
3 Pick up 4b and pass needle down through bead 9. Pick up 2b, 1g. Pass needle up through bead 12. Pull thread to tighten.
4 Pick up 2b, 2g and pass down through bead 16. Pick up 2b, 1g and pass up through bead 19. Pull tight.
5 Pick up 3g, 1b and pass down through bead 23. Pick up 3g and pass up through bead 26.
6 Pick up 2b, 2g and pass needle down through bead 30. Pull tight. Pick up 3b and pass up through bead 33.
7 Pick up 4b and pass down through bead 37. Pick up 3b and pass up through bead 40. Tighten the work. This completes the leafed-flower motif.
  You can repeat this as often as you wish. Several plain black pattern units are advisable so that the flower and leaves are clear. When you finish the length, make sure that you end with two complete plain flowers then attach the bead fastener.

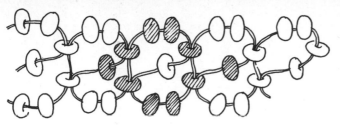

Diagram 42

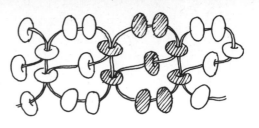

Diagram 43

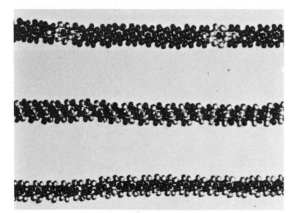

38 Pattern B variations: flowers, diagonal, centre stripe

This way the pattern will remain evenly spaced along the length. If you decide to make a matching ring in this pattern you should work it so that the flower comes at the centre front – one flower only. This pattern may be varied in a number of ways according to preference. The flowers may be closer so that the leaves touch, spaces may be greater, or there could be one central flower only on a choker as with the ring.

A modified flower with only one bead for the leaf is shown in diagram 42, and diagram 43 shows the flower without any leaves at all (see illustration 38). As with pattern A you may use a 4mm wooden bead or a size 4 Rocaille bead in the centre of the flowers. The following pattern is for a ring, but any of the articles made using the other patterns and variations are suitable.

Pattern B. Wooden bead centre. Diagram 44

Materials:
   Ninety size 10 beads in gunmetal
   Eleven 4mm wooden beads in plum
   Monofilament nylon
   Size 9 needle

Key:
   g – gunmetal
   p – plum
Pattern:
Pick up and secure first bead and count as bead 1.
1 Pick up and thread 5g, 1p and pass needle up through first bead. Pull tight.
2 Pick up 5g and pass needle down through bead 5. Pull tight.
3 Pick up 4g, 1p and pass needle up through bead 11.
4 Pick up 4g and pass needle down through bead 15.
   Continue working in this way until the ring will fit your finger when the final joining sequence is picked up. The join is worked in the same way as the normal join for B, but remember to pick up three beads for the bottom, a wooden bead for the centre, and three beads for the top. See diagram 45 and illustration 33, bracelet 2.
   The most attractive of the variations of pattern B is that known as the arrow pattern. This can be worked in a variety of ways and lends itself to the use of several colours (see illustrations 37 and 39). This is a typical North American Indian pattern and is as attractive with very bright colours as with more subtle ones. Once you have learned the sequence of the beads which make up the arrow shape you will find that this is an excellent pattern on which to base your own experiments.
   The first example of this pattern uses just two colours. Diagrams are given for several variations – begin by following diagram 46 which is the straightforward two-colour arrow pattern and also shows how to make the join.

Pattern B. Arrow. Two colours. Diagram 46

Materials:
   Size 10 beads in pearl and gunmetal
   Monofilament nylon
   Size 9 needle

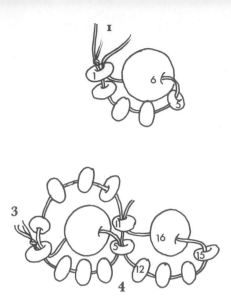

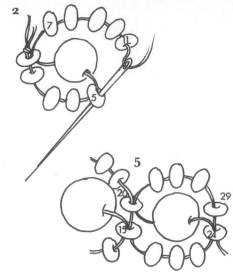

Diagram 44   Pattern B, wooden centre bead

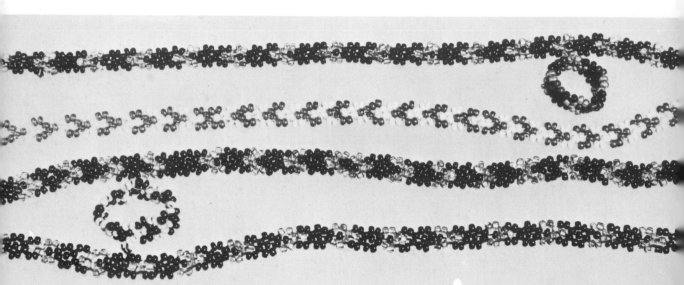

39a Chokers and rings in B arrow pattern

Key:
   p – pearl
   g – gunmetal

Pattern:

Pick up and secure first bead and count as bead 1.

1 Pick up 4g, 2p and pass needle up through bead 1.

2 Pick up 2g, 1p and pass needle down through bead 5.

3 Pick up 2p, 2g and pass needle up through bead 9. Pull tight.

4 Pick up 2p, 1g and pass needle down through bead 12.

Diagram 45   Joining with a 4mm wooden bead centre (or a size 4 Rocaille)

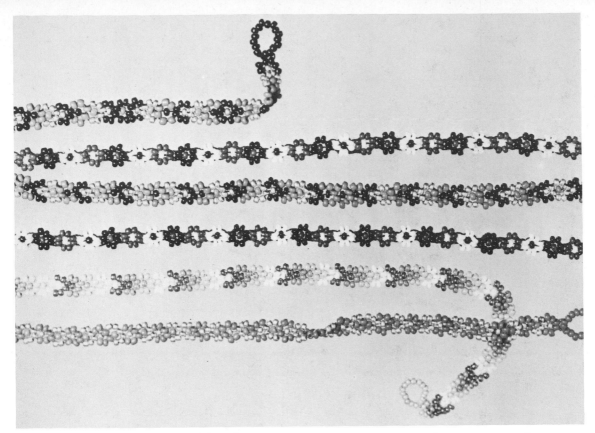

39b Chokers in A and B patterns with loop fasteners

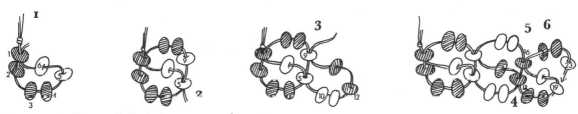

Diagram 46   Pattern B, Basic Arrow, two colours

5 Pick up 2g, 2p and pass needle up through
  bead 16.

6 Pick up 2g, 1p and pass down through bead 19.
  Pull tight. This sequence continues until the
  end of the work.

  When first learning a pattern it is a good idea
to make something that will require a join, say
a ring or a very long necklace. This way you will
learn pattern and joining sequence from the
beginning. Diagram 46 shows the join as well as
the arrow pattern itself.

The join. Diagram 46

The work began with gunmetal beads so the
join would be worked as follows.

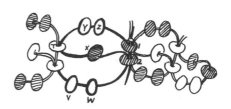

Joining Arrow

  Pick up beads V, W. Pass needle up through
bead 2. Pick up bead X (gunmetal) and pass up
through bead T. Pick up beads Y, Z, and pass
down through beads 1 and 2. Work thread back

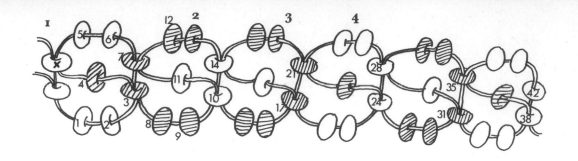

Diagram 47   Reversing the Arrow, showing detail of the movement to make the reverse

into beads making slip knots along the original working threads as you do so.

Once this basic sequence has been mastered it is easy to vary the arrow pattern. It always begins 4, 2. Pass through one bead. 2, 1. Pass through fifth bead. From there onwards the variations can start. The sequence of beads and colours following the 4, 2, 2, 1 is always 2, 2, 2, 1, until the work is joined, or a fastener attached.

Loops, fastening beads, or other fasteners are attached as for the other patterns. Variations as follows may be worked.

Pattern B. Arrow. Reversing the arrows at the centre. Diagrams 47 and 48

Materials:
  Size 10 black and gold beads
  Monofilament nylon
  Size 9 needle
Key:
  b – black
  g – gold
Pattern:
Secure first bead and count as bead 1.
Pattern is worked as for the two-colour arrow until you reach a halfway point in the work.

Reversing the pattern: the diagrams show a sequence of beads, starting with bead 1 for the reverse.

1 Pick up beads 1, 2, (b), 3, 4 (g). Pass up and through bead X. Pick up 5, 6, 7 (2g, 1b). Pass down through bead 3.

2 Pick up 8, 9 (2b); 10, 11 (2g). Pass up through bead 7. Pick up 12, 13 (2b); 14 (1g). Pass down through bead 10.

3 Pick up 15, 16, 17 (3b); 18 (1g). Pass up through bead 14. Pick up 19, 20, 21 (3b). Pass down through bead 17.

4 Pick up 22, 23, 24 (3g); 25 (1b). Pass up through bead 21. Pick up 26, 27, 28 (3g). Pass down through bead 24. The reversal is complete, and the sequence continues, 3, 1, 3, until you finish the work, or reverse again (see diagram 48). Doing this will bring you back to the pattern with which you began. The dark–light choker in illustration 39 shows this reversing clearly.

You could try reversing the design several times along the work. Each time this is done two motifs of the same colour appear, so it is a good idea either to keep these points the same colour or, if the work is to be very long, to alternate them (diagram 48).

Now you have learned to work two of the threading patterns, it is up to you to develop and

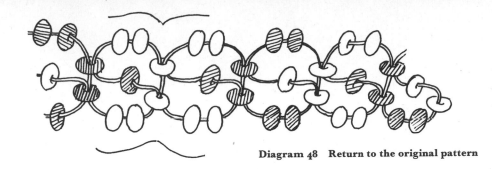

Diagram 48   Return to the original pattern

enjoy them. Combinations of A and B work well, as do alternate motifs of large wooden centres and size 10 centres (see bracelet in illustration 33). You might try several A flowers, then several B's. Use wooden beads in A, and not in B: the variations are almost endless.

Diagrams 49–55 show three-colour and two-colour patterns using B. One of these is a three-colour arrow pattern. There are several stripes and zigzag patterns and almost certainly you will find others of your own which are not shown here.

The following is the pattern for a three-colour diagonal stripe using pattern B. For the other patterns simply follow the diagrams.

Pattern B. Three-colour diagonal stripe. Diagram 49

Materials :
   Size 10 dark-blue, pale-blue and pearl beads
   Monofilament nylon
   Size 9 needle
Key :
   db – dark blue
   pb – pale blue
   p – pearl
Pattern :
Secure the first bead (p) and count as 1 in pattern.
1 Pick up and thread 2p, 1db, 2pb, 1db. Pass needle up through bead 1.
2 Pick up 1p, 1bd, 1pb and pass needle down through bead 5. Pull tight.
3 Pick up 1p, 2db, 1p and pass needle up through bead 9. Pull tight.
4 Pick up 1pb, 1p, 1db and pass needle down through bead 12. Tighten.

Diagram 49   Pattern B variations, a three-colour diagonal stripe

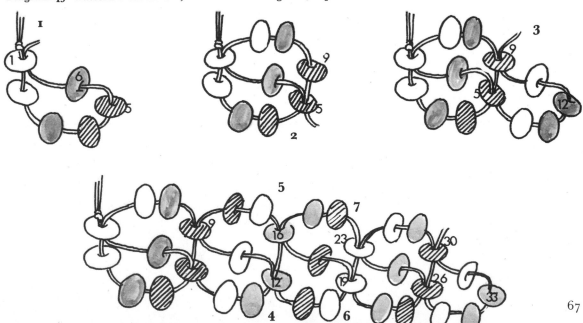

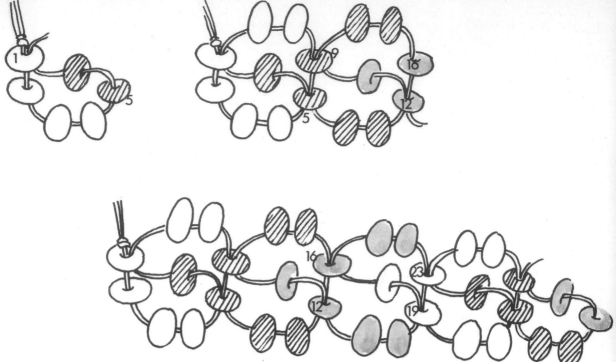

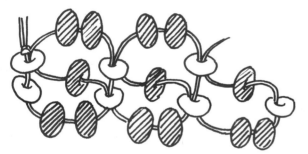

Diagram 50   Pattern B Arrow in three colours

Diagram 51   Pattern B variation in two colours

Diagram 52   Pattern B, narrow zigzag

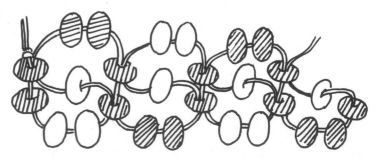

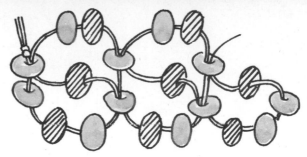

Diagram 53   Pattern B, two-colour stripe

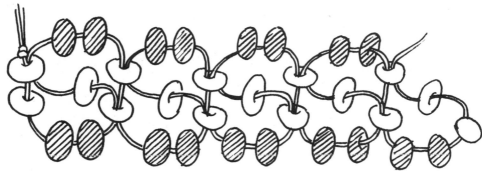

Diagram 54   Pattern B, centre stripe

Diagram 55   Pattern B, wide zigzag

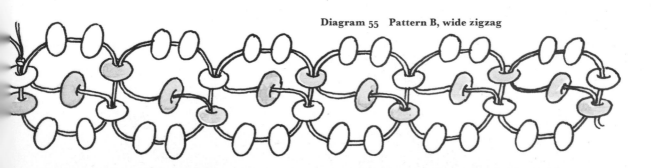

40 Rocaille bead purse using expanded C pattern

5 Pick up 1pb, 2p, 1pb and pass needle up through bead 16. Pull tight.
6 Pick up 1db, 1pb, 1p and pass down through bead 19. Pull tight.
7 Pick up 1db, 2pb 1db and pass up through bead 23. Pull tight.
Proceed from stage 2 of pattern and work until you have sufficient length for a ring.

By following the diagrams you should, once the pattern itself is easy for you to work, be able to carry out any of the colour sequences with ease (see diagrams 50–55).

Pattern C

This pattern forms a wider band of beads than A and B, and is much more complex in construction; it does, however, offer much more scope to the beadworker since in certain forms it may be extended to make a variety of large items. It is the basis for collars, mats, and for the purse in illustration 40. Once pattern C is mastered you will find endless uses for it. Initially it is a complicated pattern and when you first begin to work it the beads seem to form a meaningless tangle. It is important to hold the work firmly between the fingers and thumb of the left hand, and to roll the beads between those fingers in order to keep the tension even along the work. Once a few rows have been worked, the beads begin to fall into a definite pattern; by then you will have become used to holding the work and will be able to see quite clearly through which bead you must pass the needle for a second time.

Once you have worked this and are familiar with pattern C, you should attempt it in one colour only. As with patterns A and B, this is a good aid to learning the pattern movements and

the beads through which the needle passes for a second time, without relying on colours for reference. Eventually, as the work becomes more familiar and you are working with an even tension, you will see that those beads which are passed through twice protrude more than the others. Illustration 30 shows several rings in pattern C. You will notice that several colours and designs are possible, and that the wider band makes a very attractive finger or scarf ring.

In order to make the pattern easier for you two colours are used in the first example and the contrast (light-coloured) beads are those which are picked up twice. The first example of C is a ring. I have used rings throughout with the threading patterns, because they provide an ideal opportunity to learn how to join up the work so that the pattern is in sequence and the join does not show. The joining sequence is the same in each pattern C example, but the colour sequence depends on the design worked. The beads passed through twice remain the same.

Pattern C. A ring in two colours. Diagram 56

Materials:
  Size 10 beads in black and pearl
  Monofilament nylon
  Size 9 or 10 needle
Key:
  b – black
  p – pearl
Pattern:
Make sure you have plenty of thread in the needle. Secure first bead as for other patterns and count as 1 in pattern instructions.
1/2 Pick up and thread 1b, 1p, 1b, 1p, 1b, 1p, 1b, 2p, 1b, 1p. Pass needle up through bead 5.
3 Hold the work firmly between finger and thumb so that it will not twist out of shape. Pick up 1p, 1b, 1p and pass needle up through bead 1. Hold firmly and pull thread to tighten.
4 Pick up 2p, 1b, 1p and pass needle down through bead 13. Pull tight.
5 Pick up 1p, 1b, 1p and pass down through bead 10. All beads through which the needle passes twice are contrast or b beads.
6 Pick up 2p, 1b, 1p and pass up through bead 20. Pull tight.
7 Pick up 1p, 1b, 1p and pass up through bead 17. Pull tight and continue pattern from stage 4, making sure that you keep the

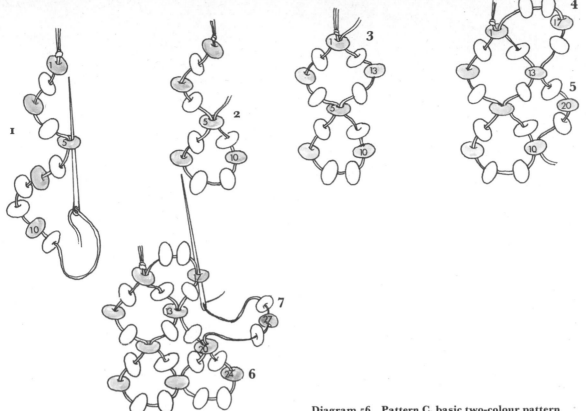

tension of the work even and that the beads passed through a second time are b beads. The pattern should have begun to form by the time you reach stages 5 and 6 of the diagrams and the contrast beads should protrude. This pattern has a certain amount of built-in stretch due to the diamond formation. When you have enough length to join the work (that is, when the work fits your finger) you should bend it round your index finger so that you can see exactly how the join is made. To begin the join, the start (first bead) should be at the opposite side of the work to the working thread.

The join. Diagram 57

Bring the work around the finger so that the two ends are almost touching. Pick up 2p and pass needle up through bead 7. Pull tight. Pick up bead V (b) and pass up through bead R. Pick up bead W (p) and pass through bead 3. Pick up bead X and pass up through bead O. Pick up beads Y and Z and pass down through bead 1. Work into the ring making slip knots to secure the thread then trim tail and working thread close to the work. All the beads in the join are main-colour beads.

Diagram 56   Pattern C, basic two-colour pattern

You can use this pattern for bracelets and chokers as with A and B, and it is also ideally suited for a headband to be worn Indian fashion around the forehead. It is not possible, however, to make a loop at the start, as it is with A and B, so this has to be attached at the end when the work is complete but before the working thread is cut off (see diagram 58). The bead and stem are attached with a new working thread.

Fasteners C. Diagram 59

If two loops are used and the corresponding number of fastening beads attached at the other end of the work, a new thread is used and

Diagram 57   Join for Pattern C, and fastening off thread

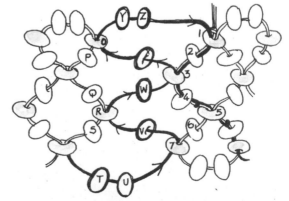

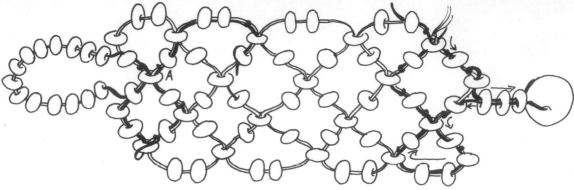

Diagram 58   Pattern C fastener, using a single bead and loop

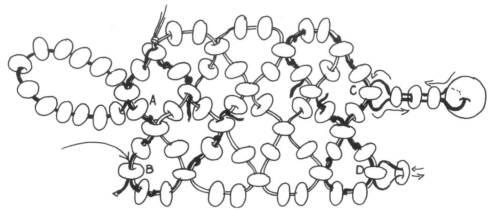

Diagram 59   Pattern C double fastener

attached at a point back in the pattern. This thread is secured by slip knots between the beads as it is worked to point A in the diagram. Point A is bead 3. Take thread down through this bead and pick up 12 size 10 beads. Work back into bead 3 and down the pattern making slip knots until point B is reached. Point B is bead 7. Make another loop using 12 beads and work thread into beads making slip knots. Secure and cut off.

To make the bead fastenings, attach new thread as for the loop and work to point C. Take needle down through this bead and pick up three size 10 beads and one 6mm wood bead. Take needle back through three size 10 beads as shown and pass through point C again. Work down to point D making slip knots as shown and make another fastener. Take thread back into the work and fasten off making slip knots between beads as you go. Cut off excess thread. This method should be used for most items made with pattern C, unless an alternative method is given.

The two-colour ring is perhaps the simplest pattern since the contrast beads form an easy guide to which beads have to be passed through twice. Other designs for this pattern also have some kind of reminder for the uncertain and inexperienced beader. In the next pattern the sequence of beads is less regular and so the diagram should be followed initially. The design is much more striking than that of the first ring, and it forms a good introduction to the three-colour pattern which follows. (See illustration 41.)

In the following pattern a ring is used as an example once again so that the joining sequence may be learned. Two colours are used for the pattern.

Pattern C. Zigzag. Two colours. Diagram 60

Materials:
    Size 10 beads in red and black
    Monofilament nylon
    Size 9 needle (use size 10 if the beads are small

with tiny holes, because at the point where the ring is joined the thread passes more than three times through one of the beads and if this is broken the whole pattern is spoiled)

Key:
  r – red
  b – black

Pattern:

Secure first bead and count it as 1.

1 Pick up and thread 2b, 3r, 4b, 2r (11 beads in all). Pass needle up through bead 5 and pull tight. Keep hold of the beads so that they do not twist out of shape – if the wrong beads are picked up at this point the pattern will not join properly.

2 Pick up 3b and pass needle up through bead 1, keeping hold of the work so that it stays in the position shown in part 2 of the diagram.

3 Pick up 4b and pass needle down through bead 13. Pull thread to tighten.

4 Pick up 1b, 2r and pass needle down through bead 10. At this point the work will not appear to form any particular pattern. The shape of the red beads should now look rather like a reversed tick.

5 Pick up 4b and pass the needle up through bead 20, pulling the thread to tighten; this draws out the base of the tick and the zigzag begins to take shape.

6 Pick up 2r, 1b and pass needle up through bead 17.

7 Pick up 2b, 2r and pass down through bead 27. Pull tight. The first part of the zigzag shape should now be completed.

8 Pick up 3b. Pass needle down through bead 24 and pull tight.

9 Pick up 4b and pass needle up through bead 34 and pull tight.

10 Pick up 1b, 2r and pass the needle up through bead 31.

11 Pick up 4b and pass down through bead 41.

12 Pick up 2r, 1b and pass down through bead 38, pulling the thread tight.

13 Pick up 2b, 2r and pass up through bead 48. Pull tight. The first complete zigzag sequence should now be clear.

14 Pick up 3b and pass up through bead 45.

15 Pick up 4b and pass down through bead 55. Pull tight.

16 Pick up 1b, 2r and pass down through bead 52.

41 Pattern C: wide C choker in three colours, wide C bracelet, zigzag C, three-row zigzag in wide basic C pattern

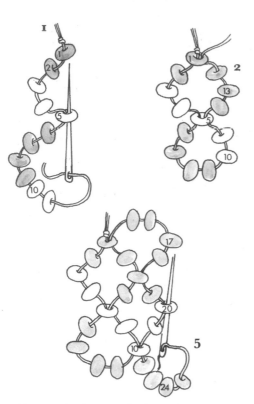

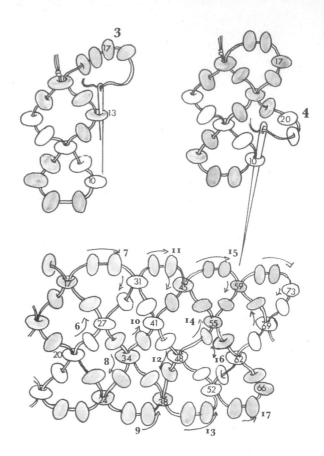

Diagram 60   Pattern C, zigzag in two colours

17 Pick up 4b and pass up through bead 62. Pull tight.

The work is repeated from stage 6 until there is enough length to fit the finger. The zigzag must join accurately for the pattern to be complete around the circle of the ring. The first bead must be at the opposite side of the work to the working thread. A certain sequence of beads is required for the join so that the zigzag is completed. (See diagram 57 for basic two-colour C join, but refer to text for colour sequence.)

Joining the zigzag C

Pick up 2b and pass needle up through bead 7 as shown in diagram 57 for joining first C pattern. Pull tight. Pick up beads V and pass up through bead R as shown. Pull tight. Pick up bead W and pass needle up through bead 3. Pick up X (r) which is part of pattern and pass up through bead O. Pick up 2b and pass down through bead 1. Work back into pattern making slip knots and

cut thread. Work in the tail of the thread at the start and snip off ends.

Anything made with this pattern should be joined in this manner, unless of course you intend to use a loop and bead fastener, in which case the method shown in diagram 59 should be used.

Joining a new thread

Join a new thread by starting several rows back in the work. Leave the old thread in the needle and thread a new needle for the new working thread. Make a slip knot and work into pattern towards the end of the old thread; make slip knots between beads at intervals as you go. Work several rows of pattern with the new thread and then, with the old thread, work into the newly-worked patterns making several slip knots across all the threads at intervals.

The ends of the old and the new thread should be cut off very close to the work.

Pattern C has many variations. It is not possible to include wooden beads because they are too big and the pattern does not form correctly if they are included among the small beads, but a floral pattern may be worked and the previous pattern is part of this.

Pattern C. Floral. Three colours. Diagram 61

Materials:

Size 10 beads in brown, gold and pink
Monofilament nylon (approximately 1·5m)
Size 9 or 10 needle

Key:

b – brown
g – gold
p – pink

Pattern:

The numbers in the pattern correspond to those in diagram 61. Secure first bead and count as bead 1 in the instructions.

1 Pick up 2b, 3g, 4b, 2g and pass up through bead 5.
2 Pick up 3p and pass needle up through bead 1. Hold to prevent twisting and pick up 3b, 1p. Pass needle down through bead 13.
3 Pick up 1p, 2g and pass down through bead 10. Pull tight.
4 Pick up 4b. Pass up through bead 20. Pull tight.
5 Pick up 2g, 1b. Pass up through bead 17.
6 Pick up 2b, 2g. Pass down through bead 27.
7 Pick up 3p and pass down through bead 24. Pull tight. Pick up 3b, 1p and pass up through bead 34. Tighten the work.
8 Pick up 1p, 2g and pass up through bead 31. Tighten.

The pattern with flowers set in the apex of each zigzag should now be clear. Following the previous diagrams should now be sufficient if you remember to include the beads which make up the flowers at the right places.

The join. Diagram 57

Pick up 2b and pass up through bead 7. Pull tight. Pick up bead V (p) and pass up through bead R as shown. Pick up bead W (p) and pass up through bead 3. Pick up X (b) and pass though bead O. Pick up 2b and pass down through bead 1. Complete the work by passing into the work making slip knots between the beads.

It is a simple matter, once you are able to work both this and the previous pattern, to make a choker or ring without the zigzag, so that you have a plain band with flowers along its length. Simply follow pattern and diagram 61 but ignore the g beads – that is, replace the zigzag beads with the main colour.

Once you have more experience of using this particular variation of C you could perhaps try working C with flowers of several different colours, or perhaps petals and centres of flowers in several colours. You only need to remember which beads in the pattern sequence are flower-petal beads, and which belong to the background.

When you join up this pattern it is still necessary to have the start of the work at the opposite side to the working thread, and half a flower should be complete when you start the join. This is completed as part of the joining sequence. For a bracelet or choker, loops and fastening beads should be made. Diagram 62 shows the pattern with diagonal stripes in three colours (this could of course be reduced to two if you feel that three are too complicated to begin with).

Diagram 61   Pattern C, floral pattern in three colours, with the flower placed in the apex of the zigzag shapes

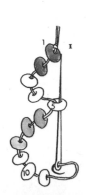 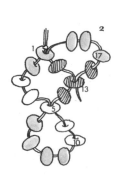 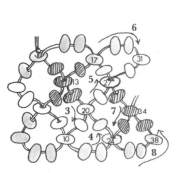 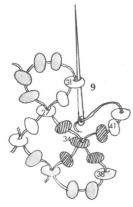

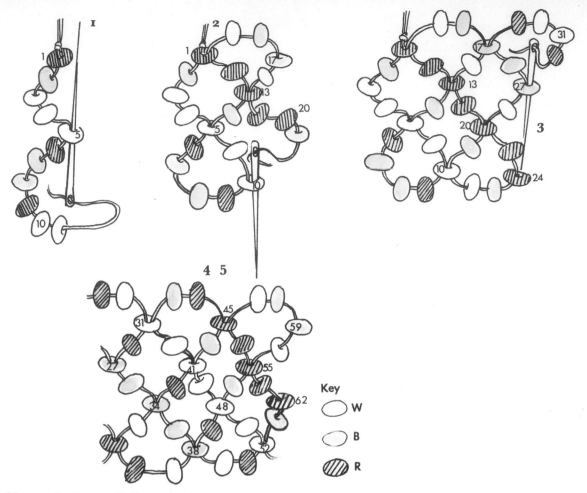

Diagram 62   Pattern C, diagonal stripe in three colours

Pattern C. Three colours diagonal stripes

Materials:
   Beads size 10 in red, white and blue
   Monofilament nylon
   Size 9 or 10 needle
Key:
   r – red
   w – white
   b – blue
Pattern:
Secure first bead and count as bead one in the
pattern.
1 Pick up and thread, 1r 1b 3w 1r 2b 1r 2w
   (11 beads) and pass needle through bead 5,
   (a white bead in this case).
2 Pick up 1b 2r pass needle up through bead one
   and pull tight. Pick up 1w 2b 1w and pass
   needle down through bead 13. Pull tight.
   Pick up 2r 1b and pass down through bead 10.

3 Pick up 1w 1b 2r and pass up through bead 20,
   pull tight. Pick up 1w 2b pass up through bead
   17 and tighten. Pick up 1r 2w 1r pass down
   through bead 27.
4 Pick up 2b 1w pass down through bead 24,
   pick up 1r 1w 2b pass up through bead 34,
   pick up 1r 2w pass up through bead 31, pick
   up 1b 2r 1b pass down through bead 41. Pick
   up 2w 1r pass down through bead 38. Pick
   up 1b 1r 2w, pass up through bead 48 pull
   tight.
5 Pick up 1b 2r pass up through bead 45 pull
   to tighten. The pattern should now be clearly
   visible and from here it is simple to follow it;
   it may be worked from stage two again.
Join pattern as follows, and follow diagram for
First C using the beads in the following sequence.
   Pick up 1r 1w pass up through bead 7, pull
tight, pick up 1b (x) pass up through bead
r pick up w (r) pass up through bead 3, pick
up bead x (w) pass up through bead 0, pick

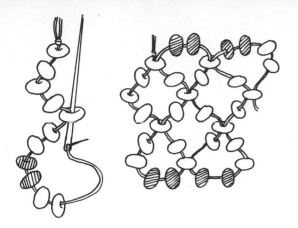

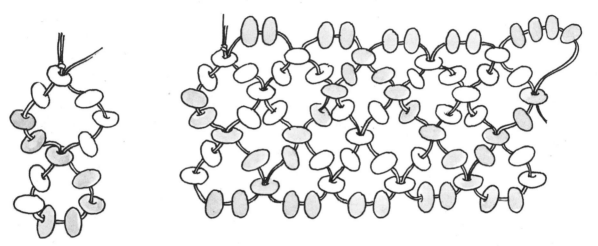

Diagram 63   Variation for Pattern C

Diagram 64   Variation for Pattern C

up y and z (b and r) and pass down through bead 1 and on into work. Secure the working thread as described and cut off.

Diagrams 63 and 64 have no instruction in the text but it should be a simple matter to follow them once the pattern itself is familiar to you. Other variations include, dots of colour where the centre of a 'flower' would normally be. A multicolour stripe or zigzag. Or for diagram 64 different colours in the 'spaces' whilst the surround is of uniform colour.

The pattern is particularly effective as a hat band, its slightly stretchy make up is ideal for putting around rigid articles and no fastener is required to keep it in place. Diagrams 62–4 show some attractive variations.

Braids for clothing or for home accessories are also possible with this pattern and you yourself will think of other ways to use it.

You are not even restricted to this particular width: the pattern may be extended almost indefinitely as follows. Illustration 41 shows a wider version of the pattern with three rows of zigzag. More sequences of three beads are added between the top and bottom sequences of four beads to make the pattern wider.

Pattern C. Extended (wider) version. Diagram 65

Materials:
    Size 10 beads in blue, pale green and pearl
    A double length of monofilament nylon 2 or 3m long
    Size 9 or 10 needle
Key:
    b – blue
    g – pale green
    p – pearl

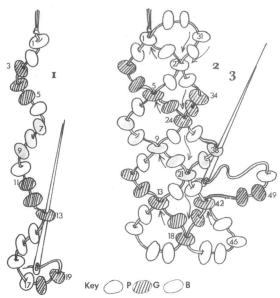

Diagram 65   Wide Pattern C making three zigzags

Key ⬭ P ▨ G ⬭ B

Pattern:

Secure first bead and count as bead 1.

1 Pick up and thread 2p, 3g, 1p, 3b, 1p, 3g, 4p, 2g (19 beads in all). Pass needle up through bead 13.

2 Pick up 1p, 2b and pass needle up through bead 9.

3 Pick up 1p, 2g and pass needle up through bead 5. Pick up 3p and pass needle up through bead 1. Pull tight.

This strip of work will be difficult to hold and you should take care not to allow the beads to twist out of place. The experience you have gained by working pattern C in its narrow form will help you to see which beads you must pass through again in order to pull the pattern into the correct shape. Continue the pattern as follows.

Pick up 4p and pass down through bead 27. Pick up 1p, 2g and pass down through bead 24. Pull to tighten. Pick up 1p, 2b and pass down through bead 21. Pick up 1p, 2g and pass needle down through bead 18. Pull to tighten. Pick up 4p and pass up through bead 40. Pick up 2g, 1p and pass needle up through bead 37. The pattern should now be easy to follow. This is much too wide for a ring, but makes an attractive bracelet or, if you have the patience to work a very long strip, a very firm and useful belt.

It may be extended almost indefinitely in this form and the longer and wider it is the more designs are possible (see diagram 66). It is worth drawing the pattern out and trying your hand at designing by colouring the ovals which represent the beads. This way you can produce individual and unique designs.

Number the beads in your diagram thus making the pattern easy to follow and work from. If you wish to construct a very large flat area of beadwork, perhaps for a table mat or to fold into a purse or small bag, Pattern C may be extended by adding more beads to the basic pattern units as follows. The choker and the black bracelet in Illustration 41 on page 73 are constructed in this manner. By increasing the number of beads the pattern will grow much faster and take less time to complete. This increase of beads can be almost unlimited, but you must remember that each time more beads are put into the pattern units the work becomes more open, i.e. the diamonds get bigger. An added bonus if you are making a purse to be lined, is that the work also becomes much softer as it is opened out and the lining will show through the spaces in the pattern. Increases in this particular way are always by two's since the beads to be gone through twice are in the centre of the series, i.e. in C narrow, the sequence is always 4, 3, 4, 3, 4, etc. increasing by two gives you, 6, 5, 6, 5, 6, etc. and so on . . . 8, 7, 8, 7, 8, 7. A word of warning however, it is not successful when increased too many times, because the work becomes *too* open and unmanageable. Try using wooden beads for the versions using big diamonds, a considerable number will be required but the resulting work is very attractive.

The Rocaille bead purse in the illustration 40 on page 70 was constructed in this manner, i.e. 6, 5, 6, 5, 6, 5, 6, etc. always turning the work with 6 beads.

Bracelet using extended C (See Illustration 41 Diagram 66)

Materials:

Black beads in one colour
Monofilament nylon
Size 10 or 9 needle

Pattern:

Secure bead one and count as one in the pattern.

1 Pick up and thread 16 black beads and pass needle up through bead 7. Pull tight.

2 Pick up 5 beads and pass up through bead 1. Pick up 6 beads and pass down through bead

19. Pull tight. Pick up 5 beads and pass down through bead 14. Pick up 6 beads and pass up through bead 30.

Continue until the work is long enough to suit your purpose and finish by working the thread back and making slip knots.

Fasteners are attached in the same manner as for pattern C in its basic form.

Joining the work to make a ring is done as shown in Diagram 65. This particular extended version of C makes a successful ring but the bigger the pattern units become the less rigid it is and less suitable for this purpose.

Joining pattern C. Diagram 67

The way of working is the same as for joining the narrow C pattern, but three beads are picked up at the top and bottom instead of two, and two beads rather than one are used to make and complete the diamonds.

If you decide to make a belt from pattern C and any of the extended versions of it, make sure to use strong nylon thread, and if it is necessary for you to join a new working thread at any point during the pattern this must be attached very securely indeed.

When nylon monofilament is used the threads should be cut off very close to the work and if possible the ends eased inside a bead by pulling the work very gently through your fingers. This applies especially to chokers and bracelets which will probably be worn directly against the skin. Any protruding ends can be very irritating because the nylon is hard and quite sharp.

Collars

The collars shown in illustrations 42 and 43 look very complicated. In fact they are simply another extended and expanded version of pattern C and are relatively easy once the technique of expanding the pattern to shape the collars and holding the work is mastered.

The initial difficulty is easily remedied if a sample is worked before a full collar is attempted. The curve of the collar is no secret either. This is merely the result of extending and expanding the work towards the bottom whilst keeping it narrow at the top. Constructing the curve means picking up progressively more beads towards the bottom of the work, thus the pattern units grow larger. This may be done as many times as you like and, in common with the uniform version of C in which all the pattern units are enlarged equally, the more beads you use per unit the bigger the successive diamond motifs become. By using contrasting beads at certain points in the work you will find it is easier to see which beads to go through a second time as you work back towards the top of the collar. Once a few rows have been worked the beads to be passed through twice will become more obvious. By making a sampler you will learn how the diamonds form the pattern, and also become familiar with the technique of extending the beadwork to make the curve, and with holding the work to prevent it slipping and twisting out of shape.

Before you attempt to make a full collar remember to check the neck measurement, by measuring loosely around the base of the throat (make a note of this figure).

Diagram 66   Expanded and extended Pattern C, opening out the diamonds

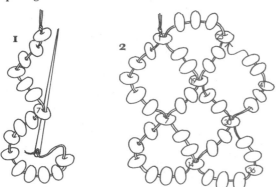

Diagram 67   Join for expanded Pattern C

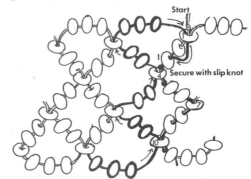

79

As the collar grows larger check the length from time to time. Once the work is half the neck measurement you should begin to reverse any design in the work, and if the collar has shaping at any point you should reverse this too so that you now begin to work back towards the end of the collar. It is better to make a collar too small than too large. Once complete it is difficult to alter beadwork if it is too big; a collar which is too small, however, may simply be extended at either side in order to make it the correct length. This way any central design is kept at the centre front.

Fastenings are added once the work is completed. If a full circle is worked then this may be a simple loop and bead as used for many of the chokers and bracelets in this section. If the collar is not to extend around the neck fully then tabs are added using basic C (see illustration 42), and a loop and bead, or some other form of fastening, attached.

Narrow collars are made simply by reducing the number of pattern units between top and bottom of the work, and by using correspondingly less beads to open it out. Collars with shaped edges (see illustration 43) have the number of pattern units reduced progressively and then increased again in certain places. This is a useful device when a collar is to be very deep, since it allows it to pass over the shoulders without lifting up. This shaping can be done in as many places as you wish.

The number of pattern units may also be increased at the centre front of the work so that the collar dips lower. This is a good idea if you want to concentrate a particular design there, or if the collar is intended to fill the neckline of a garment. Dangles and fringes can also be added to collars to extend them even further – they are attached when the work is complete. The narrower the collar the less it needs any additional shaping other than the curve which forms naturally: there is insufficient width for the collar to lift as it crosses the shoulders, and any extra shaping detracts from the effect.

Illustration 43 shows the first collar I made. It took much time and patience and was made more complicated because I shaped it in two places. Parts of it were unthreaded many times and it is by no means a perfect example.

At first you may find it difficult to hold the work and to control it because as it gets longer it also becomes heavier. Once you have learned how many beads to pick up and when and where you should do so, and once you have achieved an even tension, then the work progresses much faster. It is important to use a very strong thread to support the weight of a vast number of beads. Because the collars are so heavy I always use monofilament nylon 4lb test (breaking strain); with this it is easier to maintain an even tension and prevent the beads slipping. It is also important to cut the tails of old and new threads very close to the work so that the ends will not irritate the skin when the collar is worn. One method I use is to make a knot in the double length of nylon, and cut the tail very close to it. The knot is pulled firmly into a bead, the thread then being secured with a slip knot as in the other patterns.

Collars may be used as jewellery or as part of a garment. If you wish to make the collar part of a dress, then cuffs may be worked in the same manner – simply measure the wrist and tighten the curve. It is a good idea to stitch these to the garment and remove them only before cleaning or washing.

Fastenings

A bead loop and a larger fastening bead may be used. In order to strenghen these the thread should be passed around the loop as many times as possible and also through the stem of the bead several times (a double stem may be used). In the small open-work collar in illustration 42, a ring bolt and ring have been used. A button and buttonhole loop fasten the white collar. This came from Malawi and the fastening device is common to much African work. It is suitable also for your own beadwork and you may find that you have a special button that you can use. If you prefer, ribbon or cord ties may be sewn to the ends of the collar.

Inspiration for collars comes from many different sources. The Zulu collar in illustration 70 demonstrates a simple horizontal 'stripe'. Collars from other parts of Africa and from New Guinea make use of other patterns and techniques. Many of these collars are brightly coloured and perhaps not suited to present tastes but it is an easy matter to change colours. Collars from ancient Egypt, whilst differing in technique and materials, will provide other ideas. They are usually very deep, covering the shoulders and extending over the chest.

Before you begin what is perhaps a mammoth project, decide on the colours you wish to use and the quantities. You will require a considerable amount of beads, and if there is to be a main body of colour with only a little patterning then you should be sure that you have sufficient beads in that colour to complete the work. Nothing is more frustrating than to run out of beads halfway through a piece of work. You might find that size 10 needles are more suitable than size 9 which is more commonly recommended, but this depends largely on the size of the holes in the beads. You will also require a considerable length of monofilament nylon. It is impossible to estimate the exact number of beads or length of thread used in the collars.

Collar pattern 1. Diagram 68. Illustration 43

Materials:
 Size 10 Rocaille beads in two colours
 Monofilament nylon used double
 Size 10 or 9 needle
Key:
 m – main colour
 c – contrast

Until you are sure of the pattern sequence *count the beads*. In the first stage this is vital since the correct formation of the diamonds depends upon accuracy.

In diagram 68 only the contrast beads are given numbers; these are the beads through which the needle and thread must pass twice.

The work will draw up considerably once the second, upwards, row of beads is added. However, in order to make the working technique clear, in the second stage of the diagram the beads are shown very widely spaced and the pattern is expanded.

Pattern:
Secure the first bead which is a contrast bead (c) and count this as bead 1.

This pattern is the one used for the collar in illustration 43. The black collar in illustration 42 uses approximately half this pattern.

1 Pick up and thread 1c, 1m, 1c, 1m, 1c, 1m, 1c, 1m, 1c, 1m, 1c.
2 Pick up and thread 2m, 1c, 2m, 1c, 2m, 1c, 2m, 1c.
3 Pick up and thread 3m, 1c, 3m, 1c, 3m, 1c, 3m, 1c, 3m. (There should now be 47 beads threaded.)
4 Now pick up 6m, 1c, 3m and pass the needle

◄ 42 Collars using pattern 1: the inner collar dates from the early twentieth century, the middle collar is Milawian, and the outer collar is modern showing C extended and expanded

43 Collar 1, using Rocaille beads

up through bead 43 which is a contrast bead. (There should now be 57 beads on the thread.)

The following stages require that the needle is passed up through the beads.

  5 Pick up and thread 3m, 1c, 3m. Pass up through bead 35. Hold the work at this point.

  6 Pick up 3m, 1c, 3m and pass up through bead 27. Hold and pull thread to tighten.

  7 Pick up 3m, 1c, 2m and pass up through bead 20. Tighten and hold.

  8 Pick up 2m, 1c, 2m. Pass up through bead 13.

  9 Pick up 2m, 1c, 1m and pass up through bead 9. Hold the work firmly and pull the thread gently to tighten the work and draw the beads together.

10 Pick up 1m, 1c, 1m and pass up through bead 5.

11 Pick up 1m, 1c, 1m and pass up through bead 1. Pull to tighten.

The pattern will look strange and in fact not at all like the drawing. However, once another row has been worked *down* in sequence, a more obvious shape will start to form.

12 Pick up 2m, 1c, 1m and pass the needle down

through beads as shown in the diagram. The beads are now picked up in the reverse sequence until the bottom of the pattern is reached. The turn is then worked as follows.

Bottom turn

Pick up 6m, 1c, 3m and pass up through contrast bead. Continue working in this manner until work is half your neck measurement. Then reverse any contrasting pattern and repeat to the end.

You may wish to include bands of solid colour in the work instead of having the 'spotted' pattern. This is a simple matter. Begin the solid rows from the top and when you wish to revert to the original pattern of main and contrast colours simply do so from the *bottom* of the work. If there is to be a matching band of one colour at another point in the work be sure to commence at the bottom and end at the top in order to keep the design symmetrical.

Having worked several rows of the collar pattern you will see how the curve is formed by increasing the number of beads gradually towards the bottom. If these increases are not

Diagram 68 Collar 1 in extended and expanded C Pattern ▶

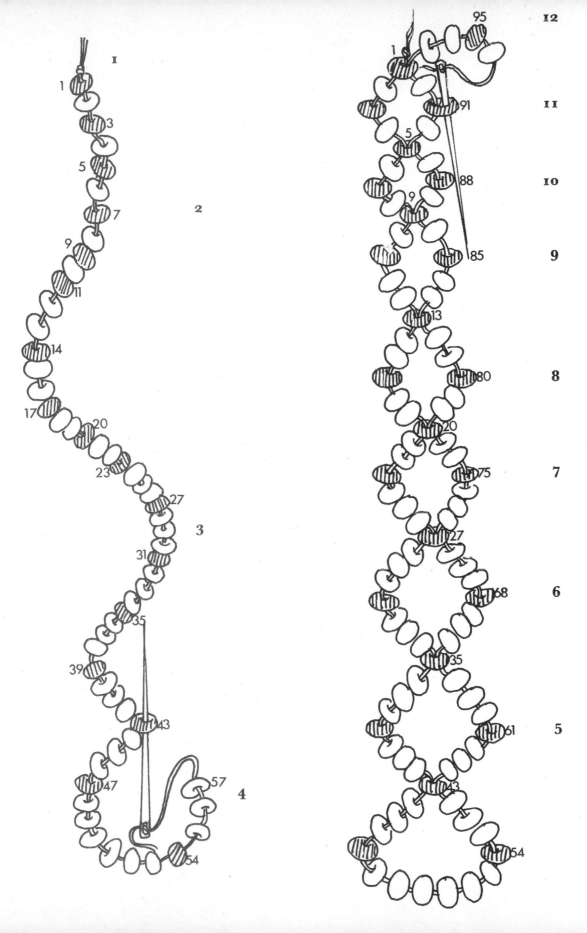

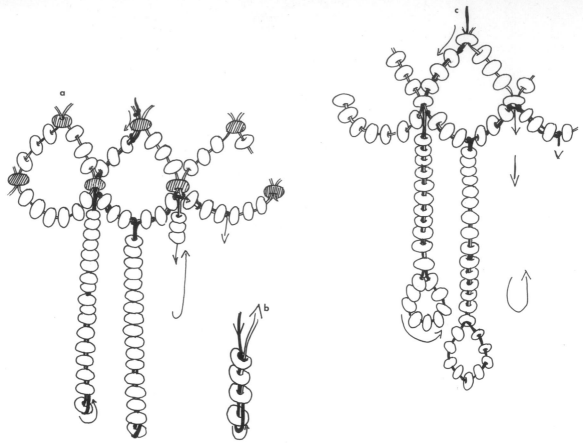

Diagram 69   Decorative dangles for collar, attached to bottom of centre front

graduated in two's, the work becomes too curved and the result is a close band of slightly-curved work with a 'fluted' edge caused by too great an increase in the number of beads.

Once you have tried your hand successfully at this first collar you will be able to experiment more freely with your own ideas. Shaping or using several colours may be your next objective. With careful preplanning a wide range of colours may be used and quite complicated designs worked, most of which are based on the diamond. Narrow collars lend themselves to bands of colour, and a wider version with increasingly wide bands in three colours is also pretty. The first few pattern motifs are basic C for this collar and so one of the C patterns could be used for this part of the collar. If you decide to make a narrow version of the collar, use part of the pattern for the first collar; pick up beads as far as bead 31 (c); pick up 6m, 1c, 3m; pass up through bead 27 and continue as for pattern 1 (see p. 82).

If the work is turned after a sequence of 2m, 1c, 2m, you will only require four beads to make the bottom of the turn, otherwise the base of the collar will be too wide. The top of the work remains the same however.

To make the collar longer at the centre front, work to the point where you would normally add six beads to make the turn, but instead begin by adding a further extension and expansion of 4m, 1c, 4m to increase the length and the curve. If you do not wish to extend the curve, simply add more sequences of 3m, 1c, 3m, and the turn for the latter will be the same. To make the turn after a 4m, 1c, 4m sequence you must use eight beads at the bottom. If you are going to make the work very deep and in so doing increase the number of beads in the pattern units at intervals, you must remember to increase the number of beads in the bottom part when you turn the work.

A scalloped edge is possible and very attractive. This is made simply by decreasing and increasing the number of pattern units at regular intervals along the bottom of the collar; these can of course be made wider towards the front if you wish.

Fringes and dangles may be added to the collar when you have completed it – these look best if they are graduated in length towards the centre, thus following the curved edge, and if they are worked at the centre front of the collar only (diagram 69 shows how to attach the fringe and dangles to the work). You must attach a new working thread for these and I recommend the method which eliminates prickly ends of nylon (by drawing a knot into a bead). If the holes in the beads will allow it you could use thread for the fringes so that they will hang more easily. Whichever is used – nylon or thread – the work should not be pulled up too much because this makes the long fringes rather stiff and unattractive. For a different effect, a large bead can be added to the bottom of the fringe or dangle; this is followed by another smaller bead over which the thread passes before going back into the string and on into the work. If the size of these beads is graduated along with the length of the fringe, you will have an unusual collar. Loops can also be added to the ends of the dangles. Drop beads are useful for ending dangles and for the centre of loops; you might try suspending

the drops from the centre of each group of beads which form the turn of the pattern.

The collar in illustration 44 is far more open in appearance and consequently the work progresses much faster. The method of construction and the basic technique are also quite different. This pattern can become difficult to handle because, until the final stage, the work is very long and therefore likely to get tangled. There is no built-in curve and it may look odd until you realise how the collar is made to curve to fit your neck. When complete, this collar forms a circle. As with the previous pattern, this collar may be extended, and at a certain point more beads must be added to the patterns in order to extend the bottom edge a little. Unlike most of the threading patterns there is no increase in the beads in order to turn at the top and the bottom. The whole collar is based on the diamond shape with the addition of two extra beads at the bottom of the diamonds.

To make the first attempt easier I have used two colours, and again the contrast beads indicate the beads which are to be passed through again.

44 Collar 2, open diamond pattern

Collar 2. Diagram 70

Materials:
    Size 10 beads in two colours
    Monofilament nylon or Polytwist (thread is as suitable as nylon for this pattern and the result is softer)
    Size 9 needle
Key:
    m – main colour
    c – contrast
Pattern:
Secure the first bead which is a contrast bead and count it as bead 1.

1 Thread 1c, 5m, 1c, 5m, 1c, 5m, 2c. Pass the needle up through bead 19. Pull to tighten.
2 Pick up 5m, 1c, 5m and pass up through bead 7. Pull tight.
3 Pick up 5m, 1c, 5m, 1c, 5m and pass the needle down through bead 26. Pull to tighten the work and draw it into the diamond shape.
4 Pick up 5m, 2c and pass the needle up through bead 55. Pull to tighten. Repeat from stage 2 until there are 48 points to the collar. Fasten off the thread and rethread the needle with a new length. If you use a double thread approximately 1m long there will be sufficient

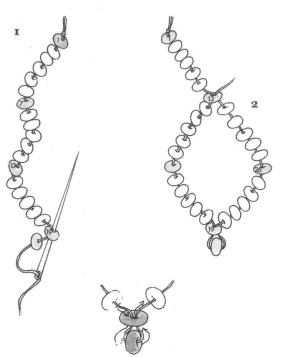

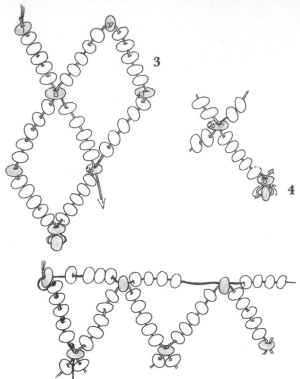

Diagram 70   Collar 2

Joining the top to make the curve

Diagram 71   Collar 2 fastener and neckband

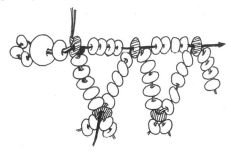

to make the loop for fastening at the end of the work.

Attach new working thread at bead 7 and pull the knot into the work (bead). Make a slip knot and pass the needle up to bead 1 as shown in diagram 70. Make a slip knot before passing through bead 1.

Fastener and neckband

This technique is used if the fastening bead is not to be attached until the neckband is complete. For joining the bead on the same thread as neckband see diagram 71. Attach through bead 7 and make a slip knot. Pass thread up to and through bead 1 as shown. Thread one 4mm and one 6mm bead to match the main colour, plus three main-colour beads. Pass back through 6mm and 4mm beads and through bead 1 of the collar. Make a slip knot and pull to tighten.

Whichever method you use to fasten the completed work the following technique should be used to make the neckband and thus shape the collar (see diagrams 70 and 71).

Pick up four main-colour beads and pass needle through the first contrast bead at the top of the first complete diamond. Pull up and pick up four main-colour beads. Pass through next contrast bead. Continue to do this until all 48 points have been linked together. Pull the

thread to draw the connecting beads and the contrasts at the top of the diamonds close together. Before continuing hold the work in the drawn-up position and try it around your neck. It should fit, since it is not meant to be worn very tightly, but if it does not, one of the following procedures should be followed.

If the collar is too small all the four main-colour beads must be unthreaded but only after you have measured it in the drawn-up state. If there is only a little difference in the length of the collar and that of your neck, a longer loop or stem to the fastening bead may serve to lengthen it. If, however, there is a difference of two or more centimetres, then unthread the beads and add one or more beads between each contrast bead. It may be sufficient only to add

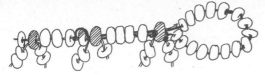

Diagram 72   Loop fastener for Collar 2

extra beads to every second group. If the work is too large, simply decrease the number of beads in the neckband.

Once the correct length is achieved continue as follows (see diagram 72). The loop is constructed without joining new thread. Make a slip knot after the last contrast bead when the collar has been drawn up into shape. Pick up and thread 16 main-colour beads and pass the needle back into the neckband of the collar for approximately 13 mm (1in) and make a slip knot to secure. Pass the needle back *over* the bead then into the work. Bring out in front of the last contrast bead. Pass through, into and around the loop. Make a slip knot and cut thread.

This is far more satisfactory than joining several new threads to make band and loop. If you have a very large neck, an extra diamond should be worked and if your neck is very small reduce the collar to 47 points.

Variations

There are several ways to change the basic

Diagram 73   Collar 2, variation 1 with Rocaille beads

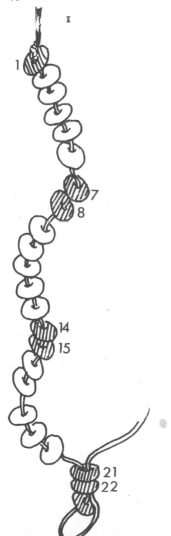

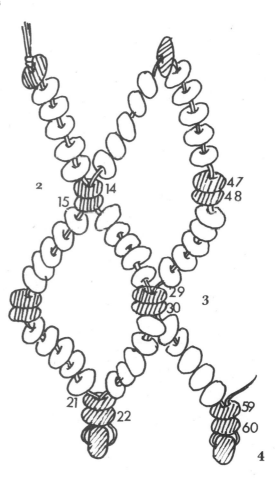

appearance of this collar without actually adding to or taking from the number of beads in the pattern. The top of the work, that is the neckband, could be worked entirely in contrast beads. All the collar may be in one colour. The upper and lower diamonds can be in different colours. Larger beads may be used as the contrast through which you pass twice, and the beads at the base of the collar can also be bigger. Small bugle beads make a pleasing change from Rocailles and may be used in place of the contrast beads.

The pattern changes in appearance when beads are added or subtracted. For instance, long bugle beads, though not reducing or increasing the number of beads used for the collar, do change the form and basic appearance (see illustration 44). This collar in black Rocaille and bronze bugle beads looks quite different to the one made entirely of Rocaille beads. Two Rocaille beads may also be used where in the first pattern there is only one (see diagram 73).

Remember that the more beads you add to the bottom of the diamonds the deeper the collar will be. At the centre front of the collar, dangles could be worked getting longer towards the centre point and then tapering off to only one or two beads. These dangles are worked as part of the pattern and not, as in the first collar, added separately. To make them, add to the number of beads at the bottom before passing over one bead and commencing the pattern again.

Bead collars have a unique quality: they are jewellery but, at the same time, easily become part of a garment. They can be elaborate, covering most of the shoulders and chest, or small, neat and suitable for everyday wear.

Some collars, like the Milawian collar in illustration 42, are threaded from a length or string of beads, as is the final collar pattern (see diagram 75). The wired collars of the Masai people are worn standing out around the shoulders and although the technique is quite different they are, like all the beadwork produced by these people, of outstanding workmanship and very beautiful.

Collar 3. Variation on collar 2. Diagram 73

Materials:
 Rocaille beads in two colours
 Nylon monofilament
 Size 9 needle
Key:
 m – main colour
 c – contrast
Pattern:
Pick up and secure first bead. Count as bead 1, a contrast bead.
1 Pick up and thread 1c, 5m, 2c, 5m, 2c, 5m, 3c and pass up through beads 22 and 21. Pull tight.
2 Pick up and thread 5m, 2c, 5m and pass needle up through beads 15 and 14. Pull tight.
3 Pick up 5m, 1c, 5m, 2c, 5m and pass down through beads 29 and 30.
4 Pick up 5m, 3c and pass up through beads 60 and 59. Pull the thread gently to tighten the work and continue working from the beginning of stage 2.
 When complete this should be finished off as in the first pattern.
The collar pattern using long bugle beads is worked exactly as pattern 1 and finished in the same way (see diagram 74 and illustration 45).

Collar 4. Worked from a string of beads. Diagram 75

Materials:
 Rocaille beads in two colours
 6mm bead to fasten
 Length of thread, or nylon if a firmer finish is required
 Size 9 or 10 needles
 Beeswax (if thread is used)
Key:
 m – main colour
 c – contrasts
Pattern:
Thread needle with a very long thread and draw it through the beeswax to smooth it. This may be used double if it is a fine thread but if Polytwist is to be used leave this as a single thread making a knot 20cm from the end. Thread as many main-colour beads as are required to pass loosely around your neck, and pass the thread back over the last bead and through the penultimate bead.
1 Pick up and thread 2c, 2m, 2c, 2m, 2c, 2m, 2c, 4m, 1c, 1m, 1c and pass needle back up through bead 18 (the last of the m beads in the series of four). Pull tight.
2 Pick up 3m, 2c, 2m and pass through 2c.

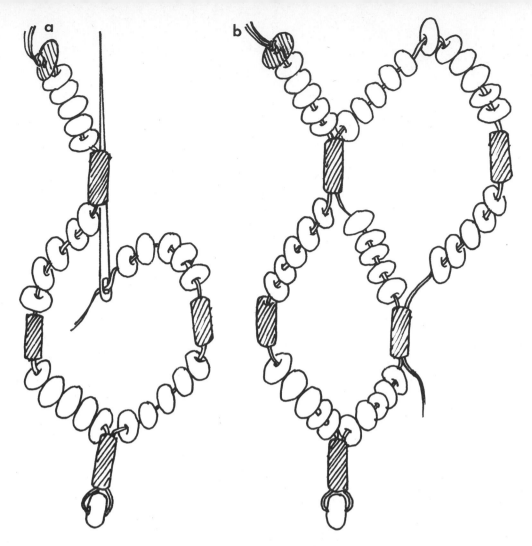

Diagram 74   Collar 2, variation 2 with bugle beads

45 Collar 3, open diamond pattern using bugle beads

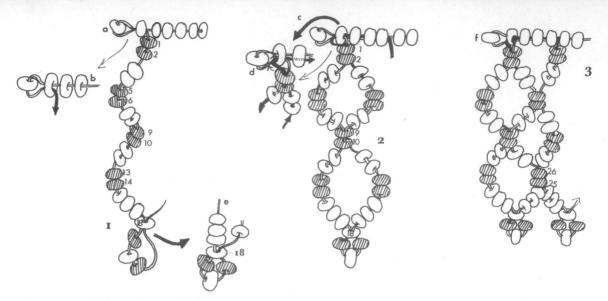

Diagram 75   Collar 3. Diagram b shows detail of the end of the string and start of the collar working, d shows how to take the thread along the string to start the second vertical, and e shows detail of the bottom of the diamond

Pick up 2m, 2c, 2m and pass up through 2c. Pull tight and pass, as shown, through the second bead of the string and through three more beads.

3 Pick up 2c, 2m and pass needle down through 2c. Pick up 2m, 2c, 2m and pass down through 2c. Pick up 4m, 1c, 1m, 1c and pass up through m bead as shown. Pull tight. Repeat stages 2 and 3 until the strip of beads is complete. Attach fastening in any of the ways already given.

You may add more beads to the series preceding the 1c, 1m, 1c, which form the turn, and to the series immediately following it, if you wish to give the collar more depth. You can, of course, use as many colours as you wish.

The finished collar will form a circle when fastened (see illustration 46). Like the previous pattern it hangs from a single string or strip of beads. Both patterns are very similar in appearance – only the technique differs.

Experiments and developments

The threading patterns which have been dealt with in this section do not limit you to the making of jewellery and accessories; they are so versatile that they can be developed into single motifs for mounting on velvet bands to be worn around neck or wrist. By freely adapting the technique of threading, many small decorative motifs are possible which may be used on shoes, bags, hair slides and the like (see illustration 47). These flowers are made by working from a circle

of beads. In order to make them it is best if you experiment with the shape, perhaps starting with a very basic pattern like the one shown in diagram 76 and illustration 48, and going on to develop your own ideas. By adding the petal loops in front and behind the basic ring, and attaching more loops to the petals themselves, three-dimensional shapes are easily worked (as centre flower in illustration 47). Earrings and brooches become possibilities: the shapes should be mounted on the special jewellery mounts available at most craft shops. I have worked these in gold, silver and some other very shiny beads, and used them as Christmas-tree and parcel decorations. They make a change from ribbon decorations and also form an extra gift.

Working from a circle lends itself most readily to the flower shape. Scattered over the pocket or yoke of a plain garment these are unusual and eye-catching accessories. The flower motif may be developed into large, flat shapes and here you must experiment to find out the number of beads per petal and how many petals can be used before the work starts to curve. These larger shapes make excellent small mats for glasses or plant pots or, if worked in wooden beads, unusual table place mats (see illustration 49). Whichever kind of beads are used you will need a large amount. Even wooden beads are used up at a considerable rate. One advantage of using larger beads, even size 7 Rocaille, is that the larger holes allow the passage of far more thread so that you are able to pass a needle several times through the same bead.

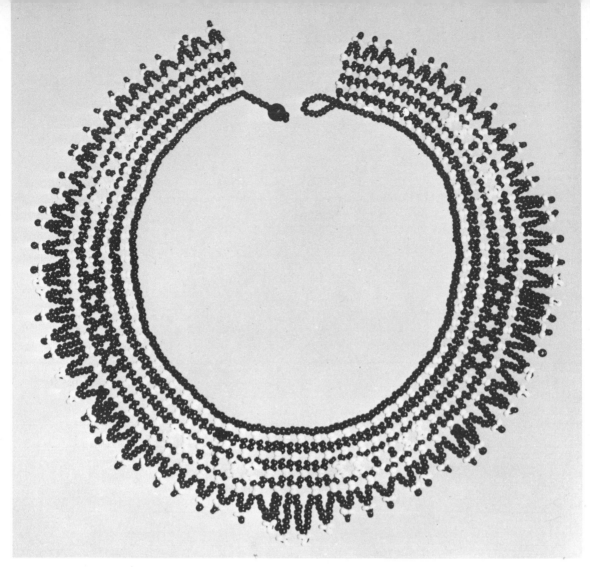

46 Collar 4, worked from a string of beads

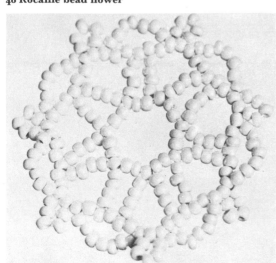

48 Rocaille bead flower

Flower. Diagram 76. Illustration 48

Materials:
  Size 10 Rocaille beads
  Size 10 needle
  Monofilament nylon (this holds the shape
  more firmly than ordinary thread)

Pattern:
Make a knot several centimetres from the end
of the thread (double thread) and thread the
first bead in the usual way. Count this as bead 1.

1 Pick up and thread 21 beads and pass needle
  through bead 1 pulling the thread tight to
  make a circle.

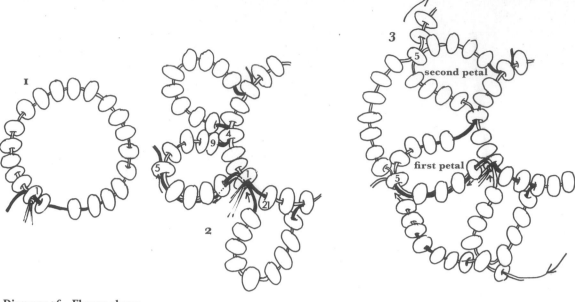

Diagram 76   Flower shape

47 Flowers from the threading patterns

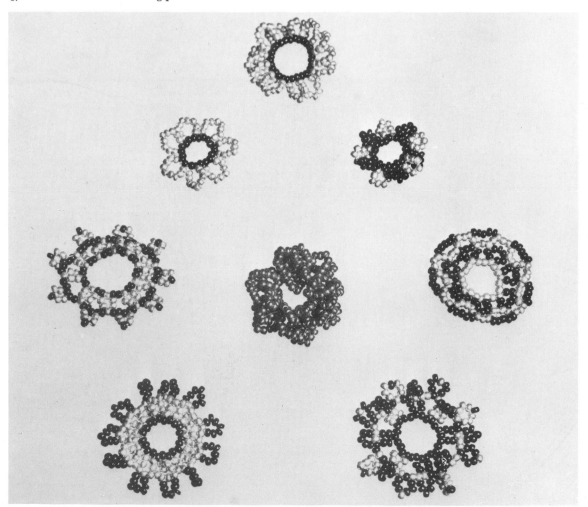

Strung chokers with wooden centres, demonstrating the variety
of effects possible with a very simple technique

Simple strung necklaces with wooden bead centres

2 Pick up nine beads and pass needle through bead 4. Pull tight. Do this six more times until there are seven petal shapes. The last time a petal is worked the needle passes through bead 1 again, up into the first petal and through bead 5 of this.

You may wish to finish the work here and make several simple flowers to sew onto a dress or sweater. If so, do not pass the needle up into the first petal but make a slip knot and take the thread around the circle again, making slip knots. Then cut off, thread the tail, work this back into the flower and cut off excess thread.

If you wish to enlarge the flower shape continue to follow part 3.

3 Pick up and thread seven beads and pass needle through bead 5 of second petal. Do this six more times around the work, linking the top of each petal with seven beads. Pull tight when the penultimate bead has been worked. Pick up the last scrics and pass needle through bead 5 of petal 1 again.

Continue to enlarge the shape by adding more petals. These must contain progressively more beads so that the work stays flat. Experiment will soon show you how many beads will keep it flat. The flower shapes in illustration 48 and 49 were all begun from a similar circle of beads and, as you can see, there are several ways in which the flower can be developed. You can also try using several sizes, perhaps increasing the size of the beads as you work towards the outer edge of the pattern.

Having used some of the threading patterns you will find that you can adapt them quite freely for many other purposes. The purse in illustration 40 demands time and patience simply because a large flat area of beads must be constructed. Were this worked in wooden beads it would take less time.

You will find many ways in which your bead-work may be used. The lampshade in illustration 50 uses a variation of the threading technique. It was constructed directly onto the frame, which was first wrapped with hem tape and, for the sake of a firm base, was placed on the lamp base so that I could have both hands free. The pattern does not follow any of those in this section, but as I worked down the separate divisions of the frame I linked each row to the one above and at the halfway stage I began to work the beads into converging lines. Part of the beauty of the shade lies in the shadows cast when it is lit from inside. The fringe used on this shade can form an unusual addition to any lampshade or could be attached with equal effect to a window blind of the roller type. Any kind of beads can be used; if they are small you will either need to use more of them or you can simply use more loops and dangles. New threads are joined in the same way as those in the threading patterns: you should begin with a very long double thread and, if possible, use nylon so that it will be less obvious.

If you contemplate a bead curtain, be warned; unless you are prepared to spend a considerable amount of money on beads, or already have a very large quantity, you should think very care-

49a African mat

49b Victorian mat

49c Mat

49d Mat

fully about the project. Try threading a length to correspond with the measurements of the drop from top of the door frame to just above floor level and you will soon see what I mean. You could try using the knotted-thread technique from Section One, so that the beads are spaced by lengths of thread, perhaps coloured carpet twine or cords. A heading of threading pattern or looped fringe would add interest to this. However, remember that you will still require a great many beads.

Nothing should be considered too improbable or impossible – even a garment. If the open-diamond pattern is used, a smock yoke, or even a short overblouse, are not too ambitious. The latter requires just two large squares or oblongs of beadwork which are then joined at the shoulders leaving a slit for the head to pass through. Or they can be joined with straps of threaded beads.

50 Lampshade using Victorian tubular glass beads

section three beadstringing two needles, two threads

This section should not be confused with 'strings' or with 'double stringing', although the patterns could easily become part of the latter technique.

Beadstringing is a different technique altogether. It may be known by different names, it is, in fact, sometimes called 'threading'. Usually larger, often wooden, beads are used to work the patterns.

This technique has, in the past, been used particularly well with jet beads. Many bracelets dating from Victorian and Edwardian times have beads with two sets of holes and two sets of threads or cords linking the pieces. Others use ordinary beads with one hole but two cords. The technique is particularly suited to elasticated work, and many children's hairbands and bracelets are constructed in this fashion.

The technique

Initially this is much simpler than the threading method, but the more complicated designs do have similar attendant complexities. The positioning of the beads depends entirely on passing needles and threads through some of the beads so that they cross in opposite directions. However, all the patterns are based on one very basic and simply worked pattern. Once this becomes clear it will be relatively easy for you to follow the others.

One of the biggest problems with this technique is learning to control the working threads so that they do not tangle. It is desirable to use thread rather than nylon, although one or two of the more complex patterns may require nylon, and indeed you may find that until the technique is familiar it is easier to use nylon. The threads cross over each other inside a bead, and it is easy to pass the second needle through the first thread and so tangle and spoil the work. With nylon this is not possible. It is quite possible to use the tiny Rocaille beads for beadstringing, either exclusively or together with other sizes and kinds of beads, but you will find it less frustrating to use larger beads while you are learning the pattern (most of the patterns state that wooden beads should be used). The patterns in Section Two were built up along the width or depth of the work as the work progressed along the length. With the stringing method extra width is produced by adding another row to the completed length of an article.

Materials

Wooden beads are required in a variety of sizes and shapes: 4mm, 6mm, 8mm, 10mm and 12mm; long and short ovals; many-sided; small lice; square beads; pony beads; and size 4 Rocaille, any odd or unusual beads, beads from old necklaces and grained and shiny wood beads can also be used.

Polytwist thread (Gütermann). Beading needles and long darners. A tapestry needle or needle-shaped bodkin. Scissors. Beeswax. Fine piping cord or twine. Crotchet cotton. Tubular macramé cords and, of course, nylon monofilament fishing line. PVA glue (for stiffening the ends of cord to prevent fraying when a needle is not necessary).

Finally, you need a very important item – a small, heavy cushion to which you can pin the work. Making one of these 'anchor cushions' is simple. Mine is filled with beans – hundreds of them – but sand, leadshot, or anything really heavy will suffice. The cushion need not be large, no more than, say 15cm square. You will also need a long, large-headed pin. For the larger beads with big holes a hatpin is an excellent idea, for the smaller beads a darning or even beading needle with a large bead stuck over the eye is suggested.

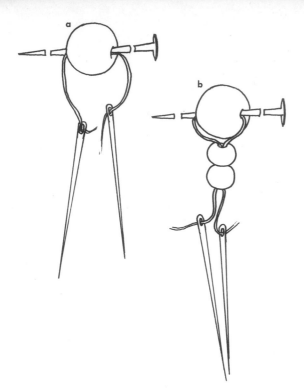

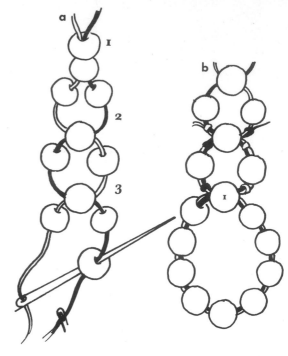

Diagram 77   Securing the first (fastening) bead to the cushion

Diagram 78   Basic pattern

Some general hints

1 Unless otherwise stated, the thread is a single strand with a needle threaded onto each end, so that a long loop forms between them.
2 Bracelets are fastened with either a 'T' bar or a bead with 'ears'.
3 The loop is worked last and is always constructed from 4mm beads unless an alternative is suggested. A loop to fit over an 8mm bead uses nine 4mm beads. Eight 4mm beads form the loop to fit over a T bar made of two 4mm and one 6mm bead.
4 A good deal of the working thread will be visible, no matter how closely you draw the beads together, so it is advisable to match thread to beads. The beads should sit closely together and the threads pulled taut. Ease the beads along so that they fall into the pattern shape by pulling both threads together until the work is evenly shaped.

5 Remember to measure wrist, neck or waist and to keep checking this when you are working. Once completed, beadwork is difficult to take out without ruining it completely. Diagram 77 shows how to secure the work to the cushion. Do this when the large fastening bead has been threaded and drawn to the centre of the double thread.

The basic stringing pattern. Diagram 78. Illustration 51

This is the basis of all other patterns.
Materials for a bracelet:
   Seventy four 4mm wooden beads in turquoise and lime green
   One 8mm or 6mm to match either colour (this is for the fastening and is threaded first)
   Turquoise Polytwist thread (approximately 1m)

51 Bracelet with 4mm wooden beads showing pattern for stringing

Two needles (beading needles or fine darners)
Anchor cushion

Key:
  t – 4mm turquoise
  l – 4mm lime
  L – left-hand needle
  R – right-hand needle

Pattern:

Before commencing, run thread through beeswax, thread a needle onto each end of the Polytwist and pull it into an even loop. Thread the large wooden bead, draw it down to the centre of the loop and pin through the hole to the cushion (see diagram 77).

1 With *both* needles pick up and thread 2t. Slide them up to the large bead. This is the fastener.
2 Pick up 1t on L, 2t on R. Pass L through second bead on R. Make sure these beads sit against the two t picked up in stage 1 (see diagram 77).
3 Pick up 1t on L, 2t on R. Pass L through second bead on R. Pull tight.
4 Pick up 1l on L, 2l on R. Pass L through second bead on R. Pull tight.
5 Pick up 1l on L, 1l, 1t on R. Pass L through t on R.
6 Pick up 1t on L, 2t on R. Pass L through 1t on R.
  Pattern repeats until bracelet will fit your wrist.
  In this pattern the last 4mm bead to be picked up and passed through is part of the fastening loop.

The loop. Diagram 78 (stage 2)

Count the last pattern bead as bead 1. Pick up on R eight 4mm beads either in one or both colours used in the pattern, to make nine beads. Pass L through all beads including bead 1. Pull tight to form the loop. Pass R through the loop again and make a slip knot after bead 1 has been passed through. On the opposite side of bead make a slip knot with needle and thread L. Work back into the last pattern section of the bracelet and make slip knots with each needle. Cut threads when you are sure the fastening is secure. This is the basic stringing pattern, using only one size. The beads should lie close together but the work should remain flexible.

The start and finish are the same for all patterns unless otherwise stated. The same pattern may be worked using 6mm or 8mm beads throughout and will be equally effective this way. Should you use the larger beads, however,

the stem of the fastening bead and the loop should still be made with 4mm beads, unless you are making a belt, otherwise it will look rather large and clumsy. The pattern in this very basic form may be worked with two sizes; the central line of beads – those through which the threads cross – can be of larger beads, while 4mm beads are used for the sides.

To make the basic pattern wider you must add a second row of beads along one side. This means that the work must be turned at one end. There is no need to add a new thread for this if the original working threads are long enough. You will find the second row easier to work if both ends of the bracelet are pinned to a cushion. The fasteners are added separately to a two-row bracelet because adding them as part of the work means it is asymmetrical.

The turn. Diagram 79. Illustration 52

Work one row of basic pattern. Remove the work from the cushion and turn so that both ends are pinned and you are working horizontally.
1 Pick up three beads on L and pass R through the last one so that the needles and threads are now at the side of the first row of work.
2 Pick up three beads on L. Pass R through the last one. Pass L into bead on first row as shown. Pick up one bead on each needle. Pass L through bead on R needle and on into bead on first row as shown.

Diagram 79   Turn for second row on basic pattern

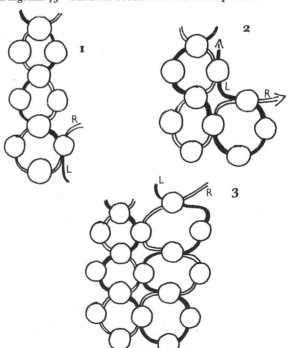

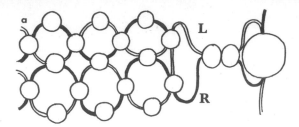

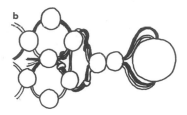

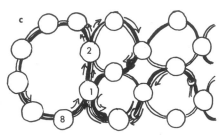

Diagram 80 Bead fasteners for two-row basic pattern, and loop

3 Continue until the work is complete. Fasten off the working thread securely.

Fasteners. Diagram 80
Fasteners are attached separately or as follows (diagram 80a). Do not cut off threads. When the end of the bracelet is reached the two needles will be at the side of the work. Pass needle L on through the first bead of the first pattern row. Using both needles pick up two beads. Pin a 6mm bead to the cushion and pass the needles through it in opposite directions. Pull tight. Pass both needles back down the two 4mm beads and pull tight. Separate the needles and work

back in the pattern rows making slip knots. Cut threads. Diagram 80b shows method with new working thread. Turn work and pin. Attach a new working thread using one needle only. Make slip knots up to the end of the work. Pass through both end beads of double pattern (diagram 80c) and pick up six 4mm beads counting the first two pattern beads passed through as 1 and 2, to make a total of eight beads. Pass thread around the loop twice. Work thread back into work making slip knots and cut off.

If you wish to begin with a fastening bead and have several rows of pattern, these are worked on either side of the first row and the work becomes symmetrical around this. Thus the fasteners are kept central to the work. The pattern makes a very pretty choker in single or double form, and with 6mm or 8mm beads a most substantial and strong belt. You will require several hundred beads for the latter.

The second pattern is a variation of the first and simply requires that you pick up and pass through more than one bead at certain points.

Variation of the basic pattern. Diagram 81. Illustration 53

Materials:
Size 4mm beads – 39 black, 28 rich brown and 24 light brown or orange
One 6mm black fastener
Black Polytwist thread (approximately 1m)
Two beading needles size 9
Anchor cushion and long pin
Beeswax

Key:
b – black
br – brown
O – orange
L left-hand needle
R – right-hand needle

52 Bracelet showing double row of basic pattern

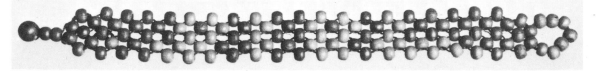

53 Variation of basic pattern

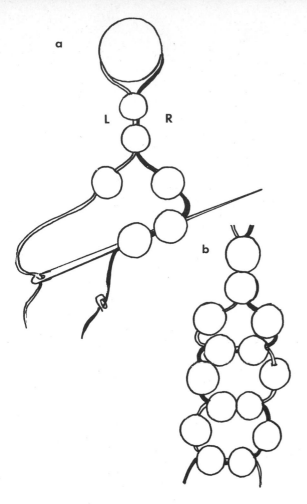

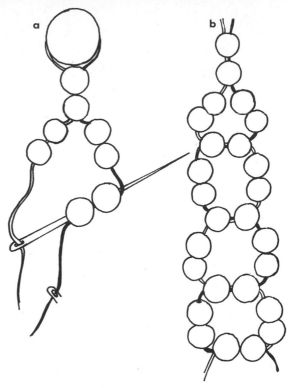

Diagram 82   Variation on the basic pattern, two beads down and two across

Diagram 81   Variation on the basic pattern, one bead down and two across

Pattern:

Run the thread through the beeswax and thread needles. Thread 6mm bead, pull to centre of the thread and secure to the cushion as shown in diagram 77.

1 Pick up 2b on both needles. Slide down until they rest against 6mm bead. Pick up 1b on L, 3b on R. Pass 1 through last 2b on R. Pull tightly to draw the work together.

2 Pick up 1O on L, 3O on R. Pass L through last 2O on R. Pull to tighten. Pick up 1O on L, 1O, 2b on R. Pass L through 2b on R.

3 Pick up 1b on L, 3b on R. Pass L through 2b on R. Pull tight.

4 Pick up 1b on L, 1b and 2O on R. Pass L through 2O.

5 Pick up 1O on L, 3O on R. Pass L through 2O on R.

6 Pick up 1O on L, 1O and 2br on R. Pass L through 2br. Pull to draw pattern together.

7 Pick up 1b on L, 3br on R. Pass L through last 2br on R.

8 Pick up 1br on L, 1br, 2b on R. Pass L through 2b.

9 Pick up 1b on L, 3b on R. Pass L through 2b on R.

10 Reverse pattern to finish.

To make the loop, count the two end beads of the pattern and thread 7b onto L. Pass through two end-pattern beads. Pull to draw up. Pass R around the loop. Finish loop as in basic pattern.

Diagram 82 is for the basic pattern with two beads in each stage: two beads are picked up on L and four on R. L is passed through two on R. One or several colours may be used as desired.

Cord or a fine string is used to thread the beads for the next pattern, which again is the basic pattern but used with different shapes of beads. It is most suitable for a belt and, if string or cord is used, is very strong when complete. Carpet twine is suitable since this is both strong and fine. The finished belt is approximately 45cm (26in) long.

The movement of the needles is exactly the same as that for the basic pattern with size 4mm beads.

Ladder belt. Diagram 83

Materials:
  8mm brown beads (165)
  Long ovals in orange (27)
  One 10mm bead in orange or brown
  Crotchet thread or cord in orange or brown
  Two large-eyed needles
  Long pin
  Cushion
Key:
  b – 8mm brown beads
  O – ovals
Pattern:
Cut length of crotchet thread approx. 2m (72in) long and thread needles. Thread 10mm bead. The 10mm bead is secured to the cushion in the same way as the first bead in the basic pattern.

Pick up 2b on both needles to make the stem of the fastening bead. Pick up 1b on L, 1b and 1O on R. Pass L through O. Pick up 3b on L, 3b and 1O on R. Pass L through O. Continue until the belt is long enough to fit you.

To make the loop see diagram 83. At the end of the pattern, after completing a sequence of three b on L, three b 1O on R and passing L through O, pick up 1b on L, 3b on R and pass L through 2b on R. Pull tight.

On L pick up 5b. Pass L through two beads at end of pattern. Pass R in the opposite direction around the loop. Pull tight and make slip knots

54 Section of ladder belt 2 with ovals and 8mm beads, showing the loop start, and using basic movements

on either side of the two beads. Work thread back into the pattern making slip knots at intervals. Trim ends. This belt is very simple to make and can be varied by using more or less 8mm beads to make the sides of the ladder. Another version of the ladder belt is shown in illustration 54.

Ladder belt 2 with fastener. Diagram 84

Materials:
  Fifty long ovals in black
  Thirty-two 8mm beads in olive and purple
  Six 6mm black beads
  One 10mm bead to fasten
  Two large-eyed needles
  Black thread or twine
  Cushion
Pattern:
Thread needles with a length of thread approximately 2m (72in) long. Thread one 8mm black bead and draw to centre. Secure to the cushion.
1 Pick up three 6mm black on L, three 6mm black on R and one 8mm olive. Pass L through 8mm on R. This forms the loop for fastening.
2 Pick up one oval on L, one oval and one 8mm purple on R, pass L through 8mm on R. The pattern continues in this way until the belt is long enough to fit you. When the last section of pattern has been worked, pick up one 8mm on R, pass L through this and pull tight. Pick up one 10mm bead on R, and pass L through. Pull tight. Pass both needles through 8mm bead again as shown and work back into the pattern making slip knots.

Diagram 83   Ladder belt 1

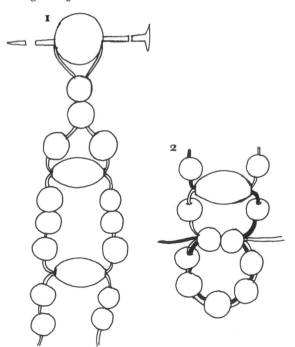

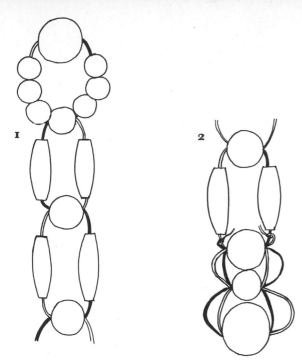

Diagram 84   Ladder belt 2, showing loop and bead to fasten

This pattern and the preceding one are also suitable for bracelets. The larger the ovals and the connecting beads the thicker the cord or thread may be and, if you wish, it is not necessary to use a needle at all. The ends of the cords may be stiffened by dipping them into a PVA glue and rolling them between finger and thumb until the glue is dry. This makes the ends stiff enough to pass through the beads without the aid of a needle.

Rocaille beads may be used for the stringing patterns with great effect. You will find that it is easier if you use monofilament nylon with these beads because there is a danger of splitting the threads as the needles cross inside the beads. Almost certainly the work would have to be taken apart if that happened. If you use nylon, do not pull too hard on the two threads when drawing the beads into the pattern shapes – a gentle tug is enough. Work threaded onto nylon which is pulled too tightly is very inflexible.

Single rows of basic pattern may be worked into very attractive long necklaces, but as bracelets they tend to be rather insubstantial although in small pieces they may be suitable for a child.

Several rows of the basic pattern look very pretty. The following example uses a multiple basic pattern, and the three rows carry the theme further.

Three-row bracelet using Rocaille beads. Diagrams 85–88. Illustration 55

Materials:
    Size 10 Rocaille beads in black and gold (approximately 600)
    One 6mm black wooden bead
    Nylon monofilament line
    Two size 10 beading needles
    Small, heavy anchor cushion
    Long large-headed pin
Key:
    g – gold
    b – black
    L – left-hand needle
    R – right-hand needle
Pattern:
Thread two needles and pick up 6mm fastening bead. Draw to the centre of the threads and secure to the cushion as shown in the diagram.
1 Follow diagram 85. Pick up and thread 3b on L, 3b on R, and 2b with both needles together.
2 Pick up 3b on L, 3b, 3g on R. Pass L through 3g on R.
3 Continue using this sequence until the length will fit around your wrist.

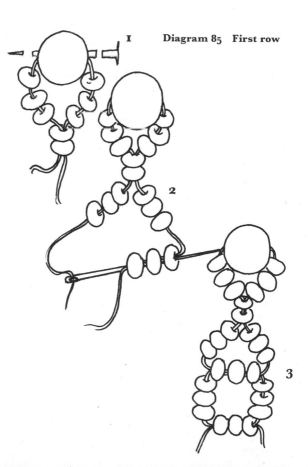

Diagram 85   First row

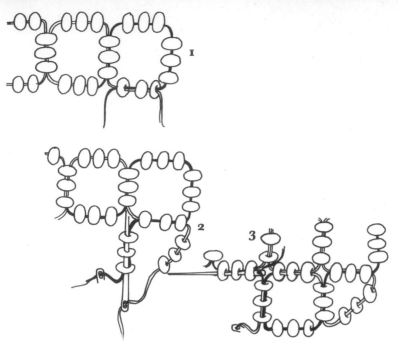

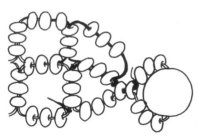

Diagram 86   Turning to start row 2, showing the ending of row 1, making the turn, and beginning work on row 2 after the completion of the turn

Diagram 87   Completing row 2 and fastening off old thread

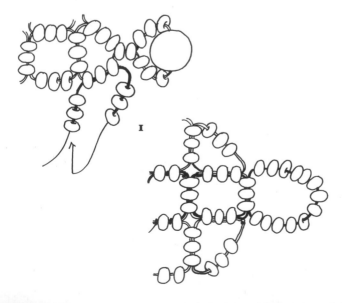

Diagram 88   For row 3, thread two needles onto one long thread and pass into side bar of the fastening bead, knot together, then take right-hand thread into the work and secure. Work the loop with the left-hand thread

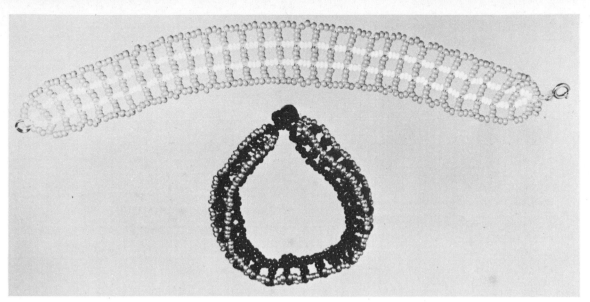

55 Three-row bracelets: the fastened bracelet has been worked into a three-dimensional shape by adding a fourth row after the bracelet is completed

Second row (diagram 86).

1 You must now make a turn to commence the second row of the bracelet. The manner in which this is done is the same as for a single three-bead basic pattern, but the number of beads is increased to correspond with the pattern being used and a slanting, not a squared, end is made.

Turn the work and pin so that the length faces you. Work the pattern so that the threads are also facing you – that is, the last pattern sequence of row one. (On R pick up 3b, 3g and 3b on L. Pass R through 3b on L. The thread should now be as in part 1 of diagram 86.)

2 Pick up 3g on L, 3b on R and pass R through 3g on L. You will see how the second row uses the side bars of row one as the third row of the pattern.

To complete the movement, pass the R needle through the three beads on row one which are to form the side bar of row two (see diagram). This movement continues along the row until the final pattern square is reached.

Diagram 87. To complete the row pick up 3g on L, 3b on R. Pass R up through 3g on L and on into the three beads which form the first sequence of row one. On L pick up 3b and pass into first bead of same sequence. Secure these two threads with slip knots and cut off. Rethread the needles with a new working thread for row three.

Turn and pin the work. Row three begins at the fastening bead end as shown in diagram 88.

1 Secure new threads as shown (one thread, with two needles). Repeat as row two until end is reached. The loop is made before fastening off the working threads.

Last pattern square. Pick up 3b on L and knot together with R thread. Leave R thread until fastening loop is complete. Take L through three beads forming top of centre row as shown. Pick up 13b and pass needle back through three beads of pattern and around the loop again. Take thread into pattern rows making slip knots at intervals and cut. Work R thread back into pattern making slip knots and trim ends.

This pattern makes an excellent choker or can be sewn to a small stand-up collar on a dress as added decoration.

Illustration 55 shows this bracelet pattern in two forms. The black and gold pattern can be joined so that there are four sides, making a hollow band. To do this bend the edges (rows two and three) up and, having secured a working thread, bring it out at the start of the first side bar of pattern on row two. Pick up three beads and pass down three beads of side bar on opposite side. Pick up three and repeat by passing needle down three beads in side bar on opposite side. Continue until the whole length is filled like this. To draw the rungs of this fourth row into line pass thread back along the bars just made in the opposite order to the first. Pull into shape and fasten off thread.

The following patterns are developments of the basic patterns.

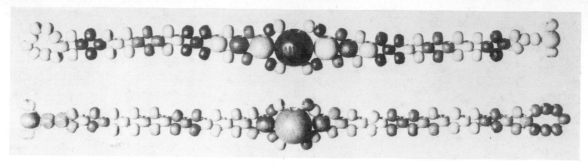

56 Bracelets with large bead centres

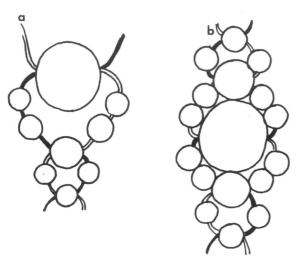

Diagram 89   Stringing with a large 12mm centre bead, 4mm and 6mm beads

Bracelet with large centre bead. Diagram 89. Illustration 56

This uses the basic pattern for the first nine sequences. Use any colour or combination of colours you like, matching the larger centre bead to one of them.

Work nine basic pattern units and then continue, using diagram 89.

Pick up one 4mm on L, one 4mm and one 6mm on R and pass L through 6mm. Pull tight. Pick up two 4mm on L, two 4mm and one 12mm on R and pass L through 12mm. Pull tight.

Reverse sequence from here: two 4mm on L, two 4mm and one 6mm on R. Pass L through 6mm. This may be varied and, if you wish, only one 4mm bead need be used with the centre bead. However, a considerable amount of thread will be visible in this case whereas two beads plus the large centre bead reveal far less.

Graduated centre. Three colours. Diagram 90. Illustration 56

Materials:
  4mm beads in black, rich brown and light brown
  6mm beads in the two browns
  8mm bead in light brown
  12mm bead in black
  Black Polytwist thread
  Two needles
  Cushion
Key:
  b – black
  lb – light brown
  db – dark (or rich) brown

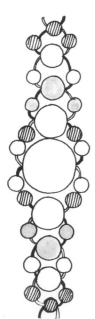

Diagram 90   Stringing 12, 8, 6 and 4mm beads in three colours

  L – left-hand needle
  R – right-hand needle

Pattern:

(Use 4mm beads in the following pattern unless larger sizes are specified.)

Thread 6mm lb and secure to cushion. With both needles pick up and thread 2lb and slide them down to the 6mm bead. The basic pattern is alternate colours in an lb, b, lb, rb, lb sequence.

Pick up and thread 1lb on L, 1lb and 1b on R and pass L through b on R.

Pick up and thread 1b on L, 2b on R. Pass L through 1b on R pull tight.

Pick up 1lb on L, 2lb on R. Pass L through last lb on R.

Pick up 1lb on L, 1lb and 1db on R. Pass L through db on R.

Pick up 1db on L, 2db on R pass L through 1db on R. Pull threads evenly to draw the pattern into shape.

Pick up 1lb on L, 2lb on R. Pass L through 1lb on R.

Pick up 1b on L, 2b on R. Pass L through 1b on R. Pull tight.

Pick up 1b on L, 1b and 16mm lb on R. Pass L through 6mm lb. Pull tight.

Pick up 1lb on L, 1lb and 1 6mm db on R. Pass L through 6mm db on R.

Pick up 1db on L, 1db on R and 1 8mm lb. Pass L through 8mm lb on R.

Pick up 1b and 1lb on L, 1b, 1lb and 1 12mm b on R. Pass L through 12mm on R. Pull to draw pattern into shape. The centre is now half completed.

Repeat the pattern in reverse until the bracelet fits the wrist.

Make loop in the manner previously described.

You may like to try working this pattern with larger centre line of beads right from the start – these may be all one colour or may match the outer rows of beads. If the bracelet is too small then add more 4mm patterns to either end of it or perhaps another 8mm bead pattern will give sufficient length. Remember, however, that the centre pattern should increase and diminish evenly for the bracelet to be really effective.

Square beads which have been used for other patterns in previous sections are useful for the stringing patterns, either in combinations of round and square beads, or alone. Those known as small square are useful for the previous pattern and those which are true cubes are very effective if used alone for the basic pattern. The flat sides of the beads lie closely and neatly together and make a solid strip of work.

It is difficult to make a fastening loop with these particular beads; the square shape does not lend itself to this construction. Small Rocailles should therefore be used for this unless you are able to match the colours with those of the 4mm wooden beads. A loop of 16 size 10 Rocaille beads will fit snugly over one square bead. This loop is added last without attaching a new working thread, as with all the patterns. Be careful not to pull the threads too tightly (see illustration 57).

Many-sided wooden beads fit well into the centre of the stringing pattern. They are an unusual addition to the work, and a graduated design may be worked in the same manner as that used for the round beads of different sizes. A many-sided bead is used where the 12mm bead was used. Small lice may also be used with success (see illustration 58).

The three bracelets in the illustration show how well different shapes and sizes may be combined and how they are equally effective with beads of the same colour or of several colours. Try a few experiments of your own: for instance, some odd beads may be suitable for the centre of stringing patterns, especially if they are used with only one other colour.

Floral stringing pattern. Diagram 91. Illustration 59

Materials for Flower Bracelet:
  Size 4mm turquoise wooden beads
  Size 6mm wooden beads in purple, turquoise and olive green
  Turquoise Polytwist thread or nylon
  Two needles
  Anchor cushion
  Large pin
  Beeswax for waxing thread

Key:
  t – 4mm turquoise
  p – 6mm purple
  o – 6mm olive green
  tu – 6mm turquoise
  L – left-hand needle
  R – right-hand needle

Pattern:
Wax thread, and thread the two needles. Pick up one turquoise 6mm bead and slide to the centre of the thread. Fasten to the cushion with pin. Pick up 1t on R and pass L through. Pull tight. Repeat this so that there are two 4mm turquoise beads forming a stem to the fastener.

57 Cube bead bracelet using basic pattern, with Rocaille bead loop

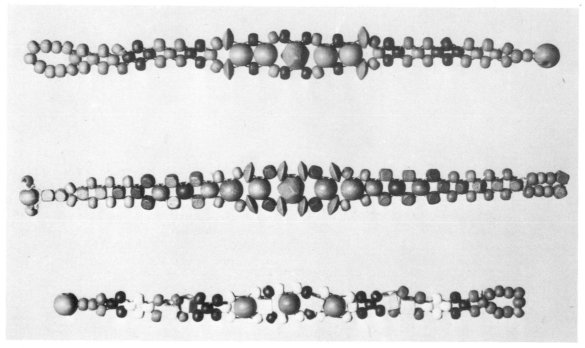

58 Bracelets with basic pattern movement, using several shapes and sizes of beads

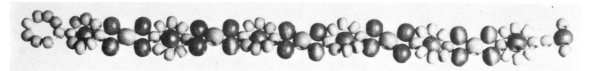

59 Floral pattern, using 6mm flower centre

1 With the left needle pick up 7t and pass the needle through bead 1 as shown. This makes the circle which forms the eight petals of the flower.

2 Pick up 1p on L and pass R through it.

3 Pull tight and pass R and L through the bottom petal bead in opposite directions. Pull tight. This makes the flower.

4 Pick up 1o on L, 1o and 1tu on R and pass L through tu on R. Pull tight.
Pick up 1o on L, 1o and 1t on R and pass L through t on R.
Pick up 7t on L and pass L back through first bead. The pattern of flower and connecting

pattern now repeats until the work is sufficiently long. A loop is formed in the usual manner (see diagram 91). Pattern ends with a flower. This pattern works as well with 6mm and 8mm beads or with all 4mm beads. If larger beads are used, a very attractive belt can be made.

In the illustrated bracelet the loop was too large, so on either side of the first bead a 4mm bead was added to form a T bar.

A collar made by the stringing method

The collar in illustration 60 was made by the

stringing method. This technique will produce collars which are as lacy and attractive in appearance as those made by the threading technique in the previous section. By increasing the number of beads in the rows of stringing a curved band is produced, the basic principle being exactly the same as the threading. However, if the number of beads is increased in each unit of the pattern too much fullness results, so only certain pattern 'squares' are increased. The work *must* be firmly pinned to a cushion when in progress otherwise it becomes very difficult to handle. The tension should be kept even throughout. Increasing the number of beads so that a perfectly flat collar emerges is very difficult and the more usual result is a frilled edge to the work. This can be very pretty although too much of a frill is rather overpowering and fussy. By only increasing the number of beads in the centre patterns, and very gradually at the sides of the work, a shaped collar with a gently-frilled edge may be produced; the frill will be almost imperceptible when the collar is worn unless, of course, you require it to be more pronounced. More beads are added to the bottom row of the work than to any other, and a very open effect is possible. The first row of the work should be as long as your neck measurement when measured loosely around the base. Allow a little more if you anticipate wearing the collar over a sweater or dress. A loop and fastening bead may be worked before you commence the second and subsequent rows since the collar is not worked on either side of the first row, as in the wide bracelets, but each row is joined to the last one worked.

The length of the rows, that is, the number of pattern squares, does not increase; only the number of the beads. The depth, however, may be increased as much as you wish, so if you want to work a very lacy collar then the larger the pattern units become the faster the work will progress and the deeper it will be. Remember that too many beads in the patterns will make a large frill. The collar in illustration 60 has three rows.

Strung collar. Diagram 92. Illustration 60

Materials:
Size 10 (or 7) Rocaille beads in two or more colours

Diagram 91   Loop for floral stringing, fastening off with slip knots, with the right and left-hand threads around the loop

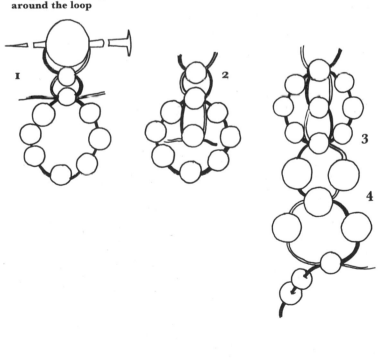

6mm bead to fasten, or a hook and eye
Polytwist thread or nylon monofilament
Two size 10 or 9 beading needles
Beeswax if thread is used
Cushion and several glass-headed pins for
securing work

Key:
  m – main colour
  c – contrast
  L – left-hand needle
  R – right-hand needle

Pattern:
The example is worked without fastenings.
These are added later.

   Thread the needles and pick up 2m beads,
slide them to the centre of the thread and pin
through them to the cushion.

1 Count the 2m beads as the first rung of the
  pattern. Pick up 2m on L, 4m on R. Pass L
  through 2m on R. Pull tight.
2 Pick up 2m on L, 2m and 2c on R. Pass L
  through 2c on R. Continue this until the work
  is the same length as your neck measurement.
  End with a solid main-colour pattern and turn
  the work as shown in diagram 92. The threads
  should now face you when the work is turned
  and pinned so that the first row is in a horizontal position.

You will find that the work is easier to handle
if you also pin it at intervals along the first
pattern row.

3 Make the turn and work four pattern units
  as row one.
4 Increase. Pick up 4m on L, 3c on R. Pass R
  through 4m and on into bar of main-colour
  beads on first row. Continue until there are
  four pattern units left to work and work them
  as row one.

You may turn the work over each time if you
wish so that you always work in a R to L direction as in the diagrams (there are no right–wrong
sides). Work the turn and commence row three
with four pattern units as row one and four as
row two. If you wish to make the work deeper
in a short time then increase number of m beads
on the needle: this adds depth but does not
influence the curve of the work or the amount of
frill – this is achieved by the increases made in
the contrast colour beads which now form the
horizontal bars of the collar.

  Increase row three from the ninth pattern by
adding two beads to the main colour and one to
the contrasts. When the last eight pattern units
are reached, work four as row two, four as row 1.

  If you would like the depth of the work to be
greater towards the centre front of the collar
then you should make a note of the number of
units it takes to work a whole row, find the centre
and work several patterns on either side of this
increasing the number of main-colour beads by
one or two each time: the third row has five
main-colour beads; increase 6, 7, 8, 9 to centre

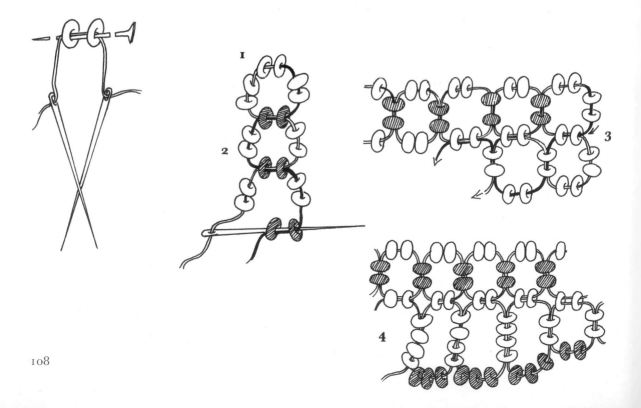

60 Collar using Rocaille beads, with three rows

then decrease 9, 8, 7, 6, 5 on opposite side; revert to normal pattern. This may be done on each, or alternate rows, so that the collar has a greater depth at the centre.

Now that the shape is forming it is up to you to develop the collar to your own liking. If you wish to make this a narrow collar, three or four rows of pattern will be sufficient and at the end of the last of these rows you should secure the working threads and cut them. Attach the fasteners, either a loop and bead or a commercial ring bolt and split ring, or even a hook and buttonhole eye. The fastening for the collar may be a ribbon tie. The ribbon is threaded through the last square of the pattern on the first row and is either stitched into place or used double. Alternatively, the ribbon can be woven through the whole of the first row and the ends used to fasten the collar.

The larger wooden beads are rather clumsy for the collar and look their best if they are additions rather than the only beads used. Four millimetre wooden beads and 4mm Rocaille beads are suitable for this pattern. If you wish to increase the depth of the work quite rapidly use Rocaille beads plus long bugles in the contrast or vertical bars of the pattern. The bottom row of the pattern might include drop beads or particularly beautiful beads; alternatively, several rows might have this additional interest.

Any beads can be used to add interest in this way. Adding fringes and dangles to strung work, especially to the collars, is not a great success. The slight frill on the complete collar does not lend itself to this additional decoration.

Once you have mastered the technique of increasing the number of horizontal beads to make a curve or frill you will be able to experiment easily. The collar may be worked so that the rows of pattern are close together; this is done by adding only to the horizontal bars and not to the vertical ones which produce the depth. To make a very open and lacy collar many more beads are added to the vertical bars than to the horizontal ones. The frill is as adaptable as the threaded collars in Section Two. Edgings for a variety of household objects can be made and sometimes the more frilled the work is the better. A complete circle on a smaller scale would provide you with a set of cuffs, to match a collar perhaps, and so complete a garment. Large flat pieces of the basic stringing pattern can be made into purses or table mats. The variations of the basic pattern may also be used this way and the work will grow faster if more and larger beads are used to make up the pattern units.

The stringing technique is versatile and useful to complement the threading and 'strings' and to add more to your enjoyment of beads, as well as to your knowledge and understanding of them.

◀ **Diagram 92   Securing Rocaille beads to the cushion, using Collar Pattern, showing the turn for row 2, and the lengthening and widening of row 2**

part two
section one beadweaving
the woven fabric of beads

Background

The previous techniques should rightly be called 'handwork' since the only tool, other than needle and thread, is the hands, but loomed work or beadweaving utilizes other tools. Beadweaving is quite different in appearance to the threading and stringing techniques. When woven, the beads form parallel rows which make a solid band or ribbon of beads as flexible and closely woven as cloth – thus the title of this section. The technique of beadweaving was popular during the Victorian and Edwardian eras when woven chains, purses, bags, panels for mirror backs and the like were worked with beads similar to those in use today. Miser purses, a curiously Victorian invention, often included a woven section in the centre. Pincushions and stool tops were other popular items. Woven on an Apache Loom, modelled on those used by the Apache Indians and similar in construction to the loom described later in this section, many examples survive and may be seen in museums throughout the country. In 1909, beadweaving was speeded up by the introduction of the Square Bead Loom, a compact wooden contraption.

Traditional North American Indian Bead-work, as in illustration 61, has been made for generations by the weaving technique. Some of the work produced is used for personal decoration, although nowadays a great deal is produced specifically for the tourist trade. In the past the work was significant as part of the high tribal ceremonial dress, the colours of the beads and the designs employed being symbolic and rich in meaning. Today much of this remains, in that designs which are part of a symbolic and complicated mythology, closely interwoven with Indian life and traditions, are still used in the modern work. Illustration 62 presents designs symbolizing the four divisions of the earth and

other common Indian symbols. Many of these designs are used traditionally in beadwork and some, which are more commonly used for embroidered beadwork, are still useful to the modern worker who wishes to adapt the traditional. Indian designs nearly always translate well into geometric pattern, and many of these designs formed the basis for my earlier work.

As with beads used in other parts of the world, whatever the techniques employed, the early American Indians made their beads from the objects nearest to hand. The tribes of the interior used seeds, berries, small pine cones and pebbles; those of the coastal regions, and in particular the east coast, perfected the art of making shell beads, called wampum, which – via trade, exchange and capture – gradually found their way to other tribes. In order to obtain the dark and light beads required for the symbolic patterns, the shells of the whelk and the clam were used, one producing a deep purple-grey colour, the other a white. These shells were made into small cylinders of almost glass-like smoothness, drilled and then either used as currency (for which they are most commonly known) or woven into belts. Belts such as these were an important part of tribal ceremonial, used to record transactions between the various Indian nations, to record treaties between them, and often, such was their significance, used as tokens of peace (see illustration 63). Sometimes the beads were dyed so that intricate patterns could be created: not only are the designs themselves significant but also the colours and their relationships within the designs.

Woven belts are part of Zulu tribal life and they, too, have a deeper significance than being a mere item of dress. These message belts were often carried over vast distances by runners to give (as the name implies) messages to other tribes. To make the belts the Zulu weaver would at one time have manufactured his beads from

61 Apache beadwork collar

62 North American Indian symbols

1

2

3

4

5

63 Wampum belt with tortoise-shaped medicine bag attached (courtesy British Museum)

stone or shell. To produce the required shape suitable for weaving he would have had to pierce them through the centre, thread them onto a stick and then grind them, by rolling them many times backwards and forwards on a flat stone, until they became cylindrical and smooth.

Generations ago, Arab traders introduced Venetian glass beads to the wandering Masai people of Kenya. Later explorers offered beads as tokens of friendship and peace, and then as items for trade and exchange. The Masai people are exquisite craftsmen, applying a high degree of skill and understanding of materials to their work; they still use beads which originate from the outside world, but the designs and the workmanship are uniquely Masai. Men and women alike wear an incredibly complex mass of beaded jewellery. Much of it is a significant part of their lives, and much of it passes from generation to generation. Their huge stiff collar discs are made up from thousands upon thousands of tiny seed beads threaded onto wire and bent into shape; bands of woven beads sometimes link the sections of the discs together. Wide bands of wooden beads and narrow bands of seed beads adorn the

necks, ankles and wrists of both sexes; long looped earrings made from tiny beads are worn by the women. Clothing is supported by beaded straps, sandals are secured by them and plaited straps of beads used to carry burdens. The work of these people is a never-ending source of inspiration.

To mention all the nations of the world who use beads for weaving would take a whole chapter and still hardly do them justice. However, as a source of inspiration, some of the patterns, the colours and the articles made are invaluable. In our modern mechanized society we are conventional in our usage of personal adornment, and so a glimpse of how other peoples use a craft can open up new avenues for exploration and give us original and sometimes surprising insights. In her book, *Beadwork from North American Indian Designs,* Marjory Murphy provides patterns and working instructions for a variety of traditional North American Indian necklaces and bracelets. These designs, some adapted to suit modern tastes and others purely traditional, are revealing in their complexity.

Although a loom is usually employed for the weaving technique it is not an absolute necessity, rather a convenience. The threads which carry the beads can be fastened to any firm bar of wood, a belt buckle or a ring, and anchored securely at the other end to an immovable object such as a belt around one's own waist. The method is admittedly somewhat tedious and the tension, even for the most experienced weaver, difficult to maintain, thus producing uneven and often slack work. Once the actual mechanics of weaving have been mastered, though, it is worth trying, if only to gain an insight into the difficulties encountered by past craftsmen, or for the sake of experiment and variation. If the beadworkers of still-primitive tribes can produce exquisite work by the clumsiest of methods, so can the modern worker.

section two
what is beadweaving?

Beadweaving resembles wool weaving in that it is based on taut warp, that is, vertical threads. In place of the shuttle used in fabric weaving a needle and thread are used and strung with a number of beads; these form the weft, the horizontal threads. However, the over and under movement used in conventional weaving techniques is not used in this craft. The needle and thread which carry the beads is passed *under* the warp threads from right to left or left to right (whichever is more comfortable) and then back through the beads but *over* the warps in the opposite direction (see diagram 100).

The thread carrying the beads must therefore be strong and also fine enough to pass twice through the centre of the beads. Fine synthetic threads are strong enough to support small beads, although the warp threads should always be thicker. If the work is to be of great length or width, and therefore very heavy, a thicker thread should also be used for the weft.

I always use a synthetic buttonhole twist (Gütermann Polytwist) for both warp and weft; it is manufactured in a wide range of colours, it is strong and the finished work remains flexible and retains the characteristics of other woven materials. It is also thick enough to plait or knot by the macramé technique if desired.

Developing your own rhythm and working process will take time and experience. Learn not to look for the holes in the bead and always keep your beads in separate shallow containers to facilitate picking up, (under artificial light it is often very difficult to spot a wrong-coloured bead). You *will* miss warp threads as you pass the needle back through the beads and you *will* bend needles so that they become useless; beads will break, threads *will* split and you will be tempted to give up. In a very short time, however, the rhythm will come and the work will progress as smoothly as the techniques you have already mastered.

Tools

The Beadloom. This is the major tool. In diagrams 93–5 you can see how a beadloom may be made.
Beading needles. Sizes 9 and 10 and, for very tiny beads, size 12.
Threads. Gütermann Polytwist synthetic thread. Fine polyester thread of the same make is also useful for finishing the work and for weaving when extra-fine, but strong, thread is desirable. Monofilament nylon is not suitable for weaving.
Beads. Size 10 and 7 Rocaille beads.
An assortment of wooden beads in various shapes and sizes. Ceramic and glass beads of different kinds.
Beeswax for waxing the threads.
Graph or squared paper. Pencils and/or fibre or felt-tipped pens.
Fasteners. An assortment as for the previous techniques: hooks and eyes, ring bolts, buttons, studs, buckles and brass or plastic rings.
Hem tape, in a variety of colours if possible, but certainly black and white. Width should be 13mm ($\frac{1}{2}$in) and 25mm (1in).
One or two large *bulldog clips*.

The loom

Several commercially-made looms are available from craft shops, but they tend to be expensive. If you intend to take up the craft seriously it is worth investing in one, but initially a home-made loom like those in diagrams 93–5 will be adequate. Home-made looms do, however, have limitations. It is not possible to adapt all of them for longer weavings, and the cardboard box loom will only be suitable for relatively short items. A child's wool weaving loom has been used by many of my adult students; the only adaptation required to make this loom suitable for beadweaving is

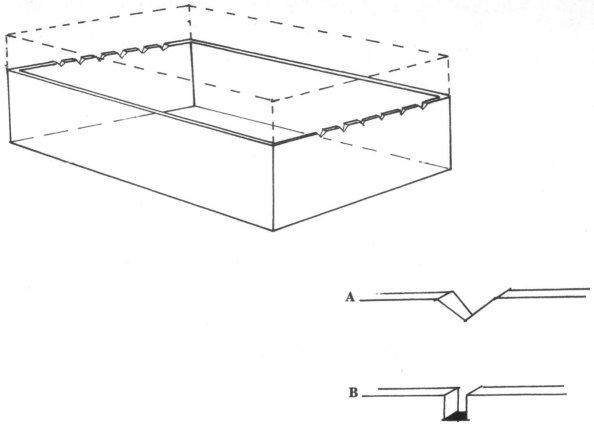

A

B

Diagram 93   Cardboard box loom made from shoe box or other firm card box. The box can be halved to make it less likely to bend inwards. Details A and B show notches

the cutting of extra grooves between the existing ones.

To begin with think of the loom simply as a vehicle for carrying and supporting the warp threads. Making a loom is easy and materials for its construction should be available around your home. A simple loom is constructed from a shoe box or some other cardboard box which is fairly strong and rigid. It should not be too wide or long otherwise the tension necessary for the warp threads will pull it out of shape. If the box is deep, cut it down to half the depth as indicated in diagram 93. This is such an easy loom to make, and so easy to come by, that once the technique is familiar it can be discarded in favour of a more durable one. If you have a wooden box which is easy to adapt by notching the ends, so much the better.

A picture frame which is not too big, is also a suitable vehicle for the warp threads. The advantages of a frame are many, easy accessibility to the threads being one of them. My first loom was an old frame. Panel pins were hammered into the short edges at approximately 3mm ($\frac{1}{8}$in)

intervals to provide spaces for the threads of the warp. On my current loom (illustration 64) the rollers have metal combs set into them; the teeth of the combs are used to space or separate the warp threads. Notches or slits cut into the card or wooden looms serve the same purpose, as do panel pins hammered along the edge of frame or home-made wooden looms. Whether you use notches, grooves or pins they should be evenly spaced and, when threaded, the warps should run parallel to each other.

To make a simple yet effective loom only three pieces of wood, a few panel pins and a little glue are required (see diagram 94). The base board should be approximately 13–25mm thick and the wood fairly heavy; if fabric or a piece of felt is stuck to the underside of this it will not scratch furniture. The raised ends should be at least 25mm high to enable the fingers to pass beneath the weaving with ease. These ends should be stuck to the base with a good wood glue, or pinned from beneath. Only shorter pieces of weaving are possible with this loom. Do not make the base too long with the idea of producing longer

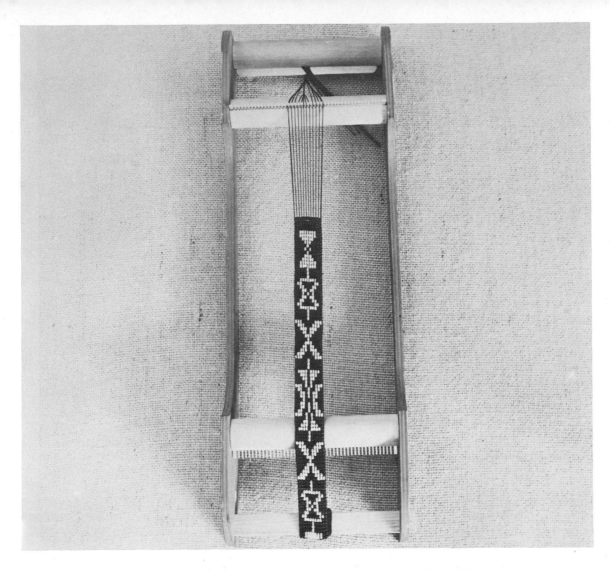

64a Loom with weaving in place

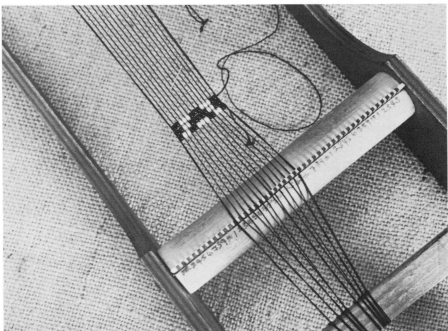

64b Straight weaving on loom showing the double outside warps and the numbering in the spaces

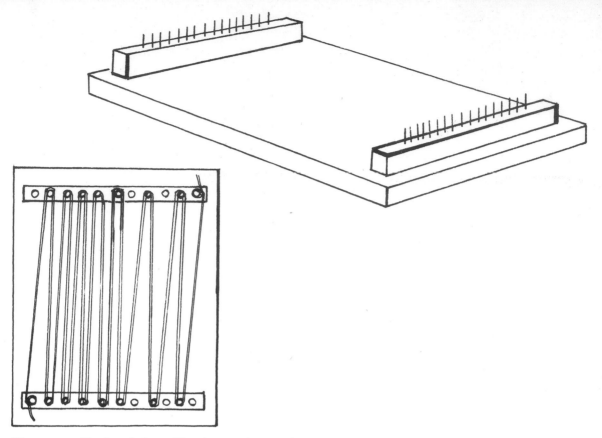

Diagram 94 Hand-made loom. The pins stand on platforms at least 1″ high and 1″ wide, and the base is ½–¾″ high

weavings; if it is very much longer than 30–43cm you will find it difficult to maintain an even tension without some device to hold the warps. The pins are hammered into the raised ends along a centre line and should be approximately 3mm apart. Modifications to the loom which will allow you to make longer articles are plained on p. 117.

Setting up the loom. The warp

The warp threads are the vertical or downward threads which support the weft (horizontal bead-carrying thread). These threads must be very strong in order to take the considerable weight of the beads and, if the woven item is intended for wear (a belt, bracelet, or choker), then the warps must be able to withstand considerable handling. The length of the warp threads depends on the item.

The loom in diagram 94 is set up with a continuous warp; this is tied to the first pin with a secure knot, wound backwards and forwards around the pins and tied again at the last one. The diagram shows two versions of the continuous warp. For very small (size 10) beads the first

method of winding around each pin is used, for larger (size 7) beads the warp is wound around alternate pins as shown. The box loom should be set up with a continuous warp which is also wrapped around the base of the box. The loom used to weave all the examples is ideal for making longer articles of woven work. The warps can be moved along many times and with practice there is no limit to the length which can be woven.

It is easier and quicker to set up the warps if all the threads are cut at once. If the work is to be 30cm (12in) long the threads are cut 30cm for the length of work plus 75mm (3in) which makes up the length of the loom, plus 16cm (6½in) to allow for the work to be wound on. The total length which can be woven without this being done is 25cm thus the threads would be cut 53cm × 5 = 265cm – the threads are cut double so that they can be attached to the bar on the loom with a half-hitch mounting (see diagram 96).

In the same way that the length of the warp determines the length of the work, so the number of warp threads determines the width. Each space between the warp threads represents a

Bracelets based on the chevron pattern woven in several widths,
worn with a woven, fringed choker

Abstract beadwoven hanging. The staggered lines of weaving are
the result of using several sizes and shapes of bead in both wood and
glass, which require the weaver to insert extra beads in places in
order to maintain an even tension

bead. To make the work stronger and to give it a neater, firmer edge, the outer warp threads are doubled by adding an extra thread. These double threads go through the same notch or space between the pins.

For example, to make a choker 32cm long and 25mm wide using size 7 beads you would have to have 14 warp threads. This means cutting seven lengths of thread double the required length, plus the necessary length to wind on the work and finish it off. Each thread is folded in half so that there is a loop at one end. I have avoided giving a specific length, since home-made looms are likely to be of different lengths. Once the work is completed and removed from the loom, however, the remaining lengths of warp thread have either to be tied, knotted or threaded individually onto a needle and woven back into the work, so you should allow sufficient thread for this.

Setting up the different looms

The home-made loom uses a continuous warp

Diagram 95 Picture frame loom with each warp thread tied individually so that the weaving can be moved around the frame in order to make larger articles

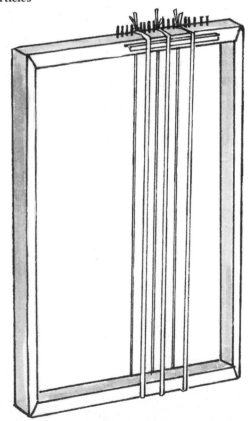

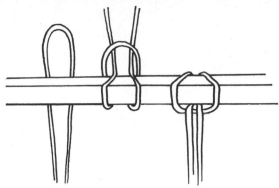

Diagram 96 Attaching warp threads

thread which is secured at either end or wrapped around the whole loom so that the threads run underneath the wooden base. Moving this warp so as to make a longer weaving (a belt, for instance) is only possible if each warp thread is tied separately (see diagram 95). This is also suitable for the frame and the box loom, but there are difficulties in keeping the threads taut. To ensure that the threads are kept as tight as possible, a piece of wood or dowel rod is slipped under them and drawn back so that it is caught between the threads and the side of the box, frame or wooden loom; this lifts the threads slightly and effectively tightens them (see diagram 95). The wood is easily removed if the work is to be moved around the loom and replaced before weaving is recommenced. Great care should be taken when easing the work around the loom: once the warp is filled and the wood removed take all the threads in one hand and ease them around the loom so that unfilled warps are brought from the bottom of the loom. Try not to drag the threads too hard through the notches or grooves which separate the threads because rough edges will fray the warp threads and a broken thread is difficult to repair (see page 132). If the grooves are rubbed with wax or varnished before you begin weaving they will be smoother. Panel pins, if used, should be removed from one end so that the woven part slides around the edge; these are not replaced since the beads will keep the warp open.

Diagram 96 shows how to attach the warp threads to the loom used for the examples. This is also suitable for the frame loom since the threads may be fastened around the end and, providing the frame is not too wide, a bulldog clip can be used to secure the ends of the warp at the opposite end. Otherwise they should be tied around the whole frame singly.

On the commercial (Apache) loom used throughout the weaving section, the warp threads

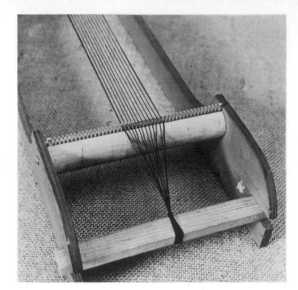

65a Warp threads attached separately to the bar of the loom by a half-hitch

65b Warp threads attached all together in a half-hitch to the bar of the loom

66 Warp threads secured into a grooved roller

are attached to the wooden bar at one end of the loom and at the opposite end are secured into a grooved roller by means of a slender length of wood (illustration 66). This grooved roller can be rotated in either direction in order to decrease or increase the tension of the warp threads. When the loom is relatively new this method is very secure and the threads stay firmly stretched between the two ends. Once the loom has been in use for some time, however, the groove and wood wear away so that there is less tension and the threads slip from beneath the wood. To counteract this, I use an ice-lolly stick in place of the original wooden slat and find this sufficiently

thick to hold the threads in place. Alternatively, a piece of paper or foil can be wrapped around the wood to thicken it. On all the looms, whatever the means of guiding, the warps are spaced equal distances apart. Whether pins, grooves or notches are used it is helpful to pencil in numbers in groups of 10 so that the threads always run through directly opposing spaces (see illustration 65 where this is clearly shown).

Beads

The beads used in the previous sections can all

be used successfully in the weaving technique, but until you are more proficient, larger round beads and beads of different sizes in the same piece of work should be avoided. The beads used throughout are of regular shape and size and it is especially important that this should be so for weaving. They must lie close together, not only along the length of the weaving, but also across the width. Uneven and oddly-sized beads, even if only slightly so, will create uneven and unattractive work which is not only difficult to control but a disappointment for the beginner. The beads used, unless otherwise stated, are size 10 or 7 Rocaille beads in either a lustre, opaque or transparent finish. For the first attempts I would recommend using size 7 beads because they are larger, have bigger holes and are less likely to cause problems. These are supplied in similar colours to size 10 although the lustres are not available. Since they are larger the work will grow faster. The thread will pass easily several times through the larger holes in the size 7 beads and, although it is usually only necessary to do this twice, when new threads are joined or when the work is strengthened it must be done three times. Once you have become proficient it is possible to include much larger beads in the work; special techniques are required for this and are described in detail on pp. 153–159.

Old jewellery containing evenly-sized beads will add to your store of beads; junk stalls, jumble sales and perhaps your own attic will supply others. However, it is most important to remember, as with the other beadwork techniques, that a considerable number of beads is required. Weaving uses perhaps more than any other technique. Wherever possible and practicable I have given the approximate quantities of beads required to make specific articles in the text. Nevertheless, wrists, waists and necks do vary a great deal, and so it is not always possible to be accurate. A way of calculating quantity fairly accurately is given on p. 144. Ways and means of augmenting your beads are possible and some of these are shown on pp. 165, 178. Beads and other tools are shown in illustration 67.

Containers and storing the beads

Containers are an important part of your working equipment. Many of my containers are typewriter-ribbon boxes with transparent lids which enable me to identify colour and size without opening the box and also provide an ideal working container. Another advantage is that they hold exactly 3oz of beads which is one of the quantities in which they are supplied. Boxes sold in anglers' supply shops (see illustration 67) which have one or two divided trays make excellent storage containers for wooden beads.

Needles

The techniques in the previous sections will have made you familiar with beading needles, but some of the information given in the first section about tools is worth repetition. The needles used for beadwork are generally fine with a long slender eye which will take thicker threads. They are purpose made for beadwork. Several sizes exist and a supply of each is necessary if you are to cope with variations in the size of the bead holes. These needles may be bought at haberdashery counters and other non-specialist shops but, in general, are supplied in only very small and relatively expensive quantities. The suppliers listed on p. 182 will be able to supply far larger quantities and are more likely to stock all the sizes. More than one packet of needles is advisable: they are so fine and flexible that during the course of weaving they become bent by the pressure of the fingers and it can then be difficult to pick up the beads and to guide the needle through them. Bent needles are, however, adequate for making strings and for the basic threading patterns. When very bent they become almost useless but it is perfectly possible for them to be straightened and used again. Anything which can be recycled in this way should be. If you *must* throw the needles away take care not to toss them into the rubbish bin or into a plastic rubbish bag because small children and animals often find rubbish irresistible, and indeed at some point *someone* will handle it. So wrap the needles in several layers of paper and put the paper into a strong container which is to be thrown away. This way the risk should be eliminated.

Some general hints

Several of the very basic rules, plus a few more, are also well worth repetition.

1 Always use more thread than you think you will need – warps must be long enough to allow the work to be: rolled on if a long article is being woven; finished off in one of the ways are given on p. 128.

2 The weft, or working thread, is used singly unless a very fine thread is being used in which case a double strand is advisable.

3 Check the tension of your weaving from time to time; each row should be pulled tight so that the beads lie close together.

4 If the beads have sufficiently large holes, the working thread should occasionally be taken back into the work for perhaps 3 rows then returned to the starting point of a new row in order to strengthen the weaving.

5 The rows of beads must be pushed close together so that there are no spaces between them. A comb, slotted over the warp threads and pulled up against the beads, will help.

6 Knotted threads will cause the loom to jerk sideways if it is not very heavy, so avoid knots by waxing the working thread with beeswax before the weaving is started.

7 Keep the working space clear. A cloth or piece of thick felt over the table helps to prevent the beads rolling too far if spilled.

8 Use a pin cushion for needles and pins.

9 Make sure you have sufficient beads to complete the work *before you begin.*

10 Keep your working materials away from small children and animals.

11 Use nail scissors with curved blades for trimming threads close to the woven beads. This will allow you to cut very close indeed to the work but to avoid important threads like warp and weft.

12 *Never* begin a working thread by making a knot and starting from the edge of the work because this is untidy and impossible to cut off. See p. 127, diagrams 101–2 for the correct procedure.

All the looms illustrated are as childproof as it is possible to make them and are intended for use by children and adults alike. Toddlers, however, do not possess the necessary manual dexterity to use the looms so, if they wish to join in, a large blunt needle, large wooden beads and instructions to make a necklace will keep them happy.

Design: planning the work

Before attempting any complicated patterns, or planning, you may feel you would rather master the technique itself by working several rows, or even a bracelet length, of plain weaving. Starting, attaching the new working thread, removing from the loom and finishing off the ends of the work could all be practised in this way on one piece of work. However, it is much more satisfying and interesting to work a pattern, even if only two colours are used. This is partly due to the way the pattern emerges as each row is completed. Woven beadwork allows many extremely complex patterns to be used and many colours as well. If you are attempting a pattern of several – or even only two – colours, some kind of plan provides a handy guide and is a good reference for future work. As you become more proficient and confident, you will need a pattern less and less. However, no matter how experienced you become, a pattern may sometimes be very necessary when a great many colours are being used, or when a weaving is done in several separate parts to be joined later.

Planning the work means knowing which bead goes where and what colours to use; in order to plan successfully a grid is required and graph or squared paper is used for this. You may wish to copy a pattern from another source or perhaps one based on one of the illustrations herein which is not given in the text, or it may be entirely your own. Cross-stitch patterns, in particular, provide the beadweaver with a wealth of ideas, based as they are on a grid system. Other patterns may come from weavers' pattern books (many of these employ a similar grid), and Florentine, Bargello, tapestry, petit point and Berlin woolwork patterns from embroidery books are all based on geometric, squared designs. Many European peasant costumes are richly embroidered with cross-stitch patterns, and are easily adapted to the technique of beadweaving, as are blackwork and some other old English embroidery patterns. The traditional symbols of the North American Indian, used by them for centuries, are superb examples of geometric pattern. All the above are easily adapted to your work. You may require only sections of these or you may decide to put together several from different sources.

Whatever the form of the final design it is not always possible to have direct access to the original source, so if you record the patterns on paper you can use them several times. Each square on the paper represents a bead. It is therefore a simple matter to add a colour or a symbol to represent the bead and so build up the pattern. However, if you use graph paper which has very tiny squares, two squares vertically should be used; this is because the Rocaille beads are longer than they are wide, so that the planned pattern in squares will not give a truly accurate picture

67 Weaving equipment: beads, containers, needles, thread and scissors. The beads include 4mm to 12mm wood in matt, shiny, and wood grain; small square, lice and cubed wood; sizes 10, 7, and 4 Rocaille; long, short and large ovals; and flat discs ▶

of the complete design. Using two squares (vertically) and so expanding the pattern will give a better, though still not perfect, idea of how the work will look when woven. Remember that the warp spaces represent beads: an even number of spaces will not allow you to make patterns which come to a point, because two beads will be central – an odd number of spaces will allow this. Any curved lines in a chosen pattern will be represented by steps both on paper and in the weaving because of the nature of the technique and the beads. Patterns are as varied and almost unlimited as beads themselves, and if there are limitations they are set only by the weaver and by the nature of the materials.

Two colours will be sufficient for the first attempt. Make a rough design and indicate the colours by darkening some squares and leaving others blank. You may well feel disappointed with your first weaving but be reassured that the more you do the better you become and what you learn whilst making the first one will be valuable experience for subsequent weavings.

section three how to weave

Weaving a choker 25mm (1 in) wide in two colours

First measure your neck to ascertain the actual length and make a note of the measurement. Add this to the amount of thread you will require to fasten the warp to the loom you are using, plus sufficient to finish off the choker in one of the ways shown on p. 129. Bear in mind that woven chokers look their best when worn fairly close about the neck.

For the loom in illustration 64 and for the frame loom *the threads are cut twice this length*, that is they should be the calculated length when folded in half. For others, a continuous warp or single lengths are used. You will need to cut seven lengths – 14 threads when folded. To make a choker 25mm wide you need 11 spaces for 11 size 7 beads, therefore 12 warps are needed, plus an extra one at each side. Thus 11 spaces = 12 warps + 2 extra = 14 threads.

If you are using a loom like the one in illustration 64, or the picture frame loom, double threads are attached as shown in diagram 96 and illustration 65. If one of the other looms is being used you should carefully calculate the thread needed and cut single lengths then attach in one of the ways given in setting up the loom on p. 116 or use a continuous warp.

Secure the threads when you have spaced them and tighten them so that tension is even over all the threads. If you are working on a dark surface with dark thread, place a sheet of light paper beneath the loom (or, in the case of a loom with a solid dark base, on the base beneath the warp). The threads will then be clearly visible and the risk of eye strain lessened. Your pattern should be placed in front of you where it is easy to refer to. The warp threads and the working (weft) thread should match as closely as possible the colour of the background beads. Thread is used as a single strand if it is Polytwist and double if finer polyester thread is used.

Securing the Working (Weft) Thread

The working thread is secured in one of the following ways.

Diagram 97. Knot the working thread to the double outside warp and weave several rows of close weaving with the thread only. Take care not to pull the warps together and distort them. This is repeated when the end of the weaving is reached and folded to the back of it, after trimming the warps to finish off.

Diagram 98. Weft thread sewn to outside warps. Leave approximately 10cm (4in) of thread in the tail – this can be woven into the work later. The thread should be stitched through the warps.

Diagram 99. Knot to the outside warps. Tie a firm double knot with the working (weft) thread, around the warps. Leave approximately 10cm (4in) thread in tail to be woven in later.

I use the second method of attaching the working thread, but if you experiment you will find which is the most suitable method for you. All the diagrams and photographs in this section show a right to left working method. This way of working is most comfortable for me, but some of my students find that working from left to right suits them better, and some prefer to turn the loom once it is set up and work towards themselves rather than away.

Choker in two colours 25mm (1 in) wide

Materials:

Size 7 black and yellow Rocaille beads (black is the main colour)

Polytwist thread to match main (black) beads

Beeswax

Size 9 beading needle

Run the working thread through the wax to

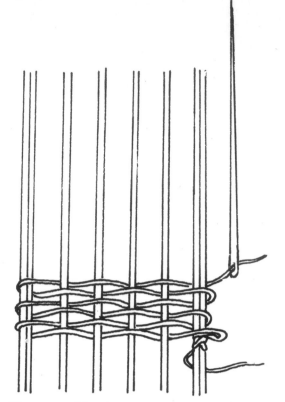

Diagram 97   Weaving with thread

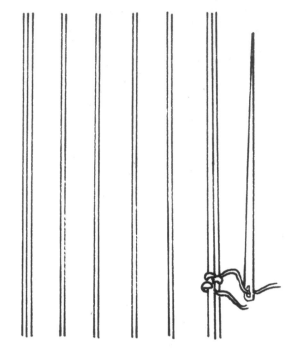

Diagram 98   Thread stitched to warp

Diagram 99   Thread knotted around warps

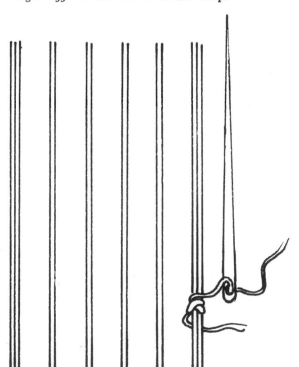

smooth it. Using approximately 1 metre of Polytwist, thread the needle and attach it to the double outside warp threads with one of the methods shown, or weave a few rows of over and under darning and bring the thread out at the side where you will begin weaving.

Written directions for the choker pattern are given as well as a graph. You may prefer to use one or both of these as you work. The graph shows you how a pattern for weaving may be worked out in symbol form.

Key:
    Text: b – black beads
              y – yellow beads
    Graph: x – yellow beads
    Clear squares – black beads

All weavings are given a number for reference purposes.

Weaving (see diagram 100):

To weave, pick up 11 black beads on the needle and slide them down the thread.

1 Pass the needle and thread under the warp threads. Diagrams show right to left but whatever is the most natural to you should be used.

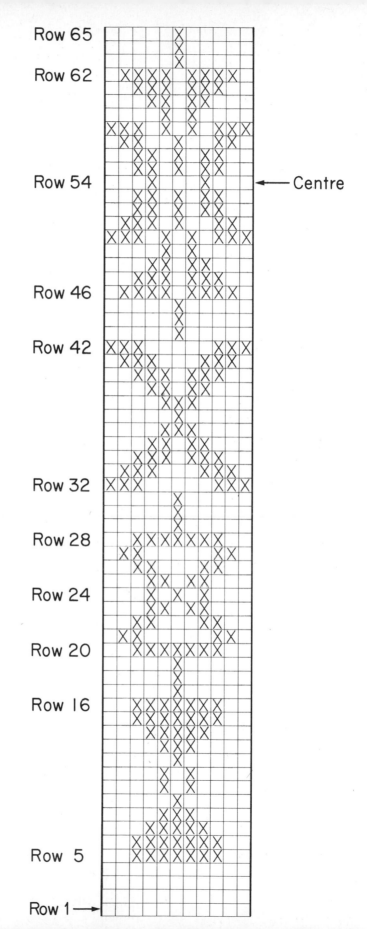

Row 65

Row 62

Centre

Row 54

Row 46

Row 42

Row 32

Row 28

Row 24

Row 20

Row 16

Diagram 99a   Weaving 1, two colours, black and yellow. Blank square = black, x = yellow Four rows plain black weaving – to lengthen, increase number of plain rows, to shorten, omit one or two, or all black rows, and continue pattern at row 1

Row 5

Row 1

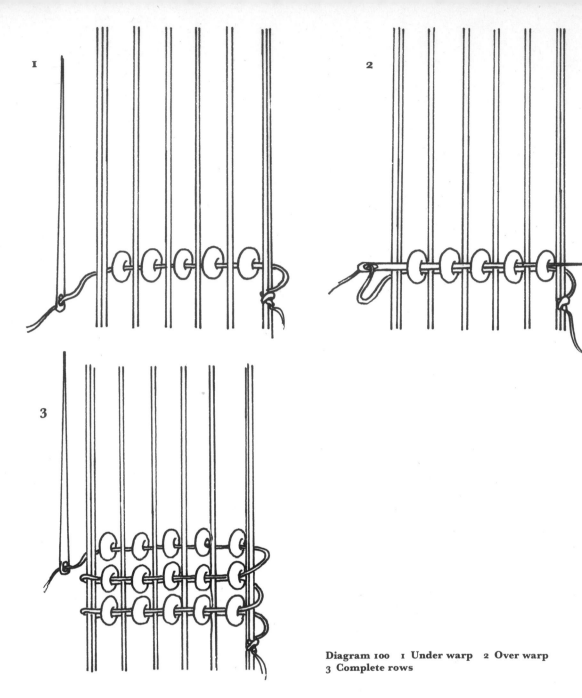

Diagram 100 1 Under warp 2 Over warp
3 Complete rows

2 Pull the working thread taut enough to bring the 11 beads into line with the 11 spaces in the warps, but not so tight that the inside warps are drawn. Take needle in left hand, place a finger of your right hand beneath the warp and press the beads up into the spaces. Hold them and pass the needle and thread back through the beads and over the warp threads. It will soon become automatic for you to press the beads up into the spaces and work back through them.

Make certain that all the threads now lie beneath the needle because if they do not they will lift between the beads and look untidy and the work will also be loose. If you miss a thread at this stage it is likely that you will continue to do so since it will be out of line with the others, so check that the weft covers the warps on its return through the row of beads. If the gleam of the needle is visible between the beads, with no thread running over it, then you have covered all the warps. Take needle in your right hand and pull the working thread gently to tighten the weft. If this is not done sufficiently the work will be slack and a lot of the thread will show between the beads; too tight and the beads will be forced out of line. You will soon acquire the knack of tightening the weft correctly. All it requires is practice. It may be difficult to maintain an even tension through the work when you first begin, but you will find that as you progress the ability to keep the work firm and even develops very quickly.

The pattern is for a 30cm (12in) choker. If you have a larger or smaller neck you should either add several rows to the plain weaving at either end (do this so that there is an equal number of rows at each end) or miss the plain rows out altogether. Size 7 beads down the work measure 25mm (1in). Count the row already worked as row one.

Pattern, Weaving 1 (with graph):

Rows

1–4	11b
5	2b 7y 2b
6	2b 7y 2b
7	3b 5y 3b
8	4b 3y 4b
9	5b 1y 5b
10	4b 1y 1b 1y 4b
11–16	Repeat rows 10–5
17–19	5b 1y 5b
20	2b 7y 2b
21	1b 2y 5b 2y 1b
22	2b 2y 3b 2y 2b
23	3b 2y 1b 2y 3b
24	3b 1y 1b 1y 1b 1y 3b
25–31	Repeat rows 23–17
32	3y 5b 3y
33	1b 3y 3b 3y 1b
34	2b 3y 1b 3y 2b
35	3b 2y 1b 2y 3b
36	4b 3y 4b
37	5b 1y 5b
38–45	Repeat rows 36–29
46	1b 4y 1b 4y 1b
47	2b 3y 1b 3y 2b
48	3b 2y 1b 2y 3b
49	4b 1y 1b 1y 4b
50	3y 1b 1y 1b 1y 1b 3y
51	1b 2y 2b 1y 2b 2y 1b
52	2b 2y 1b 1y 1b 2y 2b
53	2b 2y 1b 1y 1b 2y 2b
54	3b 1y 3b 1y 3b

55–65 Repeat rows 53–43. This completes the centre pattern of the choker. The rest of the pattern is now worked in reverse order to row one.

This choker is shown on the loom in illustration 68.

During the course of the work you will almost certainly need to begin a new working thread. Never allow the working thread to get to the point where it is so short that it must be left hanging at the side of the weaving. When there is about 10cm (4in) of thread remaining, leave it and the needle hanging at the side of the work. Thread a new needle with a waxed thread (1m) length and pass it into the work, several rows back in the weaving, draw the tail of the thread into the row if possible and then work into the next row. Never knot the thread and leave a knot at the side of the work. Never at this point sew to the outside warps, this also will leave an unattractive lump of thread which cannot be removed. If it is difficult to hide the tail of the thread begin in the centre of a woven row, as in diagram 101, and pull the tail to the back of the work where it may be trimmed when the weaving is removed from the loom. Work into the rows of beads towards the point where you must begin to weave once again, making a slip knot in each row over the weft and warps as you work to the new row (diagram 101). The old thread is worked into the new weaving when several rows

Diagram 101   Starting a new working thread (shown as black)

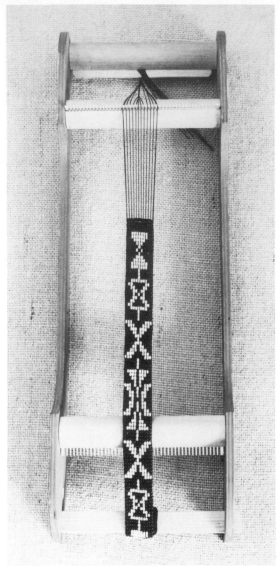

68 Weaving 1: the choker is rolled onto the bar to allow more weaving space

Diagram 102 Securing the old thread (shown in black) by passing it into the weaving with the new thread

have been completed (diagram 102). Pass through several rows and make a slip knot over the weft between the beads to secure the thread, pass halfway into a row and take needle through to back of the work, unthread and leave any tail hanging. This is cut off when the weaving is finished.

Alternatively, the old thread is worked back into the rows of weaving and taken through the middle of a row to the back of the weaving where it remains until the work is removed from the loom, when it is trimmed off close to the work. The new thread begins two rows back in the work, from the centre of a row as in the first method.

If you began the choker with the weaving or darning method then you should finish it in the same way. If you began with one of the other techniques the thread should be woven back for several rows, returned to the end of the final row and cut approximately 6cm (2½in) from the work.

Remove the work from the loom once you have completed the weaving part. *Do not* trim the ends of the warps at either end yet. Do not trim any ends of thread from the reverse side of the weaving.

Finishing off and fastenings

The following ways of finishing the ends and making fasteners may be applied to any of the woven examples in the text, but some are more suitable for certain items than for others. Most of these methods are visible in the illustrations, others you will no doubt invent for yourself.

There should be sufficient thread left at the ends of the weaving when it is taken from the loom to allow you to finish off in any of the given ways.

Method 1:

You may thread each separate warp thread onto a needle and weave it into the work for several rows. However, even if you do not weave complete rows with this thread you will soon find that it is becoming difficult to pass the needle into the beads because of the amount of thread already there.

Method 2:

Finishing a choker with a hook and loop fastener is a neat and almost invisible way of completing it. This is because the fasteners are attached to the underside of the weaving.

1. Tie the warp thread off close to the last row of beads. Do this in pairs. The knots should be very firmly tied. Cut the threads approximately 13mm ($\frac{1}{2}$in) from the knots (see diagram 103).

Fold the threads onto the back of the weaving (the threads left hanging there when new threads were attached during weaving will tell you which side is which – in fact there is really no right and wrong side to the weaving but when work is to be backed at the ends this is a useful point of reference).

Backing the whole of the work is possible if you wish, but one of the beauties of this kind of beadwork is that it forms a solid fabric of beads which can be seen to be woven. This is why all the examples in this section which have any kind of backing only have it at the ends.

2. Cut approximately 28mm ($1\frac{1}{4}$in) of 25mm (1in) hem tape (black) and fold the cut ends to make hems. Place this tape – folded edge to the work – at the end of the weaving, covering the cut ends of the warps and making sure the knots are drawn under the tape and so hidden (see illustration 69).

3. Use thread which matches tape and warps. With very small stitches sew the edges of the tape to the weaving by picking up the side warps, those between the beads, and the weft and warp as you work along the width. Fasten this off securely and pass the thread into the row of beads beneath the tape. Cut close to the work. When working along the bottom of the tape, catch the warp and weft threads which show slightly between each bead but take care not to pull the stitches too tightly otherwise the weaving will be distorted. Treat the opposite end of the weaving in the same manner.

Use a strong but small dress hook and sew this on to the tape at one end of the weaving (diagram 104). The hook should be covered with a small piece of tape so that only the end is showing (see illustration 69 and diagram 104).

Diagram 103   Tying off the warp threads in pairs   2 Placement of tape   3 Tape sewn to back of weaving

I

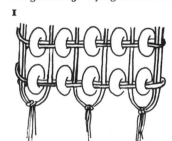

2

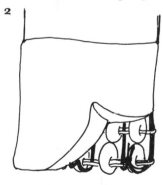

3

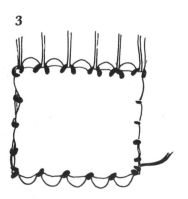

69 Choker with hook and loop, choker showing hook and loop fastened, and choker with beads and loops, showing the ends backed with tape

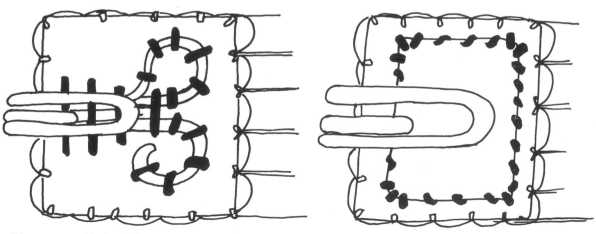

Diagram 104 Hook and loop

130

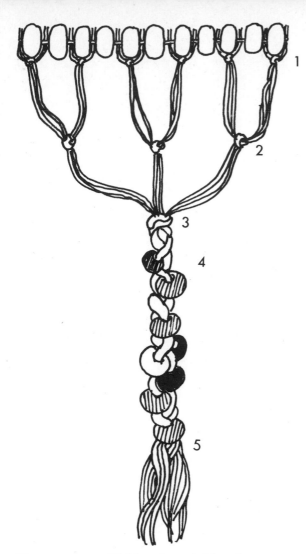

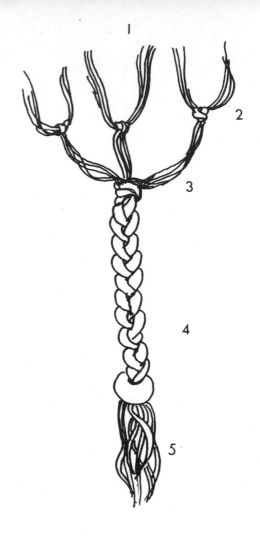

**Diagram 105   a 1 Tied in pairs, 2 tied in pairs,
3 overhand knot, 4 plait with beads, 5 tassel**

**b 1 Centre group halved, 2 tied in pairs, 3 overhand
knot, 4 plait, 5 tassel**

Make a buttonholed loop across the full width of the other end of the weaving (hand made loops are more suitable than the metal loops supplied with the dress hooks). To make the loop attach a working thread and make several long loops across the very end of the work (take care that they are not too stretched); buttonhole across these until the loop is complete. Secure the loop, pass needle between tape and weaving, bring thread out through tape and trim ends. The hook and loop are positioned so that when the choker is fastened they are hardly visible (see illustration 69).

Method 3:
An alternative method of fastening the choker is by using the warp threads themselves. For this the looped ends of the warp at the beginning of the choker should be cut through so that single threads remain. To finish the work in this manner there must be at least 15cm (6in) for the thread at each end of the work when it is removed from the loom (diagram 105).

1. Knot each pair of warp threads together, counting the outside double warps as one thread. There should be six knots. Make the knots as close to the last row of beads as possible but do not pull so tightly that the warp is drawn up and puckers the weaving.

2. Knot again in pairs so that there are three groups of threads; a pattern to the knotting should now emerge.

Knot so that there is a space between the first and second groupings. The remaining three groups may be plaited or, perhaps, if you are

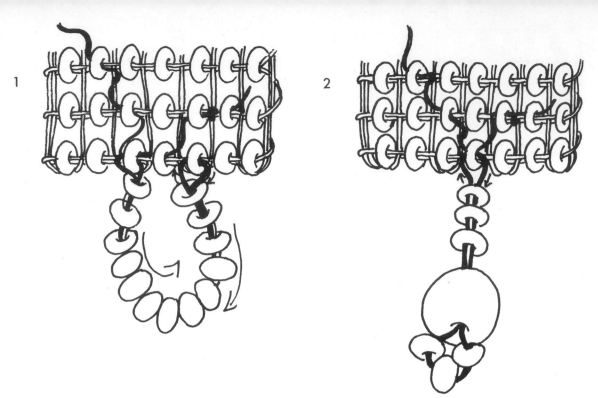

Diagram 106   Making a bead and loop fastener after completing choker and backing the ends

familiar with the art of macramé, you will use a square knot to make a fastening 'string' or 'cord'. As the threads are plaited try threading them with a variety of beads in several sizes and in the colours of the weaving. This will make a more substantial cord with which to tie the choker around the neck. If the cords are long enough to tie in front, the addition of beads on the cords adds interest and makes the choker an unusual piece of jewellery.

If you prefer a tie fastening you may still back the ends. This strengthens the ends which are subjected to more strain than the rest of the weaving. The ribbons or cords can be sewn to the tape and the choker tied at the back or front of the neck.

Method 4:

1. The bead and loop fastening which has been used throughout the previous sections of the book is also suitable for some of the woven work. The ends of the work are backed with tape as described and a loop is made by passing the needle and thread through the three centre beads of the last row of weaving. This thread is secured in the weaving as are threads for working (see diagram 106).

The loop is made in the usual manner, and if you are using a 6mm bead to fasten through the loop you should pick up 13 black beads to make up the 16 required for this bead to pass through. Make the loop and pass the needle and thread around as many times as you can. Fasten the thread off in the weaving, using slip knots to secure it (see diagram 106).

The bead fastener will require a stem of three beads. Attach working thread as for the loop; bring out at one side of the centre bead in the last row of weaving; pick up three beads, the 6mm bead, plus three beads and pass needle back through 6mm bead and three stem beads. Insert the needle through the other side of the centre bead and pass around stem and 6mm bead a second time if possible. Fasten off as for the loop. This fastener is as strong as the hook and loop. On p. 149 there are instructions for weaving the loop and fastening bead as part of the weaving whilst on the loom.

Dealing with a broken bead or broken warp

At some time you will almost certainly break a

bead as you are weaving. Or perhaps as you are attaching a new working (weft) thread. If this does happen while you are in the process of weaving a row there is no problem: you simply unthread the remaining beads and pick up the correct pattern sequence again. Alternatively, take out that row of weaving if it is already complete. If, however, the bead breaks as you begin a new working thread, usually because of the strain imposed by attempting to pass the needle through a bead already filled with threads, there are two ways of dealing with it. If the bead is in a place where it will not show when the work is complete, or is part of the main colour/background, simply leave it. The effect on tension and continuity of pattern will be minimal. If, however, it will be obvious in the finished work, perhaps coming in the centre part, then it is worthwhile removing the rows leading back to it. There should not be too many rows to remove since the new working thread is attached only 3 or 4 rows back in the work.

A broken or very badly-frayed warp thread, caused possibly by the friction of notches in a home-made loom, or through having been split with the needle, is more difficult to deal with, more especially if the weaving has progressed some way. It is possible to make a repair, but exceptional care must be taken and you will need patience to insert a new warp thread. Leave the work on the loom with the broken warp in place. Thread a needle with a single thread the length of the original warp – to help you see the new thread a length of very fine contrasting thread should also be threaded. The needle is passed along the line of the broken thread so that the new warp passes between the weft threads which hold the beads in place on the warps (use the eye end of the needle to do this). The contrasting thread will show you whether the warp is correctly inserted. When the thread is in place release the weaving and draw the new warp through the work so that it matches the others in length. Pull the old warp and the contrasting thread gently out of the work. Secure warps, check tension and continue weaving. This is a laborious, time-consuming task and not always entirely successful – taking the weaving apart and starting again is often less tedious.

If you do wish, for any reason, to take a piece of beadweaving apart, it is not necessary to waste the thread of either warp or weft. If the work has already been finished off then the resulting threads will be shorter than those of work you have not completed. Fasteners should be removed from the complete work and where possible reused. The salvaged short threads from such work are useful for sewing on the tape and fasteners of other work so save them by winding onto an empty cotton reel.

Taking a weaving apart

In a completed article begin by cutting off the first row of weaving at one end of the work (if it is unfinished there is no need to cut). It should be possible to pull off the next few rows of beads without cutting any threads. You will have several ends of warp threads and a longer length which is the working (weft) thread. Beginning with the centre warps, take hold of them at the loop end and, holding the weaving in your other hand, pull them firmly away from the work. The weaving will probably gather up as you do so but this does not matter. The warps should now slide from the work quite easily providing that during the course of weaving they have not been split by the needle when the wefts were woven. Continue until all the warps have been pulled from the work. The beads will begin to fall off the work before all the warp threads are removed, and so those remaining will be easy to remove. The threads will be shorter than those normally used for the warps, but useful nontheless.

Using fringes

The next pattern is for a fringed choker. Fringes may be added to any of the examples and can also be used to give articles a new lease of life. There are two ways in which a fringe may be added to the weaving. Both techniques are successful but if you have used very small beads you may find the method used in the following choker better (the second method is shown on p. 135, diagram 108, illustration 70).

The fringe on the following choker is worked along with the woven pattern. The beads which form the weft are picked up in the normal manner but before the needle passes back into the work and across the warps more beads are picked up to make the length of the fringe. Press the beads for the weft into the spaces between the warps and then pass the needle back over the last bead picked up and into the beads of the fringe *and* weft. Pull to tighten. Make sure the fringed part is not too rigid otherwise the work will not lie flat. (See diagram 107 for securing fringe.)

70a Fringed choker

As with the woven part of the work the sequence in which the beads of the fringe are picked up dictates the pattern which will appear. If you find it difficult to work the fringe simultaneously with the weaving it may be worked once the choker band is complete (see diagram 108). The choker is left on the loom and moved (if necessary) so that the part which is to be fringed is central and easy to handle. A working thread must be attached by running the thread into the work several rows before the beginning of the fringe. Secure this thread in the same way as you would secure a new weaving thread. The thread emerges from the work on the edge from which the fringe is to hang and the beads are picked up according to the sequence in the pattern (fringe part). The needle is passed *over* the last bead of the fringe and back along the length. Pass the needle back into the beads already woven. It is not absolutely necessary to work into the whole of the row: passing the needle into the first bead and then down the first bead of the next row is sufficient (see diagram 108). The fringe pattern is followed until the whole of the fringe is complete and the thread fastened off in the manner described for fastening

off working threads. Alternatively, when making a shaped fringe the work can be begun with the centre strand – the longest part of the fringe – and first one half, then the opposite side, worked in the manner described above. The following choker pattern uses method 1. The fringe is worked as the weaving progresses.

Weaving 2. Fringed choker

Materials:
   Size 10 black, gold and red Rocaille beads
   (black beads form the main colour)
   6mm black wooden bead to use as fastening
   Size 10 needles
   Black Polytwist thread
   5cm ($\frac{1}{4}$in) × 13mm ($\frac{1}{2}$in) hem tape
   Beeswax
Key:
   b – black
   r – red
   g – gold
Pattern for fringed choker, Diagram 107 shows how to work the fringed part as the choker is woven.

**70b Fringed choker using a
different pattern**

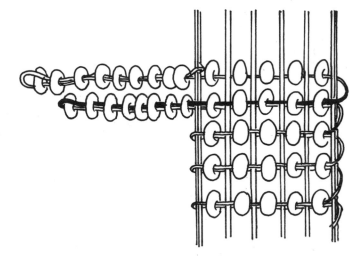

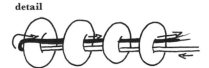

detail

**Diagram 107   Fringe,
weaving 2, showing how to
make the fringe as the
weaving takes place**

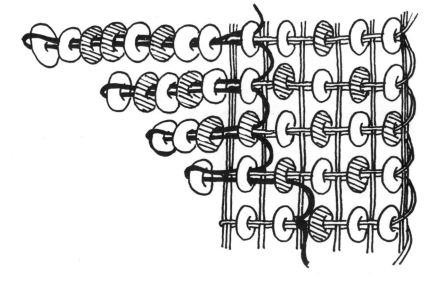

**Diagram 108   Adding
fringe after completion,
showing how the pattern is
made. The new thread
(shown as black) secures
fringe after the band is
woven**

Set up the loom with enough thread to finish the choker, plus the measurement of the complete choker.

You will require seven spaces for a 7 bead width; 7 spaces = 8 threads + 2 extra (to make the double outer warps) = 10 warps.

Thread the needle with a long waxed length of Polytwist and attach the working thread to the outside warps or weave a few rows with the thread only.

Pattern, weaving 2:

Rows

1–10	Weave 10 rows of plain black
11	3b 1r 3b
12	2b 1r 1g 1r 2b
13	1b 1r 3g 1r 1b
14	2b 1r 1g 1r 2b
15	3b 1r 3b
16	2b 3r 2b
17	2b 1r 1g 1r 2b
18	1b 1r 1g 1b 1g 1r 1b
19	1r 1g 1b 1r 1b 1g 1r
20	2r 1g 1b 1g 2r
21	2r 1b 1g 1b 2r
22	2r 1g 1b 1g 2r
23	1r 1g 1b 1r 1b 1g 1r
24	1b 1r 1g 1b 1g 1r 1b
25	2b 1r 1g 1r 2b
26	2b 3r 2b
27	1b 2r 1g 2r 1b
28	2r 1g 1b 1g 2r
29	1r 1g 3b 1g 1r
30	1g 2b 1r 2b 1g
31	2b 1r 1b 1r 2b
32–36	Repeat rows 30–26
37	3b 1g 3b
38	2b 1g 1r 1g 2b
39	1b 2g 1r 2g 1b
40	1g 1b 3r 1b 1g
41	1b 1g 3r 1g 1b
42	2b 1g 1r 1g 2b
43–47	Repeat rows 41–37

Rows		Fringe
48	2b 1r 1b 1r 2b	+ 1b
49	1b 1r 1g 1b 1g 1r 1b	+ 2b
50	1r 1g 3b 1g 1r	+ 1r 3b
51	1g 1b 1g 1r 1g 1b 1g	+ 1g 2r 4b
52	1b 1g 3r 1g 1b	+ 1b 2g 2r 5b
53	2b 1g 1r 1g 2b	+ 2b 3g 3r 6b
54	2b 1r 1g 1r 2b	+ 4b 3g 3r 7b
55	1b 1r 3g 1r 1b	+ 6b 3g 2r 1b 2r 8b
56	1r 2g 1b 2g 1r	+ 2r 6b 4g 2r 1b 2r 9b
57	1r 1g 1r 1b 1r 1g 1r	+ 1g 2r 6b 2g 1r 2g 2r 1b 2r 9b
58	1g 2r 1b 2r 1g	+ 1r 2g 2r 6b 2g 1r 2g 2r 1b 2r 10b
59	2g 1b 1r 1b 2g	+ 2r 3g 2r 6b 2g 1r 2g 2r 2b 2r 10b
60	1b 2g 1r 2g 1b	+ 3b 2r 3g 2r 6b 3g 1r 3g 2r 1b 2r 11b
61	2b 3g 2b	+ 3g 4b 2r 3g 2r 6b 3g 1r 3g 2r 1b 2r 11b
62	3b 1g 3b	+ 3b 3g 4b 2r 3g 2r 6b 3g 1r 3g 2r 2b 2r 12b

Repeat fringe from row 61 to row 48 where fringe began. Repeat from row 47 to row one to complete the fringed choker.

Once you have mastered the technique of fringing, try making fringes of various shapes. Long fringes which become even longer only in the centre of the work, for instance, or perhaps a straight fringe. You will find that fringes with loops on the end are also very attractive, and when the technique of using the wooden beads has been mastered it is possible to use these as part of the fringe on a choker. You might also try making a flower (see threading pattern) at the end of some of the fringe strands. Fringes are not suitable in the above form on some of the woven work, but a decorative edging can be added to beadweaving in many other ways.

Edgings

Instead of a fringe, a 'bobble' border can be

Diagram 109 Weaving in loops at the edge with five beads, return the needle to the same row and complete

71 Loop-edged belt

added or woven in while the work is still on the loom. If woven, only one edge can be worked at a time. The bobble edge is added in exactly the same way as a fringe during the weaving but only one bead is used. This of course may be a larger bead or a bead in a contrasting colour, alternating contrasts, or a bead to match the main bead colour of the work in progress (see page 168, illustration 87).

In the same manner, loops may be added to the work as you weave. These may be as long as you wish but small loops make an attractive border when worked close together. If you want to make the loops as you weave, they must return into the same bead from which they came and must be worked only on alternate rows (diagram 109). If they are to be worked in any other way, they are attached to the weaving when it is completed but still on the loom. There are several ways in which loops can be made using different numbers of beads and slightly different methods of construction (see diagrams 127–8).

Long loops which are made while the weaving is in progress look best if they are treated in the same way as the fringe in weaving 2 – that is, concentrated in the centre of the work and gradually increased and decreased in length. To make them more effective they should be worked from alternate rows to avoid a cramped appearance. The long loops should also be taken back into the bead from which they came. Illustration 87 shows several bracelets with decorative edgings. The belt with ribbon ties in illustration 71 has a variety of different loops along each edge made when the weaving was complete.

Shaped ends and front fastening

Front-fastening chokers make attractive jewellery. A special feature can be made of the fastening and, in order to do this, a shaped end should be worked. This is not at all difficult and there are several methods which can be employed.

The loom should be set up with the warp threads in the usual way but the warps should be considerably longer than those used for a back-fastening choker so that the fastening can be made by using the thread which remains when the woven band is completed. To shape the ends of the weaving (see diagrams 110–12).

Method 1

Diagrams 110 and 111 are basically the same. The shaping in diagram 111 is elongated by working several rows before increasing the number of beads in a row while in diagram 110 the working thread is attached to the right-hand thread of the centre space in the warps. Attach the thread to the warp as you would for starting

Diagram 110   Shaping

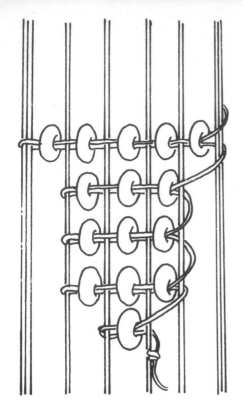

Diagram 111   More gradual shaping

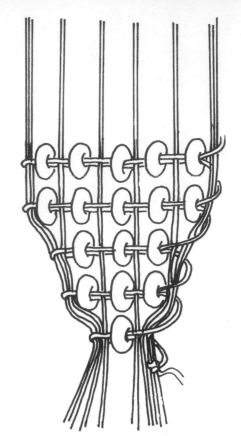

Diagram 112   Shaping over all the warps. Release tension until the work reaches full width, then tighten

72 Shaped end on loom

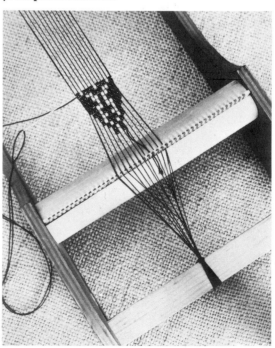

a full-width weaving. Weave one bead in the centre space and tighten the weft thread. Take the needle and thread around the next right-hand side warp thread and pick up and weave three beads; do not pull too tightly or the work will pucker. Continue to increase the number of beads by two in each succeeding row until the work is the full width. The weaving is then continued according to the pattern. The pattern may of course be extended into the shaped ends. Diagram 111 shows how to make a more gradual shaping (see also illustration 72).

Method 2, shaped ends

The loom is set up and the working (weft) thread attached to the outside warp threads in the usual manner – as for a straight-ended weaving. However, the weaving begins as method 1 with a single bead being woven in the centre warp space (see diagram 112). The outer threads are pulled into the edge of the bead. The tension on the warps should be slacker than usual to allow for this. Row two has three beads; the outer warps are pulled in again. Row three also has three beads, but if you wish to have a sharply-tapered end then this row should be increased by two beads. Continue shaping the end and filling the warp spaces until the work is the width of the choker. The warps may now be tightened again so that the tension is sufficient to begin the weaving proper.

The following choker is begun using method 1 and so it must also finish in the same manner. The longer warps allow a decorative 'tie' to be made for the front fastening. Set up the loom in the usual manner but with much longer warp threads than would usually be needed. Turn the ends of the warps several times around the bar on the loom or around whatever loom you are using, before guiding them through the teeth, or grooves. This way there will be ample thread when you finish. Make sure that there will be an equal length left for finishing the other end of the work.

Choker with front fastening and shaped ends. Illustration 73

Materials:

Size 10 Rocaille beads in black, pink and orange

73 Front-fastening chokers with shaped ends, one on wood, the other in size 10 beads

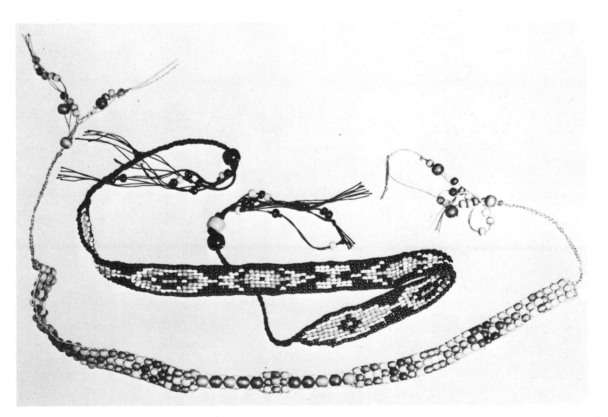

Several larger beads in the same colours as those in the pattern – these will be used when the fastening 'cord' is made.

Black Polytwist thread

Size 9 or 10 beading needles

Beeswax

Key:

  b – black

  p – pink

  o – orange

The work is 9 beads wide : 9 spaces = 10 threads + 2 extra for the double outside warps = 12.

Measure your neck and calculate the length of thread for the warps. The ends of the weaving (the points) should just meet when it is tied around the neck. The fastening will then make a decorative 'dangle' hanging at the front; if you want this to be especially long and elaborate make sure that there is sufficient thread in the warps (see illustration 73).

Pattern, weaving 3 :

Rows

1	1b (1) bead
2	1b 1p 1b (3) beads
3	1b 1p 1o 1p 1b (5) beads
4	1b 1p 1o 1p 1b (5) beads
5	1b 1p 3o 1p 1b (7) beads
6	1b 1p 3o 1p 1b (7) beads
7	2b 1p 1o 1p 1o 1p 2b (9) beads – the shaping is now complete
8	1b 1p 2o 1p 2o 1p 1b
9	1b 2p 1o 1b 1o 2p 1b
10	1b 1p 1o 3b 1o 1p 1b
11	1b 1p 2b 1o 2b 1p 1b
12–15	Repeat rows 10–7
16	2b 1p 3o 1p 2b
17	2b 1p 3o 1p 2b
18	3b 1p 1o 1p 3b
19	3b 1p 1o 1p 3b
20–21	4b 1p 4b
22	3b 3p 3b
23	2b 2p 1o 2p 2b
24	1b 2p 1o 1b 1o 2p 1b
25	1b 1p 2o 1b 2o 1p 1b
26	1b 2o 1b 1p 1b 2o 1b
27	1b 1o 1p 3b 1p 1o 1b
28	1b 1p 2b 1o 2b 1p 1b
29–30	Repeat row 28
31–38	Repeat rows 27–20
39	3b 1p 1b 1p 3b
40	3b 1p 1o 1p 3b
41	2b 2p 1o 2p 2b
42	2b 1p 1b 1o 1b 1p 2b
43	1b 1p 2b 1o 2b 1p 1b
44	3b 3o 3b
45	2b 2o 1p 2o 2b
46	2b 1o 3p 1o 2b
47	2b 1o 1p 1b 1p 1o 2b
48–57	Repeat rows 46–37
58–59	1b 2p 3b 2p 1b
60	1b 2p 1o 1b 1o 2p 1b
61	2b 2p 1o 2p 2b
62	Repeat from row 60 back to row one. Remember to shape the end as you did at the beginning.

Remove work from the loom.

There should be at least 20cm (8in) of thread at either end so that the choker can be finished with a decorative cord. Thread one of the outside warps on to a needle. Work down the side of the shaped end of the weaving, catching the free warp threads to those secured by the weft (see diagram 113). Use small stitches and do not pull too tightly otherwise the side of the work will pucker. When you reach the single bead pass through it (see detail) unthread the needle and repeat on the other side, and on the opposite end of the work. Pass through single bead each time. There should now be a bunch of 12 threads at either end, all approximately the same length. The threads can now be treated in various ways (see illustration 73). They may be plaited and a large bead attached to the ends with a tassel to finish, or a macramé knotting technique (square knots) can be used – this produces a very firm and hard-wearing cord. If you would prefer to back the ends of the work for extra strength the threads are knotted at the point of the work after they have been caught to the sides. They are either cut off and the point of the weaving is backed with tape as in weaving 1 with a ribbon, cord or other fastener being attached to the work – or the warps are knotted but not cut, the ends are taped and the warps used to make a fastener. It is much neater to use the warp threads to finish this particular design, and using existing threads to work a fastener which is part of the weaving itself gives the finished choker greater continuity. The pointed ends of the choker are in any case difficult to back neatly.

Plaited or macramé cords. Diagrams 105 and 114

Plait or knot the warp threads for 10cm (4in) and tie an overhand knot with all the threads (see diagram 105). There should be approximately 10–15cm (4–6in) of thread left. A number of larger beads in matching colours to those in the

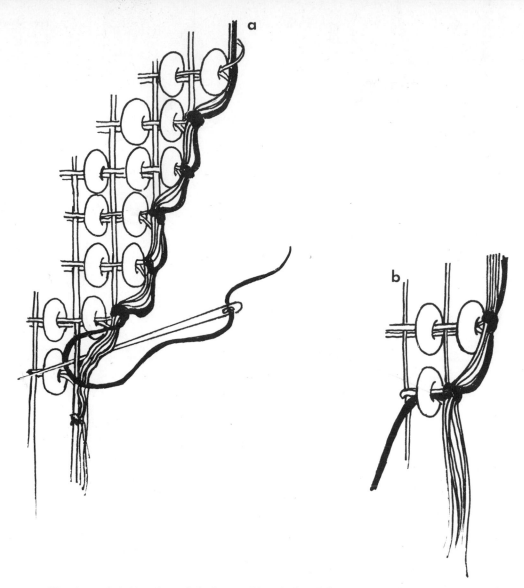

Diagram 113   Weaving 3, finishing the ends before making the 'cord' fasteners   a First outside warp shown in black   b Detail of finishing at the last single bead

pattern are used to decorate the tassel. These may be larger Rocailles, Rotelles, pony beads, wooden beads or any other suitable beads. If you want to use size 10 beads then do so. If you prefer you can use one colour only. Thread one of the largest beads, push it up to the overhand knot and tie another overhand knot very close beneath it using the technique described on p. 38. Use two or three threads each time and thread several beads on to each group of threads. Knot between each bead or group of beads until you have a beaded tassel. This may be as full of beads as you wish – for example you may choose to thread each separate thread and knot only at the ends to make a very full tasselled end.

Whichever you choose the cords with the beaded tassels make an attractive and unusual decoration. If you wish, the choker may also be fastened at the back.

The examples so far have used patterns which repeat from the centre. This is a useful way of working beadwoven patterns since it means that once the centre point is reached the weaver simply refers to her earlier work for guidance. If she has made a mistake this will be repeated which means that the final article has no noticeable error at all. The choker on the loom on p. 128 has an error but since the first half was used as reference for the second it is only noticeable when the graph is consulted.

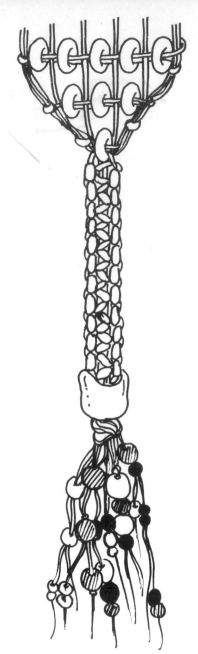

Diagram 114 Weaving 3, a decorative cord of macramé square knots with a beaded tassel

stitch pattern books must be worked out carefully on squared or graph paper beforehand.

Belts

The simpler the shape the less preplanning is required. Making a belt on the beadloom is far easier than it looks. Belts of considerable width are easy to weave and add a unique finishing touch to clothes. The wider the belt the sturdier it will be. Naturally, a considerable number of beads are needed to make a long, wide, strip of beadwork and the weaving takes rather longer than a choker length. However, part of this can be overcome if size 7 beads are used because the work will progress faster and fewer beads will be needed. The belts in illustration 75 were woven with size 10 beads. The widest took a considerable amount of time and patience to complete but because the pattern is abstract rather than formal and required no plan, it was less complicated to work than the orange belt. This is narrower, but the pattern complicated and repetitive – based on Florentine embroidery patterns, it uses similar close colour tones and 'chevron' shapes. Great care was required when repeating the pattern sections in order not to make a mistake. Because the chevrons are staggered and rather complex, a mistake would have thrown the whole weaving out of line and ruined the effect.

The fastening for this belt is quite separate from the main body of weaving and was devised because the original warp was too short to make a belt of adequate length. Thus the loom was restrung and a short piece woven. This was finished by taping the ends of the warp as described on p. 129. The fastenings at one end of the main weaving were actually made with the weft (the beginning was not treated thus since at that time it was not known that the weaving would be shorter than intended). The loops on the buckle were also constructed in this way (see diagram 115 for woven-in fasteners). This separate panel, although the result of careless planning, makes an unusual and attractive buckle which could be adapted or modified for many other weavings.

The curves, common to both the above belts, are the result of yet another accident which has been turned to convenient advantage. The warps were at some point pulled tighter on one side of the work than the other, thus making it curve along one edge. Since many belts are made

Smaller repeating patterns translate extremely well into beadweaving and they may be as simple or as complicated as the weaver cares to make them. The most simple geometric shapes – the square, diamond and triangle – look quite impressive when used with a little imagination. Solid motifs against a contrasting background, line motifs, or a mixture of both, have equal impact. More complex patterns taken from cross-

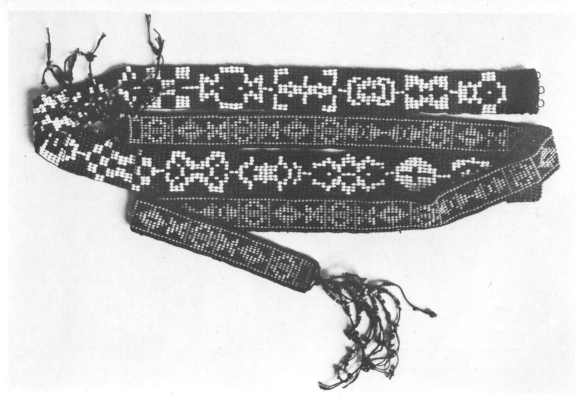

74 Belts, one with fringed ends and repeat pattern

75 Zigzag belt, and Florentine belt with bead and buckle fasteners

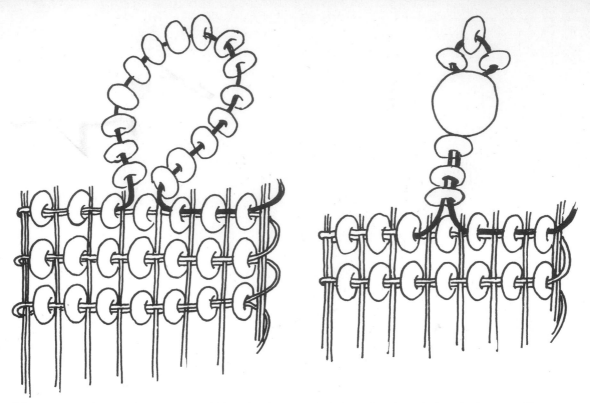

Diagram 115 Weaving in loops and bobbles, showing one single loop, but the technique is the same for two loops or more

in this way to follow the lines of the body more naturally, I now deliberately pull one side of a warp for a belt so there is greater tension there. A wide belt is also a better fit if this is done.

The belts in illustration 76 were woven with size 7 beads. Both have a white background and the patterns are of North American Indian origin with a few modifications.

Remember when setting up the loom for a belt that you will need a greater length of thread than you require for a choker, and that there should still be sufficient left when the weaving is finished to fasten off the work when it is removed from the loom. Make sure that you measure your waist accurately and that you add an inch of 'ease' to this measurement. Beadwoven belts are fairly rigid and can be uncomfortable if too tight.

Weaving 4. Belt. Illustration 76

The belt is approximately 27mm wide and there are 13 size 7 Rocaille beads across the width. If you wish to calculate how many beads you will require for your particular size, the following will provide a rough guide.

Approximately 11 size 7 beads are needed to make a belt 25mm (1in) wide. There are

approximately nine size 7 beads to 25mm (1in) along the length of weaving thus 11 × 9 = 99 beads to the square inch.

Materials:

Size 7 white, yellow, green and dark blue Rocaille beads
White Polytwist thread
Size 9 beading needle
Beeswax
White hem tape
Hook (A wide trouser or skirt hook was used for the belts in illustration 76)

Key:

w – white
y – yellow
g – green
b – dark blue

Cut 16 warp threads (eight double threads if the technique on p. 117 for attaching the warps is used).

Set up the loom so that there are 13 spaces – 13 beads = 14 warps + 2 extra for the sides = 16.

The pattern is based on North American Indian patterns. Some of the symbols have been modified a little in order to fit the width of the belt. The pattern uses the same repeating device as the chokers already described – it repeats from the centre.

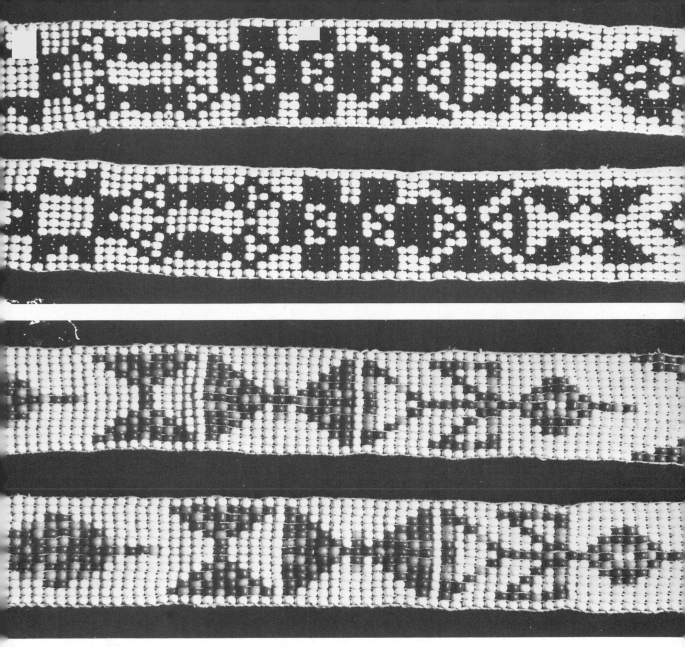

Belts with Indian patterns

The belt measures 65cm (26in). If you wish to make it larger add more plain rows of weaving at each end or where there are plain rows in the pattern (nine rows=25mm (1in)). If you need to make it much longer the extra rows should be added into the plain areas of the pattern, rather than at the beginning. To make it smaller miss out the plain rows at the start, or miss those which are used to divide the motifs in the pattern itself. When using white thread do make sure that your hands are clean, otherwise the work will have an overall grubbiness even though the beads themselves are quite clean. The thread which shows at the sides and between the beads is much more obvious with white backgrounds and so it must be kept very clean.

Pattern, Weaving 4:

Rows	
1–4	13w plain white weaving
5	6w 1g 6w
6	5w 1g 1y 1g 5w
7	4w 1g 1b 1y 1b 1g 4w

8	4w 2g 1y 2g 4w
9	3w 1g 1y 1b 1y 1b 1y 1g 3w
10	As above
11	2w 2g 2y 1b 2y 2g 2w
12	2w 2g 1y 1b 1g 1b 1y 2g 2w
13	1w 2g 2y 1g 1b 1g 2y 2g 1w
14	2g 2y 2b 1y 2b 2y 2g
15	3g 1y 1b 1y 1g 1y 1b 1y 3g
16	2g 1b 1y 1b 1g 1w 1g 1b 1y 1b 2g
17	1g 1b 1y 1g 1b 3w 1b 1g 1y 1b 1g
18	2g 1b 1y 1b 3w 1b 1y 1b 2g
19	1g 1y 1g 1b 5w 1b 1g 1y 1g
20	2g 1y 1b 5w 1b 1y 2g
21	1g 1y 1b 7w 1b 1y 1g
22	As above
23	1g 1b 9w 1b 1g
24	As above
25	1g 11w 1g
26	As above
27	6w 1g 6w
28	6w 1y 6w
29	6w 1b 6w
30	6w 1g 6w
31	5w 1g 1y 1g 5w
32	4w 1g 1y 1b 1y 1g 4w
33	3w 1g 1b 1y 1w 1y 1b 1g 3w
34	As above
35	4w 1g 1y 1b 1y 1g 4w
36	5w 1g 1y 1g 5w
37	6w 1g 6w
38	6w 1b 6w
39	1w 2g 2y 1b 1y 1b 2y 2g 1w
40	1w 1g 3w 1b 1y 1b 3w 1g 1w
41	1w 1y 2w 1b 1w 1g 1w 1b 2w 1y 1w
42	1w 1g 1w 1b 2w 1g 2w 1b 1w 1g 1w
43	1w 1g 1b 3w 1g 3w 1b 1g 1w
44	1w 1g 4w 1g 4w 1g 1w
45	5w 1b 1w 1b 5w
46	4w 1y 3w 1y 4w
47	3w 1g 5w 1g 3w
48	2w 1b 7w 1b 2w
49	1w 1g 1b 2y 1g 1b 1g 2y 1b 1g 1w
50	13w
51	1w 4g 1y 1b 1y 4g 1w
52	2w 3g 1y 1b 1y 3g 2w
53	3w 1g 1y 1g 1b 1g 1y 1g 3w
54	4w 1g 1b 1y 1b 1g 4w
55	5w 1g 1y 1g 5w
56	6w 1b 6w
57	4w 1y 1g 1b 1g 1y 4w
58–63	Repeat rows 56–51
64	13w
65	1w 1g 9w 1g 1w
66	1w 1y 1g 7w 1g 1y 1w
67	1w 1g 1y 1b 5w 1b 1y 1g 1w
68	1w 1b 1g 1y 1g 3w 1g 1y 1g 1b 1w
69	1w 1y 1g 1b 1y 1g 1b 1g 1y 1b 1g 1y 1w
70–73	Repeat rows 68–65
74	13w
75	6w 1y 6w
76	6w 1g 6w
77	6w 1b 6w
78	5w 1y 1b 1y 5w
79	4w 1g 1y 1b 1y 1g 4w
80	3w 1y 2g 1y 2g 1y 3w
81–82	2w 1g 1y 1b 1y 1g 1y 1b 1y 1g 2w
83–88	Repeat rows 80–75
89	6w 1y 6w
90	1w 1g 2w 1y 1b 1g 1b 1y 2w 1g 1w
91	1w 1g 1y 2w 1y 1g 1y 2w 1y 1g 1w
92	2w 2g 2w 1g 2w 2g 2w
93	3w 2g 3w 2g 3w
94	1w 1y 2w 2g 1b 2g 2w 1y 1w
95	1w 1y 1g 2w 1g 1b 1g 2w 1g 1y 1w
96	1w 1y 1g 1y 2w 1b 2w 1y 1g 1y 1w
97–102	Repeat rows 95–90
103	13w
104	3w 1g 5w 1g 3w
105	2w 1g 1y 1g 3w 1g 1y 1g 2w
106	1w 1g 1b 1y 1b 1g 1w 1g 1b 1y 1b 1g 1w
107	As above
108	2w 1g 1y 1g 3w 1g 1y 1g 2w
109	3w 1g 5w 1g 3w
110	13w
111	Repeat row 109–1 to complete the belt

Finishing off and attaching a fastener

Remove the work from the loom and check the size before proceeding with the finishing off. If the belt is too short return it to the loom and weave half the number of plain rows required to make it the correct length. Remove the work and turn it, keeping it right side up, and reset it on the loom. The beginning will now be in a position where you may add extra rows to it. Make sure that the finished portion of the belt is securely rolled or otherwise fastened to the loom. Weave the remaining half of the rows needed to increase the length and then remove from the loom and proceed as below. There should be enough thread left in the warps for you to tie the ends together in pairs as described on p. 129 and shown in diagram 103. Cut them and fold them back on to the belt, then back with white tape. You may find that it is more satisfactory to cover 25mm or more with tape to keep the ends of the belt neat and firm. Make the stitches you use to sew the tape to the belt as tiny and invisible as possible.

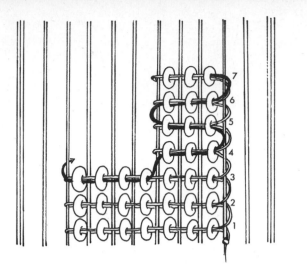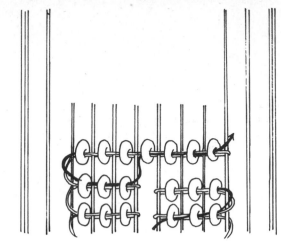

Diagram 116   Making the woven slot

Fastening

You can use two or three large dress hooks for the fasteners if you wish but a trouser or specially made skirt hook is wider, stronger and less obvious. The ends of the belt should come together without the fastener showing. If smaller hooks are to be used make sure that the loops correspond exactly with the placing of the hooks. The loop for the large hook is made so that it is almost the full width of the belt. Make sure that this loop is strongly constructed by using several strands of thread and then buttonholing over it with a double thread.

I took the patterns for the belt from those of the North American Indians, using white beads for the background colour because these give the work a more authentic look; thus the symbols used in the pattern have a more traditional look. Different colours, perhaps with a dark background, will give the belt a more modern look perhaps more in keeping with the clothes and accessories of the 1970's.

All the patterns and the colours in the examples are suggestions only. You can change them or perhaps use the colours of one pattern to weave one of the other examples, it is up to you. If you decide to use the size 10 beads, remember that the work will be narrower and shorter and so you should increase the number of beads in the weft as well as increasing the length of the warps.

Belts and chokers, in fact anything which will be taken off and put on a number of times, should have a secure and hardwearing fastener. Making these as a weaving progress is a good idea: not only does it mean that the fastener is strong

but also that the 'character' of the weaving is preserved. Making eyelets through which a thong or cord may be laced, or weaving the loop for a fastening bead, is not at all difficult. These integral fastenings can be constructed on both straight and shaped ends. Once the technique is mastered they are easily worked along the length of a choker or belt. A ribbon or tape threaded through them in a contrasting colour not only adds interest but may also be used to fasten the weaving.

Weaving 5. Choker with woven fasteners, slot and fastening band

Materials:
   Size 10 black, brown and orange Rocaille beads
   Large orange wood bead 6 or 8mm for the fastener
   Orange Polytwist thread
   Size 9 beading needle
   Beeswax
Key:
   b – black
   O – orange
   br – brown
The choker is 11 beads wide with a shaped end. Eleven spaces = 12 warps + 2 extra for the outside warps = 14 warp threads (seven if they are cut and set on double). Remember to allow enough thread to complete the work and also to roll it on if the loom is not as long as the finished work will be.

Set up the loom and thread the needle with a long waxed thread. Attach the working (weft)

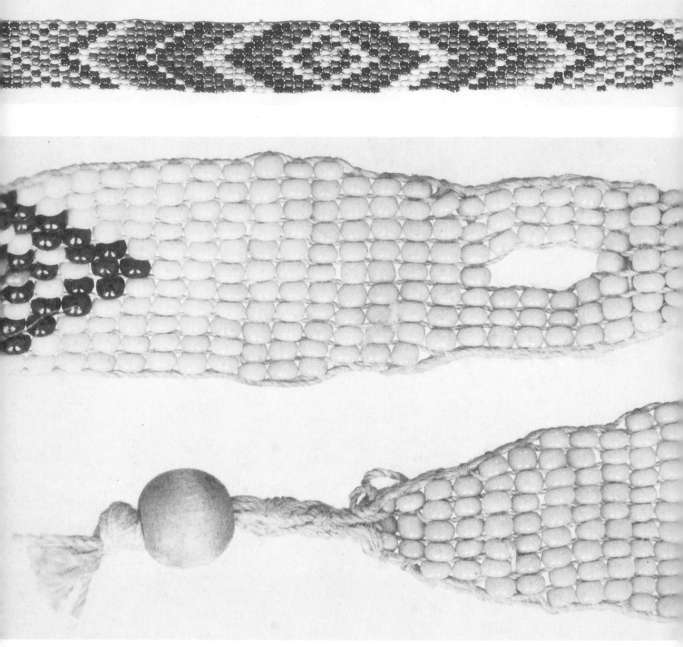

77a and b Chevron choker with woven-in slot

thread to the third warp thread from the right. If you wish use the alternative method, the thread is secured to the outside warps in the normal way and seven beads are woven; the outside thread will be drawn in as the weft is tightened. As the work widens the warps must be separated to accommodate more beads. Both methods are equally successful. The pattern begins with the rows seven beads wide. (Follow diagram 116 for the slot (loop). (See also illustration 77):

Pattern, Weaving 5:

Rows

1–3   Weave three rows of orange beads – seven beads per row.

4–7   Row four of the weaving is now divided. Weave four rows of three orange beads; take needle and thread back through all the rows and pass along row three, as shown. Working in a left to right direction work four rows of orange beads three beads wide. There should be a gap one bead wide in the middle of the two rows.

8   Working from left to right weave one row of seven orange beads across the full seven-bead width. The slot or loop is now formed. Pass needle through the row of three on left side; through the centre bead and remaining three beads of the last row, and begin next row of seven in a right to left direction (see diagram 116).

9   7O
10–12   9O
13–18   11O
19   5O 1b 5O
20   4O 3b 4O
21   3O 2b 1O 2b 3O
22   The choker is woven in a chevron pattern. It is easier if you continue from this row of the pattern working your own chevrons in the widths and colour orders you prefer. When you have woven 67 rows reverse the pattern so that a diamond shape is formed in the middle (see illustration 77a.

The choker is now completed in the following way

Rows
116–121   11O
122–124   9O
125–126   7O
127–128   5O
129–130   3O

There are three ways in which the end of the choker may be finished.

Finishing method 1:

Remove the work from the loom and secure the free warps to the sides of the work. Tie the threads of the warp in an overhand knot as close as possible to the last row of three beads. Thread an 8mm orange bead onto the remaining threads and tie another overhand knot as close to it as you can. This makes the fastening bead, and the remaining threads are trimmed to about 13mm ($\frac{1}{2}$in) in length to form a short tassel.

Finishing method 2:

Remove from the loom and treat the end as for the front fastening choker omitting the very long plaited cord and making a 13mm ($\frac{1}{2}$in) plait instead. Thread on an 8mm orange bead and finish as above or with a bead tassel.

Finishing method 3:

Weave several rows with one bead only and remove from the loom. Secure warps to the side of the work and finish with an 8mm bead as above.

The loop end of the choker is finished by securing the free warps to the side of the work as described in weaving 3. Thread each warp on to a needle and weave them back into the end of the work. This may be difficult since there is very little solid weaving here. Alternatively, tie the ends of the warps very securely, cut them approximately 7mm ($\frac{1}{4}$in) from the knot and bend the ends back. These are covered with a narrow strip of tape, or secured with a dab of clear nail varnish or glue.

For a longer choker add extra rows of chevron weaving. For a shorter, decrease the chevrons. This is an easy pattern to shorten or lengthen

Diagram 117   Adjustable fastening on plait to fit several sizes

due to its free nature. Another way of lengthening the work, if you have taken it from the loom and find it is too short, is to make a tail of 8mm beads which act as an adjustable fastener; the choker will fit several different sizes if the fastening is made in this way (see illustration 69 and diagram 117).

In a similar way the choker can be woven so that there are several loops. The same technique is used, and each slot is separated from the other by a band of four rows of seven beads. Several of these will allow the choker to be adjusted to fit different sizes.

Decorative fastenings

These add interest and individuality to the woven article and often these 'self fastenings' are more in keeping with the technique and with the nature and character of beadweaving than are commercial fasteners.

The belt in illustration 74 was finished in a way which may be used for any of the examples. Sufficient thread should be included in the warps to allow you to fringe the ends. Remember that the knots between the beads take a considerable amount of thread so allow for this when you calculate the length. The beads used for the fringe should, where possible, match those used for the weaving; otherwise use the same beads as the main colour. There should be several sizes and it is interesting if several different textures and surfaces are also used. The heavier the beads used for the fringe the better the fringe will hang and the less likelihood there is of it tangling.

Fringe for a belt 13 beads wide

Belt in black (main colour) pink and orange (13 spaces = 14 + 2 warps = 16 threads).
Beads for fringe:
    Size 10, 7 and 4 black Rocaille beads

Size 10 and 7 pink Rocaille beads
Size 10, 7 and 4 orange Rocaille beads
4mm and 6mm orange wood beads
4mm and 6mm black wood beads
The fringe is 12cm (approximately 5in) long.

Knot the warps (a) in pairs close to the last woven row (outer, double warps count as one), making seven groups of threads, (b) knot the two outer groups of threads in pairs, making two groups of threads.

The centre groups are knotted in pairs made by splitting the centre group into two. Four groups remain. Knot again in pairs. Finally knot again to leave one large bunch of threads. Divide the threads again into groups of two and three threads.

To begin the fringe thread several beads on to the threads, some in groups and some singly. Knot below each one and tie some threads from one group to the threads of another (see diagram 118).

Continue threading beads, knotting the threads together, then dividing them again. If the beads are staggered on the different threads the effect is better than if they are all at the same level. Alternate the sizes or graduate them. Use tiny beads as well, perhaps to separate the larger ones. When both ends are fringed and beaded, the fastener is added. The two ends of the work are brought together and the fringe covers the join and any of the fastener which might show. A hook and eye fastening should be made under the ends and if you wish you may strengthen the ends with tape. If you prefer to make a bead and loop fastener then this is also suitable. A front fastening choker or a bracelet may be finished in the same way and made, perhaps, to match a belt.

Fastening wide belts is sometimes a problem but this can be solved if the ends have eyelets woven into them. These are made in the same way as the slot in the chevron choker, only several more are needed (see diagram 116). For instance, a belt which is 15 beads wide would have a slot every fourth row. Thus there would be three

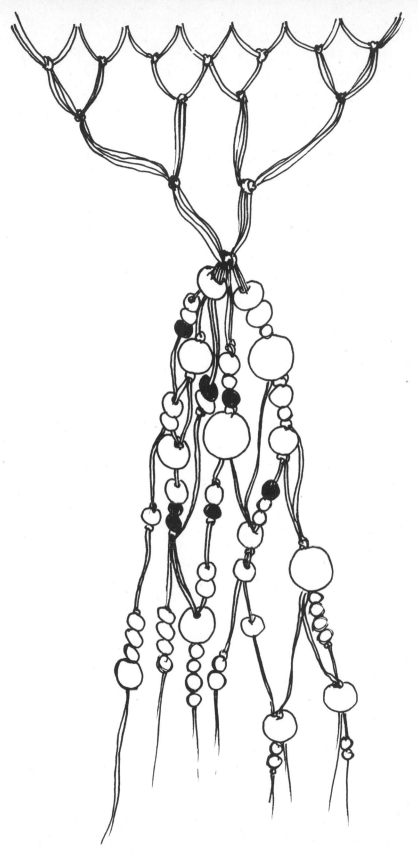

Diagram 118   Split the centre groups into two

woven rows of three beads, one slot, three woven rows of three beads, one slot and so on. When complete, the belt is laced at the front to fasten. Ribbons, plaited cords, leather thongs, or any other attractive 'cord' may be used and tied in a bow or knotted to fasten the belt. A narrow belt may of course be treated this way with only one slot at either end.

Work on the loom is not restricted to plain weaving. Decorative effects other than those in the patterns of the weaving are possible, and they make interesting and often unusual additions to your work. Plain bead stringing is one of these. Some degree of skill is necessary and since the warps must be released and then resecured into the slotted roller, make sure that you are able to keep your tension even before you attempt the following pattern.

Weaving 6. Choker with partly-strung warps. Illustration 78

This choker is narrow, only five beads wide. You will need to set up the loom with eight warps, either cut as single threads or double. For the latter cut four threads double the required length.

Materials:

    Size 10 black and gold Rocaille beads
    Black Polytwist thread
    Several size 9 and 10 needles
    Beeswax

Key:

    m – black or main colour
    c – gold or contrast colour

Pattern, Weaving 6:

Rows	
1–4	5m
5–7	2m 1c 2m
8–10	2c 1m 2c
11–13	2m 1c 2m
14–18	5m
19–20	1m 3c 1m
21	1m 3c 1m
22	1m 1c 1m 1c 1m
23	1m 3c 1m
24–25	2m 1c 2m
26–30	5m

Stop weaving. Leave the working thread and the needle at the side of the work. Release the warps at the end of the loom towards which you are working. Separate the outer warps. These are used separately. Select one and secure the rest

of the warps back onto the loom. Thread the free warp onto a needle.

String a length of beads onto the warp thread as follows.

String

1st thread:

5m	
3c	
5m	
2c	
1m	(31 beads)
2c	
5m	
3c	
5m	

Release warp threads and thread second outside warp onto needle. Secure remaining warps, plus the threaded one, back into the loom. String the second warp as follows. *Note* that the warps are released and strung one by one. Always resecure the strung and unstrung warps before you commence the stringing.

2nd thread	3rd thread	4th thread	5th thread
3m	6m	3m	Repeat thread 4
2c	5c	5c	
1m	3m	3m	6th thread
2c	3c	2c	Repeat thread 3
3m	3m	2m	
1c	5c	1c	7th thread
2m	6m	2m	Repeat thread 2
3c		2c	
2m		3m	8th thread
1c		5c	Repeat thread 1
3m		3m	
2c			
1m			
2c			
3m			

Secure all the warps, and push the strung beads firmly against the woven part of the work – they should be of equal length. Insert the needle and the working thread through the first of the strung warps to bring it to a point where you may use it to weave.

Weave two rows of 5m one row of 2m 1c 2m and two rows of 5m.

The first of these rows will be a little awkward because of the strung warps but if they are pushed back and you hold the weft beads firmly in the warp spaces with your finger it will be easier.

Stop weaving and repeat the strung section of the work. It should match the first eight strung warps.

Pass the working thread and the needle through the first of the strung warps to start the weaving again.

Repeat rows 30–1.

Remove the choker from the loom and finish the work with taped ends and a hook and loop.

This pattern also makes an attractive belt and looks particularly striking if the weaving is plain and all the strings are of different colours, either with the beads strung randomly on the warps, or each string a solid but different colour. There should be several strung sections with more substantial lengths of weaving between (10–12 rows) to make a firm belt. Remember the wider the article being woven, the more strings you will have to thread. If this technique is used on a very wide article, I suggest that the warps are strung in pairs rather than singly and that you use larger beads on these strings than in the woven section.

This particular pattern also allows you to use wooden beads of much larger size without struggling with the technique of opening and closing the warps (see diagram 122).

Weaving with larger beads

Size 4 Rocaille beads may be used for weaving. They tend to be a little more irregular in shape and size (especially in width) than the 10's and 7's so they should be selected with care, otherwise the weaving will have a very irregular edge. These beads do have several advantages however; the holes are much larger than those of the other Rocaille beads and of course the larger size means that the weaving will grow that much faster. Less of them will be required to make a wider article and so you may also need less to make up the length. Larger beads are ideal for children to use, especially for a first weaving. There is little likelihood that a needle and thread will fail to pass through them twice and initially they are safer since an ordinary long darner may be used to weave them.

Wooden beads are also suitable for the weaving process because their overall size, the large holes and the rate at which the work grows are all an advantage. These small wooden beads do, however, sometimes break very easily. Before using them to weave check that they have no hairline cracks in them. Once woven, if they break it is impossible to insert a bead and in this case the missing bead *will* be obvious. The 4mm wooden beads do, however, weave very well. They make a pleasantly flexible band and the beautiful colours look well together. Larger wooden beads may be used, but the larger they are the less attractive the finish of the woven article. They do not sit as closely together as the smaller beads and the result is a rather slack finish.

Nevertheless they have their place among the small beads: a woven combination is interesting and will serve as a good introduction to the use of various sizes of wood and Rocaille in the same piece of work.

The colours of the wooden beads are much more vivid than those of the Rocaille beads, such combinations as purple, turquoise, olive green and plum are quite striking and add an extra something to plain garments. Remember however that if you weave with wooden beads you will still require a considerable number in order to complete a weaving, even allowing for the fact that they are larger than the Rocaille beads and produce extra length.

A belt for instance will require several hundred 4mm beads. An example of numbers required for certain lengths is useful. To make a piece of weaving only three beads wide and 10cm (4in) long, you would require 72 size 4mm beads. Thus a choker 30cm (12in) long and three beads wide would require approximately 216 beads, not counting those you might use for the fastening. This may seem a small number compared with the number of Rocaille beads used, but remember that these beads are sold in quantities of a hundred and their price is similar to the many hundreds of Rocaille beads in a small box (see illustration 67). Threads should be matched as closely as possible to the wooden beads otherwise the effect will be ruined. Due to the shape of the beads more threads will be visible when these beads are woven than with the Rocaille beads. Rocaille beads are more oval in profile whereas the wooden beads are almost spherical which means that only the small area around the hole in each bead touches adjacent beads, whereas the whole side of the smaller beads fit close together.

Larger beads woven in with the smaller ones add a new dimension to the work (using larger beads with Rocaille beads is described on p. 157. Including larger beads means that you must learn the technique of opening and closing the warp threads without throwing the whole weaving out of line. The beginner will find it confusing but the experienced weaver will welcome the opportunity to experiment and learn a new dimension of the technique. When weaving with the wooden beads be careful not to pull the warps too tightly when the work is being finished off because the warp threads will pucker and the work will not lie flat if the threads are drawn up too much.

Weaving 7. Choker with wooden beads in several sizes. Illustration 73

When weaving with these larger beads the warp threads should be spaced through every alternate tooth/notch/groove on the loom. If you wish, all the warp threads may be doubled and so may the weft thread. The double warps will give you extra threads with which to complete the work. Make sure during this particular weaving that you go back through several rows of work every so often in order to strengthen and add firmness to it.

Set up the loom with a warp for three beads (3 spaces = 4 threads + 2 = 6 or 12 if all warps are double).

Materials:
   Size 4mm wooden beads in turquoise, purple, olive green and lime
   Size 6mm wooden beads in turquoise, purple and olive green
   Size 9 beading needles
   Beeswax

Key:
   t – turquoise 4mm
   O – olive green 4mm
   p – purple 4mm
   l – lime green 4mm
   Tq – turquoise 6mm
   Ol – olive green 6mm
   Pu – purple 6mm

Pattern, weaving 7: (diagram 119)

Rows

1–3	3t
4	1t 1O 1t
5	1O 1l 1O
6	1l 1t 1l
7	1O 1l 1O
8–9	1t 1O 1t
10	1t 1p 1t
11	1p 1t 1p
12	1p 1O 1p
13	1p 1t 1p
14	1t 1p 1t
15–17	1t 1O 1t
18	1O 1t 1O
19	1O 1l 1O

Diagram 119 Drawing in the outer warps for the 6mm bead, using wooden beads

20	1O 1t 1O
21	1l 1O 1l
22	1O 1p 1O
23	1p 1t 1p
24	1O 1p 1O
25–26	1O 1l 1O
27	1t 1O 1t
28	Pick up 1Tq. Insert this into the centre of the warps and draw in the side warps as you weave; pull firmly and hold so that they do not spring out again (see diagram 119).
29	1Ol
30	1Tq
31	1Ol
32	1Pu The warps must now be opened to weave three 4mm beads across again
33	Open the warps and weave 1t 1O 1t
34	1O 1t 1O
35	1t 1O 1t Close the warps again and proceed
36	1Pu
37	1Ol
38	1Tq
39	1Ol
40	1Tq
41	Open the warps to weave three 4mm beads across
	Repeat rows 27–1.

The choker may be finished off in several ways. Backing the work with tape as for chokers woven with Rocaille beads is not successful.

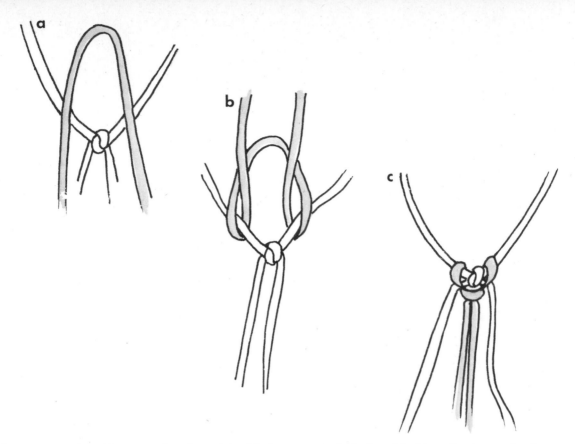

Diagram 120 Attaching extra threads to plait with the warps. A single thread is shown, but in practice there would be several warps and several threads

Remove work from the loom and check the length. If you need to make the work longer do this with an equal number of plain rows at either end.

Finishing off – the wooden choker

Tie the warp threads in pairs remembering not to pull the threads too tightly in case you pucker the weaving. Tie again in pairs some distance from the first set of knots. If you wish to make a plaited cord to tie the choker you must make it more substantial by adding several more lengths of thread to the existing warps. To do this follow diagram 120.

The new threads are attached with a half-hitch knot over the last knot tied in the warp threads. If the work is pinned to a cushion or clipped to a board while the plait is made, the task will be easier. When the length of the plait is to your liking tie an overhand knot in the threads close to the end of the plait. The plait should be

approximately 10cm (4in) and the same amount of thread should be free below the knot. Fringe these remaining threads with beads as for the front fastening choker on p. 139. This choker may be tied at either front or back. Alternatively, you can leave the threads as a tassel and simply trim them level, or cut them to make a shorter tassel. If you prefer, a loop and bead fastener can be used.

It is an easy matter to open and close the warps and insert the 6mm beads when the weaving is only three beads wide and when the beads are in any case fairly large. It is not so easy when more beads are involved and less so when the larger beads are used together with the size 10 Rocaille beads. It is a worthwhile experiment, however, since it adds a new dimension to the weaving technique and opens up even further possibilities for your work.

There are a number of ways in which the wooden beads can be inserted into the weaving. In the first method the beads are not woven in

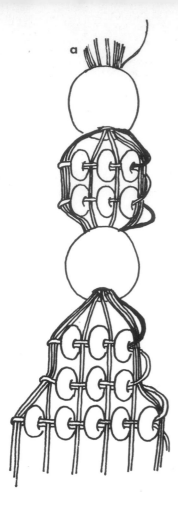

Diagram 121   a An 8mm wooden bead threaded onto the warps between woven Rocaille bead sections   b leave loop of thread at one side of bead and pass warp threads through   c pull ends of loop through bead   d warps are pulled through bead and secured in the loom

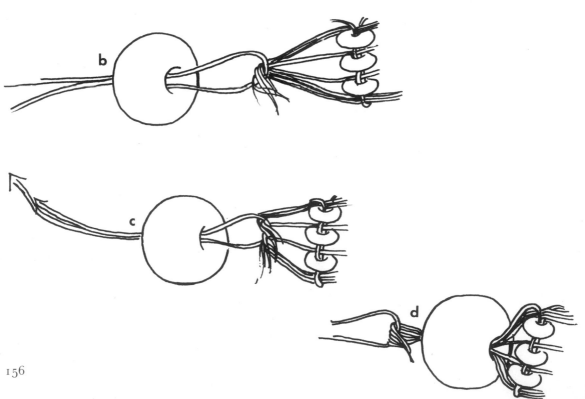

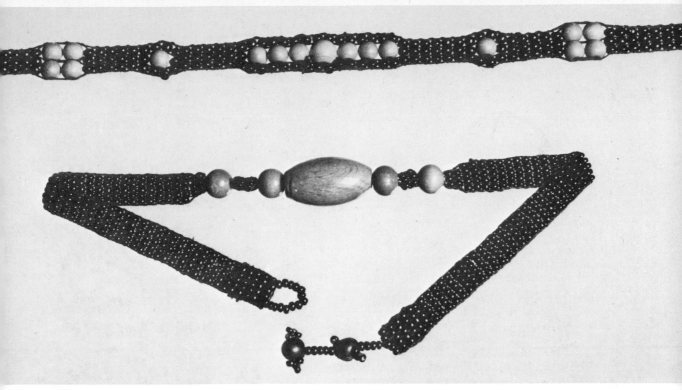

79 Rocaille and wooden bead chokers, one with the wooden beads threaded onto the warp

but are threaded onto the warps (see diagram 121).

Method One

Weaving 8. Choker with size 10 Rocaille and wooden beads. Illustration 79

Choker with size 10 Rocaille and wooden beads.

The size 10 beads provide the background colour, the wooden beads the contrast.

Materials:

Size 10 Black Rocaille beads

Four shiny orange wood 8mm beads

One large shiny orange oval wood bead

One large 12mm orange wood bead may be used instead of the oval bead, in which case use two more 8mm beads to make up the length

Two 6mm wooden beads in black (for the fastener)

Size 9 beading needle

Beeswax

Key:

b – black

o – orange

Set up the loom with eight warps: 5 spaces = 6 warps + 2 extra for the sides = 8 threads. Cut these singly or as four double lengths.

Remember to measure your neck and calculate the total length required before cutting the warps.

Pattern, weaving 8:

Rows

1–46	5b
47–48	3b insert these beads into inner three spaces and draw in the outer warps.
49	Release all warp threads and thread on an 8mm o bead. See diagram 121 for easy method of threading bead on to multiple threads. (a) Pass loop of thread through large bead leaving loop at one side. (b) Slip the warp threads through the loop, hold at both sides so they do not slip. (c) Pull ends of loop and draw warps through bead. Release from loop. Resecure the warps and lead them through the appropriate spaces.
50	Weave 3b.
51	3b
52	Repeat 49 – 8mm o bead
53	Thread oval bead in the same manner as the last 8mm bead.

157

54	One 8mm bead
55	Resecure warp threads. Open warps and lead them through the correct spaces in the loom. Weave 3b
56	3b
57	Release warps and thread one 8mm o bead
58	Resecure warps 3b
59	3b
60	Separate the two outside warps and weave 5b.
61	To finish weave 5b each row until there are 46 rows of 5b to match the first half of the weaving.

This particular way of using wooden beads is most effective when they are 8mm and above and have large holes. In fact the very big wooden beads are very difficult to use *in* the weaving. The areas of weaving between the beads are not absolutely necessary and you can simply thread the 8mm beads close together and increase the length of the plain black weaving.

The technique may be used in many ways. Wooden beads may be threaded on to the warps at intervals along the length of a weaving, or in groups. A narrow belt using this technique might be a worthwhile experiment. A bracelet to match is also a possible development of the technique.

Method Two

Using wooden beads *in* the weaving allows the use of several sizes including those beads where there would be difficulty in threading the warps through a small hole.

Weaving 9. Rocaille and wooden bead choker. Illustration 80

Materials:
  Size 10 beads in gunmetal (lustre)
  4mm and 6mm plum wood beads
  4mm, 6mm and 8mm olive wood beads
  Grey Polytwist thread
  Size 9 beading needle
  Beeswax

Key:
  g – gunmetal
  p – 4mm plum
  pl – 6mm plum
  O – 4mm olive
  ol – 6mm olive
  Ol – 8mm olive

Set up the loom with a warp for five beads: 5 spaces = 6 warps + 2 = 8.
Pattern, weaving 9. Diagram 122:
Rows

1–36	5g
37	2g 1O 2g
38	2g Pass needle through O on row 37. Pick up 2g, return through 2g. Pass through O. Pass through 2g. Tighten. This technique is used when larger beads are inserted, to avoid the rows of weaving pulling out of line and to compensate for the width of the larger beads.
39	2g 1O 2g
40	2g pass through O – 2g
41	2g 1p 2g
42	2g pass through p 2g pass back through 2g p 2g
43	2g 1p 2g
44	1g (work on one space) see diagram 122 (b)
45	1g 1ol 1g Work 1g on row 44 below (on one space) as right hand side, return needle to row 45 and complete the row.
46	1g pass through ol 1g
47	1g 1pl 1g
48	1g pass through 1p, 1g – complete by passing back through 1g, 1pl, 1g.
49	1g 1pl 1g
50	1g pass through 1p 1g
51	1g woven on one space
52	1g 1–8mm Ol 1g weave first part 52 – work 1g on 51 back to complete 52.
53	1g work through O, 1g pass back – this completes the centre.
54	Repeat in reverse to complete the choker.

The centre of the work is graduated as the beads get larger then smaller. Once you have mastered this technique, weaving wooden beads with

80 Centre pattern of wooden beads woven in

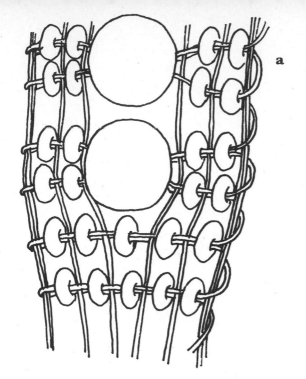
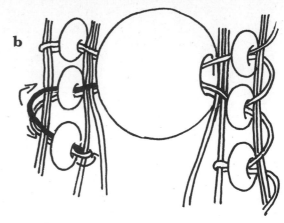

Diagram 122   a Inserting 4mm wooden beads, with two rows of two size 10 beads on either side of the 4mm beads   b Inserting a 6mm wooden bead. Work one bead on row 44, work one bead on row 45 1g 10l 1g before completion. Work 1g on row 44, return to row 45 and complete

Rocaille beads will pose few problems, simply remember to use more than one row of small beads per large bead in order to keep the work in line and compensate for the greater width of the wooden beads. When inserting a much bigger bead you should always weave one bead in a single space on one side of the work before commencing the row which contains the larger bead. This is repeated on the other side before completing the row with the larger bead. The ends may be finished in any way you wish, though a bead and loop, or a hook and loop is better than a tie, since the choker is back fastening.

These chokers, with wooden beads in the centre, look very attractive if they are fringed. Use the Rocaille beads and space them with the 4mm, 6mm and 8mm wooden beads in the same colours as those used in the weaving. Use either of the techniques described for making the fringe. In a similar manner dangles may be added from the centre front of a woven choker. Plain Rocaille chokers, or those with wooden beads, can be given this treatment with equally successful results.

Adding dangles to the centre front of a woven band

The dangles themselves are worked in the same manner as the fringes, with thread passing back over the last bead and into the string which forms the dangle. However, the dangles do not hang from the edge of the weaving but from the centre row, or rows if the work is fairly wide. Several strings are used and if these are of various lengths they are more effective. Larger beads can be added to the ends of these dangles and also used at intervals in the length (illustration 81).

Work first dangle from the very centre of the centre row of the weaving (this should be done when the woven band is complete and indeed can be used to brighten up a weaving which you have worn and perhaps grown tired of). Make this the longest; succeeding ones should be increasingly shorter. Complete the first dangle by taking the needle back into the point of entry. Continue by working into the bead next to the first or into the row below and to one side of the first dangle. Make several dangles in the centre of the weaving, but do not overload it. Dangles look better if they are beaded with several different sizes and if there are only three or four of them.

Variations on the choker theme

The weaving technique and some of the ways in which it can be used and adapted for different kinds of beads should be familiar by now; the following ideas are intended as a spur to your imagination.

159

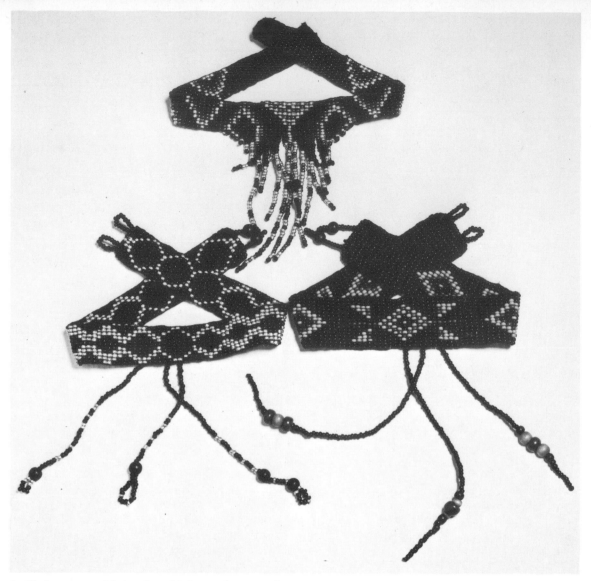

81 Chokers, two with dangles added onto the centre front

You have already seen how the warps can be manipulated to accommodate larger beads; how a loop or slot can be formed and how the ends of a weaving can be shaped. The following patterns manipulate the warps in several ways.

Weaving 10. Three-strand woven choker. Diagram 123. Illustration 82

This choker takes the decorative aspects of beadweaving a stage further. The three strands are not separate elements but part of a single weaving. The choker is wider than usual so that the three strands are clearly visible.

Materials:
    Size 10 dark-blue Rocaille beads
    Size 10 red Rocaille beads
    Size 10 gold lustre Rocaille beads
    Dark-blue Polytwist thread
    Size 9 and 10 beading needles
    One dark-blue 6mm bead for the fastening
    Beeswax

Key:
    b – dark blue

82 Three-strand choker

r – red
g – gold
c – centre

Thread the loom so that there are 13 spaces.
13 spaces = 14 threads + 2 = 16.
The choker is 13 beads wide at the widest part.
The ends of the work are shaped and the working
(weft) thread should be attached to the fifth
warp to begin the weaving.

Pattern, weaving 10:

Rows

1–2	3b
3–4	5b
5–6	7b
7–8	9b
9–10	11b
11–15	13b
16	5b 1r 1g 1r 5b
17	4b 1r 1g 1r 1g 1r 4b
18	3b 2r 1g 1b 1g 2r 3b
19	2b 1r 1g 2b 1g 2b 1g 1r 2b
20	1b 1r 1g 1r 1b 1g 1r 1g 1b 1r 1g 1r 1b
21–24	Repeat rows 19–16

Stop weaving.

Weave three b on the right-hand side, weaving
over the fifth warp thread also and drawing it in.
If you are more comfortable with the remainder of
the warps released and resting beside the loom
then this is the method you should use as long
as the tension is evenly maintained when the
left-hand side is woven.

The rows are counted from one onwards
again for this part of the work. The 3b woven
counts as row one.

2	1b 1r 1b
3–5	3b
6	1b 1g 1b
7–9	3b
10	1b 1r 1b
11–13	3b
14	1b 1g 1b
15–19	3b
20	1b 1r 1b
21–24	3b
25	1b 1g 1b
26–30	3b
31	1b 1r 1b
32–37	3b
38	1b 1g 1b
39	Repeat row 37–1.

Release the warps leaving the working thread
and needle in the work and hanging at the side
of the weaving.

Secure the left-hand side warp threads (five)
and attach a new working thread. Weave 3b,
make sure you work over the fifth thread and
draw it into the side of the three beads.

Work the left-hand side in the same pattern
as the right-hand side, keeping the tension the
same so that the rows of weaving are level
(parallel). When the left-hand side matches the
three-wide strand on the right-hand side, secure
all the warp threads and leave the working thread
and needle attached. Using the working thread

Diagram 123 Three-strand thirteen bead choker a right-hand side b left-hand side, centre and right-hand side, showing the three strands, and the new threads (shown in black)

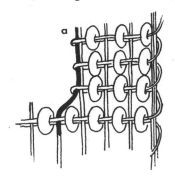

on the right-hand side, weave the end to match the first part of the work. You will have to part the threads which have been drawn into the sides of the outside strips of the weaving but if they are taken through the appropriate gaps in the teeth of the loom this should not be a problem. Secure the working thread of the left-hand by weaving it into the end and taking it out of the centre of a row to the back of the warp. *Do not remove the work from the loom.* There should be four warp threads in the centre of the weaving. Attach a new working thread and bring the needle out at the right-hand side of the centre bead (see diagram 123). Weave one red bead into the centre warps and draw the outside threads in so that a double outer warp is formed, the centre strand is one bead wide and the outer set of the four warps are drawn in with every bead woven.

Weave as follows, counting the red bead already woven as 1. (1r) g r 2 b g b r g r 3 b g r b r g 3 b r g r g r 3 b g r g 3 b (r g r g r) the last five beads are the centre pattern of the single strand. Repeat the pattern from 3b to the first bead. Secure the working thread in the solid part of the weaving. If the tension has been kept even throughout, the series of beads for the centre strand will be as taut as the outside strips. There are 75 rows of three in the side strands and there should be 75 beads in the centre strand. Remove the work from the loom and finish the shaped ends as shown on p. 141 knot the warps securely and trim them. Reverse so that the ends of the work may be backed with tape. Make a bead loop at one end of the choker and attach a bead with a stem at the other.

A plain choker with a centre strand of contrasting or even larger beads makes a pleasing variation of this pattern. In the latter case the number of beads used for the single strand of weaving should be reduced. To do this, weave to the centre point, count the beads and weave as many again (less one).

The idea of the multi-strand weaving can be further developed as follows. The choker is woven as for the previous pattern but is only 11 beads wide and in only one colour. If you wish, the ends may be woven straight across instead of being shaped.

The centre warps (four) are pulled in with the three-wide weaving on either side so that the centre space is clear. Begin by weaving a row of four wide to make this process easier, then continue the length with three beads (see diagram 124).

In addition to the size 10 Rocaille beads, you

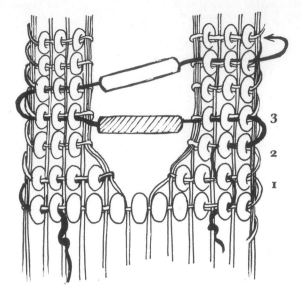

Diagram 124 The placing of bugle beads in the centre space, showing a diagonal and a straight bugle bead

will need a quantity of long bugle beads in two colours, one to match the colour of the woven part and a contrast colour (bronze lustre was used for the example in the photograph). Complete the weaving as before, securing the left-hand working thread in the solid part of the work. Take the right-hand working thread to the centre of the work and bring it out of the third row of the three-bead wide strip (see diagram 124). Pick up a bugle bead and insert the needle through the corresponding three beads in the opposite side. Insert the needle into the next row bringing it out at the centre; pick up a contrast bugle and insert the needle through the opposite three beads. Insert down into the next row, bring it out at the centre and pick up black bugle bead. Pass into opposite row. Leave a gap of three rows before commencing again with bugles. Continue along work filling in the centre space with bugle beads at intervals (illustration 83).

The sequence in which these beads are used is up to you. There are several ways in which this idea may be developed. The bugles are long enough to be used diagonally so that a zigzag pattern, a slanted, or a random arrangement can be achieved. Other beads: ovals, larger round beads, several small beads or even drop beads could also be used, and the initial idea can be developed in many ways to include several gaps with different 'fillings'.

Using cords or thicker threads for a decorative effect

This is a good way to co-ordinate a garment and a weaving when the colours of beads and fabric are not exactly matching.

To make a 'corded edge' which is thicker and more substantial than several strands of Polytwist thread a 'ply' piping cord should be used (see illustration 84). It is a simple matter to replace the outer warp threads with the cords. These are single lengths and are used in this case as the second of the double outer warps, though it is not strictly necessary to use a warp 'thread' at all. The cord is secured in the loom along with the ordinary warps and the thread of the weft passes over and under it as it would if the warp were of thread only.

These cord warps need not be restricted to the outside warps (see illustration 84, bracelet with centre cord warp) but may be used for any of the warp threads. Substituting a cord for the two centre warps works well, as does the method used for the bracelet. The centre cord was treated as an extra 'bead' with four beads at either side; the weft thread was actually passed through the centre cord each time a row was woven so that any difference in colour between thread and cord was not too obvious.

An interesting experiment involves the use of wooden beads, cords and Rocaille beads. The two centre warps are cord, with a row of 4mm wooden beads down the centre. The Rocaille beads are woven using the technique illustrated in the wood and Rocaille choker on p. 157: two rows of small beads at each side of a 4mm wooden bead to compensate for the extra width of the wooden bead. Warps and wood should contrast sharply, for example, black Rocailles, red cord and green wooden beads.

The outside warps can also be corded to match any of the colours in the weaving. Gold fingering (crotchet cord) makes an attractive edging although several strands, perhaps plaited or twisted, should be used if a very firm or thick edge is required. If all the warps are to be made of this, each should also have a yellow warp thread because the gold cord is not very strong.

Weaving 11. Choker with corded edge. Illustration 84

Materials:
   Size 10 red and black Rocaille beads

Size 9 beading needle
Red Polytwist thread
Red piping cord (one strand pulled from a 3-ply twist of fairly thick cord)
Beeswax

Key:
  r – red
  b – black

Set up the loom using cord for the outer warp. Cut the cord as a double length, secure over thread warps and separate. Place in the appropriate spaces. Make sure it is as long as the thread warps and long enough to finish with a plait.

The choker uses nine beads across the width so nine = 10 warps + 2 extra, (in this case the cords are the two extra warps). If the cord is too thick to secure into the loom in the same manner as the warps, secure thread warps, pass the cords under the roller, draw them back over the roller and clip them to each side of the loom with bulldog clips. The working (weft) thread is secured through the right-hand side warp.

Pattern weaving 11:

Weave in the normal manner working under and over the cords as you would if they were of thread only.

Rows	
1–9	9r
10	3r 3b 3r
11	2r 2b 1r 2b 2r
12	1r 2b 1r 1b 1r 2b 1r
13	1b 2r 3b 2r 1b
14	2b 2r 1b 2r 2b
15	2b 5r 2b
16	2b 2r 1b 2r 2b
17	1b 2r 3b 2r 1b
18	1r 2b 1r 1b 1r 2b 1r
19	2r 2b 1r 2b 2r
20–21	3r 3b 3r
22	3r 1b 1r 1b 3r
23	2r 5b 2r
24	2r 2b 1r 2b 2r
25	1r 3b 1r 3b 1r
26–30	Repeat rows 24–20
31	2r 1b 3r 1b 2r
32	1r 2b 3r 2b 1r
33	As above
34	2b 1r 3b 1r 2b
35	2b 2r 1b 2r 2b
36	1b 2r 1b 1r 1b 2r 1b

83 Choker with bugle beads in centre

37–41	Repeat rows 35–31
42–43	3r 3b 3r
44	4r 1b 4r
45	3r 1b 1r 1b 3r
46–47	3r 3b 3r
48	2r 2b 1r 2b 2r
49	2r 1b 3r 1b 2r
50	1r 2b 3r 2b 1r
51	1b 2r 3b 2r 1b
52	2b 1r 1b 1r 1b 1r 2b
53	1b 2r 3b 2r 1b
54	1r 2b 3r 2b 1r
55	2r 1b 3r 1b 2r
56 to end	Repeat rows 55–1

Remove from the loom and check the length.

Diagram 125   Weave over left-hand side cord, through centre cord, and through right-hand side cord

If the choker is too small resecure and add extra rows of plain red at either end.

Finishing off

Tie off the thread warps until only one bunch remains. Tie this bunch in either an overhand knot, or thread all of them, after knotting in pairs, through one large bead, using the loop of thread method (p. 156) to pass the threads through the hole in the bead.

Secure one end of the work to a firm object with a bulldog clip or with pins. Plait the cords and the threads, treating threads as one strand. If it is easier, plait the threads first, then plait the resulting 'cord' with the cord warps.

An overhand knot is too bulky for securing the end of the plait so thread a needle with matching thread and stitch through the plait approximately 13mm ($\frac{1}{2}$in) from the end of the threads, wrap the thread several times around the plait to make a neat binding and stitch through again. Cut off excess. Trim the ends of the plait to make a short tassel. Treat the other end in the same way.

Weaving 12. Bracelet with centre cord. Illustration 84. Diagram 125

This bracelet has a centre cord warp and four beads on either side. The centre warp is treated as one bead (bead 5). There is also a cord on either edge. One of the bead colours matches the cord, but the main body of the beadwork is a different colour. If you wish, however, the cord can be matched to the main bead colour.

Materials :
Size 10 black, orange, pink and brown Rocaille beads
Black Polytwist thread for the warps and orange for the weft
Beeswax
Three lengths of orange cord (one strand pulled from a 3-ply cord)

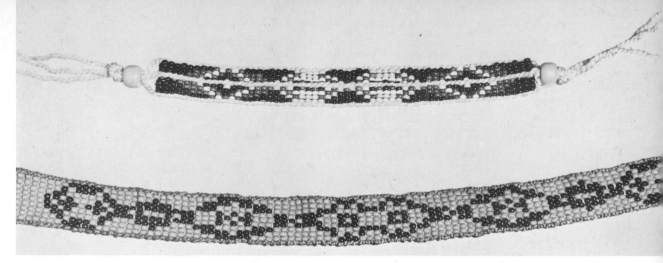

84 Corded weavings

Size 9 or 10 beading needle

Key:

b – black
O – orange
p – pink
br – brown

Setting up the loom for this bracelet

Cut the thread warps using whichever method is most suitable for your loom; there are six of these so you can cut three double lengths. Cut two double lengths of cord and attach to the loom as for a double warp thread. Turn thread and cords around the bar of the loom several times. Pull one strand of cord free and leave free (this is not used). Secure thread warps and set them in the spaces or grooves. Secure outside cord warps (there are no threads to go with these) as for the previous weaving. Secure centre warp in a similar manner, pull to one side and clip (if you find a better way of arranging this use it). Make sure the warps are secure and the tension even on both cord and thread warps.

You will need eight beads for each row of weaving. The centre cord acts as bead 5. It should form a raised ridge along the centre of the work and not be pulled down between the rows of beads. To ensure this *do not* pass weft thread back *over* this cord but *through* it as though passing the needle and thread through a bead. The needle and thread also pass through the right-hand side cord at the end of the row, but *over* the left-hand side warp cord (see diagram 125). This thread does not show between the beads,

and will not alter the final appearance of the weaving. Attach the working thread to the right-hand side cord warp.

Pattern, weaving 12:
(C = Cord)
Rows

1–3	4b pass under cord, 4b, pass back through cord as row is complete.
4	3b 1br C 1br 3b
5	2b 2br C 2br 2b
6	1b 3br C 3br 1b
7	1b 2br 1p C 1p 2br 1b
8	1b 1br 1p 1b C 1b 1p 1br 1b
9	1br 1p 1br 1b C 1b 1br 1p 1br
10	1p 1br 2b C 2b 1br 1p
11	1br 2b 1p C 1p 2b 1br
12–18	Repeat rows 10–4
19	3b 1O C 1O 3b
20	2b 1O 1br C 1br 1O 2b
21	1b 1O 1br 1p C 1p 1br 1O 1b
22	1O 1br 1p 1b C 1b 1p 1br 1O
23	2O 1p 1br C 1br 1p 2O
24	2O 1p 1b C 1b 1p 2O
25	2O 1O 1br C 1br 1p 2O
26	1O 1br 1p 1b C 1b 1p 1br 1O
27	1b 1O 1br 1p C 1p 1br 1O 1b
28	2b 1O 1br C 1br 1O 2b
29	3b 1br C 1br 3b
30	3b 1br C 1br 3b
31–59	Repeat 29–1

Remove the work from the loom and check the measurement against your wrist. Add rows of black to lengthen if necessary. Knot the thread warps in pairs and turn to the back of the work

85 Bracelets by Ann Burnell

86 Two bracelets in a freely worked zigzag pattern, using lustre beads

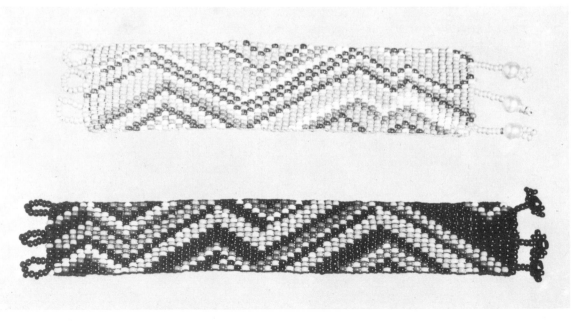

after trimming approximately 7mm ($\frac{3}{4}$in) from knots.

Back with a narrow strip of hem tape and stitch neatly in place. Draw outer cord warps into the centre (see diagram 126). Thread one orange pony bead onto the three cords. Tie an overhand knot below this. Repeat at the other end. The cords are left free (measurement approximately 2·5cm). Make a buttonhole loop under one end of the work large enough to fit a pony bead. To fasten draw opposite cords and bead through loop (see diagram 126).

There are many ways in which this idea of cording edges and using cords in place of the inner warps can be adapted and, when you are short of beads, substituting cord for several warp threads will help the beads to go further.

All the patterns so far described and illustrated would be suitable, with a few modifications, for bracelets and belts. Bracelets need a shorter warp, but enough thread should be cut so that the warps can be secured to the loom. On the loom used in the illustrations the whole of the bracelet can be woven without the work being rolled on at all. Fastenings for bracelets are similar to those already given, and I prefer the bead and loop technique to the hook and loop. The fastenings of bracelets are always much more visible than those of chokers and belts, therefore they should retain the character of the woven article.

To make a fastener part of the weaving itself simply follow the instructions for the start of the chokers on p. 148 or use the technique in diagram 115. A bracelet 25mm (1in) wide requires only one loop; if it is wider two should be used so that the work is balanced and also more secure (bracelets made by myself and various students appear in illustrations 85–7).

When I demonstrate the technique of bead-weaving I often use a bracelet pattern as this only takes a little time to weave and is easily completed in a session. I also tend to use the chevron pattern to illustrate the use of colour and repetition of pattern. The chevron is simple to work and the student learns the rule of symmetry as applied to patterns repeating around a central line of beads (when an evenly-numbered warp is used). The pattern also helps the student to acquire the knack of picking up beads in a certain sequence of colours. The bracelets in illustration 85 were made on a home-made loom. They are based on the chevron and diamond motif and fastened with loops and beads. Because bracelets are short and therefore quicker to make, they

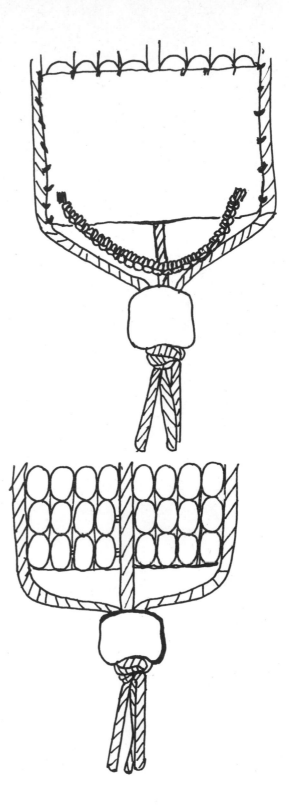

Diagram 126　Corded ends of the centre cord bracelet

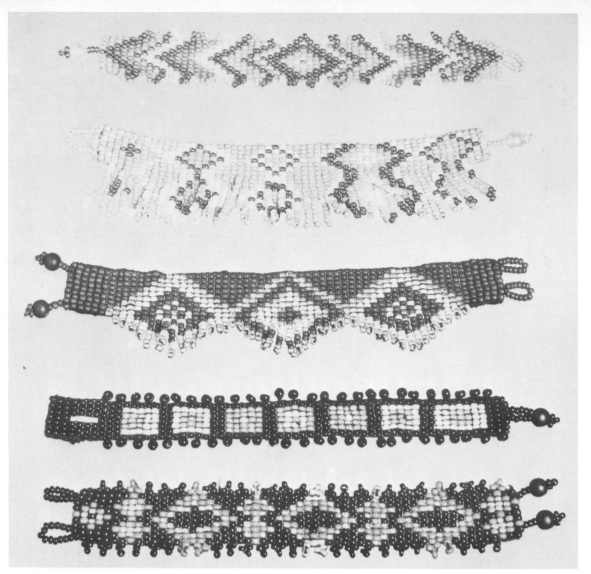

87 Edged bracelets including a three-bead bobble edge, a fringe, a shaped fringe, a single bobble, and a loop to continue the chevron pattern

are useful 'guinea pigs' when you want to try out a new pattern or colour combination, or to attempt one of the more complicated techniques.

Loops and bobbles along the edges also make pretty additions to a narrow band (see illustration 87). I always tape the ends of bracelets to strengthen them, using 13mm (½in) wide tape. The looped edge used on the following bracelet is equally suited to a belt or choker.

Weaving 13. Bracelet. Chevron with looped edge. Illustration 87

Materials:

Size 10 Rocaille beads in pale-blue lustre,

blue-grey lustre, mid-green lustre and pearl lustre

Pearl bead approximately 6mm

Pale-blue Polytwist thread

Size 9 and 10 needles

Beeswax

Pale-blue or white 25mm (1in) hem tape

Key:

m – pale blue

p – pearl

g – green

b – blue-grey

The following chevron design is given in full so that the looped edge which is an extension of the pattern itself may be worked correctly. (An edge which uses just the main colour is also appropriate.)

Set up the loom for nine beads: 10 warps + 2 for outer edges = 9 spaces. Attach the working thread using the size 9 needle for the weaving unless the beads have very small holes.

Pattern, weaving 13: chevron bracelet

Rows

1	4m 1b 4m
2	3m 3b 3m
3	2m 2b 1g 2b 2m
4	1m 2b 3g 2b 1m
5	2b 2g 1m 2g 2b
6	1b 2g 1m 1b 1m 2g 1b
7	2g 1m 1b 1p 1b 1m 2g
8	1g 1m 1b 3p 1b 1m 1g
9	1m 1b 2p 1b 2p 1b 1m
10	1b 2p 3b 2p 1b
11	2p 2b 1g 2b 2p
12	1p 2b 3g 2b 1p
13	2b 5g 2b
14	1b 3g 1m 3g 1b
15	3g 1m 1p 1m 3g
16	2g 1m 3p 1m 2g
17	1g 1m 2p 1b 2p 1m 1g
18	1m 2p 3b 2p 1m
19	2p 2b 1m 2b 2p
20	1p 2b 3m 2p 1p
21	2b 5m 2b
22	1b 3m 1b 3m 1b
23	3m 1b 1g 1b 3m
24	2m 1b 1g 1p 1g 1b 2m
25	1m 1b 1g 1p 1b 1p 1g 1b 1m
26	1b 1g 1p 3b 1p 1g 1b
27	1g 1p 5b 1p 1g
28	1p 3b 1m 3b 1p
29	3b 3m 3b
30	2b 2m 1p 2m 2b
31	1b 2m 1p 1g 1p 2m 1b
32–61	Repeat from 30–1.

Remove the work from the loom. Knot warps, trim, and back with hem tape. The loops are

Diagram 127 Weaving 13, bracelet with looped edge extending the pattern of chevrons, with new working thread shown as black

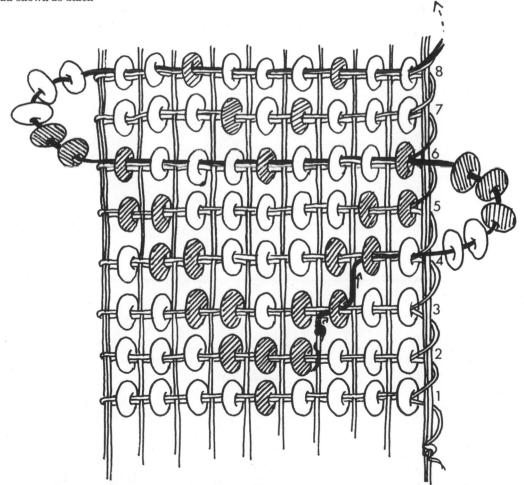

worked with the bracelet off the loom (see diagram 106). However, do not attach fasteners yet. Thread a size 10 needle with a double strand of fine Polyester thread. This should be the same colour as the Polytwist used for weaving. Wax the thread. Secure the new working thread in the weaving and bring out of fourth row.

Pattern for looped edge, weaving 13. Diagram 127:

Loops

1	Pick up 2m 3b and pass needle through row six to other side (row six has 1b at ends)	
2	2b 3g pass needle through row 8	
3	2g 3b	10
4	2b 3p	12
5	2p 3b	14
6	2b 3g	16
7	2g 3m	18
8	2m 3p	20
9	2p 3b	22
10	2b 3m	24
11	2m 3b	26
12	2b 3p	28
13	2p 3b	30
14	5b	32
15	2b 3p	34
16	2p 3b	36
17	2b 3m	38
18	2m 3b	40
19	2b 3p	42
20	2p 3m	44
21	2m 3g	46
22	2g 3b	48
23	2b 3p	50
24	2p 3b	52
25	2b 3g	54
26	2g 3b	56
27	2b 3m	58

Bring working thread out of last row of weaving at the third bead. Attach a bead loop using 12 size 10 pale-blue lustre beads. Secure the loop over the three centre beads (see diagram 115). Attach new working thread at opposite end of weaving and make a stem of three blue-grey lustre beads. Use one 6mm pearl bead and three blue-grey lustre beads to make the bobble. Work back through this and secure the thread in the rows of weaving (see diagram 115). The edging should form an extension to the chevron pattern (see illustration 87).

As the loops are formed you will see how the pattern is extended and 'turned'. This may be further emphasized by using 4 and 1 beads instead of 2 and 3 or even a greater total number. The loops can be closer together but if they are some of the effect is lost.

Fasteners for articles woven with all lustre beads sometimes present problems since the larger size Rocaille beads are not available in the lustre finish – this is when a collection of odd beads is useful. The fasteners on several of the bracelets illustrated are pearlized beads taken from old necklaces. If you do not have any suitable beads make a 'flower' using the basic threading pattern A see Section Two. Use 2 and 3 lustre beads in the centre and increase the numbers of the petal beads to accommodate these. Attach the flower with a stem to one end of the bracelet and make a loop to fit it at the other. Odd beads which are of different character to the beads used for weaving spoil the whole look and finish of the work.

Woven bracelets may be as wide or as narrow as the weaver chooses. A wider weaving has more 'body' and the appearance is somehow better if it fits closely about the wrist. Weaving is, by its very nature, a 'solid' fabric as opposed to the more open threading patterns. If you wish to weave several bracelets using the same main colour it is worthwhile setting up the loom with warps that are several feet long. To do this see below.

Weave a bracelet, leave a space in the warp long enough to finish off *two bracelets*, and start another weaving on the same warps. The first will very likely have to be rolled around the bar of the loom. The warps remain open, however, since the beads already woven keep them spaced properly. If you want to make the work narrower for the second weaving either draw in the outside warp so that there are three threads on either side, or remove one strand of the outside warp so that it hangs at the side and readjust the remaining threads to make a double outside warp. Pull the warps in for the first row and there will be no difficulty with subsequent rows. If this is done, a third bracelet need not be the same width as the narrower bracelet since the warps removed may now be reset through the teeth, and the spacing adjusted. With a warp several feet long you will be able to weave several bracelets and then finish them all off in a single operation.

You might try weaving a matching bracelet and choker using this technique. When complete, the weavings are lifted from the loom and the warps are cut, leaving sufficient thread to finish both items. Of course too much thread would be unmanageable and tangle very easily, and there is a limit to the amount of work you can wind around the bar of the loom. An alternative is to use a large amount of thread and roll this on the bar before weaving so that the weavings are done at the end of the warps. Each time one is completed it is cut off with the correct amount of thread to finish and the warp ends are resecured by the bar into the grooved roller. Alternatively, roll out more warp thread and secure in the grooved roller between the first bracelet and that about to be woven.

Bracelets to match any of the chokers can be woven by decreasing the length of the choker pattern. If the pattern is for a very decorative article make sure that you choose the centre part of the choker pattern for the bracelet. Remember also to measure your wrist and to check the length of the weaving against this as it progresses.

Fringes are as successful on bracelets as they are on chokers but they should of course be shorter, otherwise they will be a nuisance and could also be dangerous. However, since the bracelet is freer than a choker it can be fringed along the whole of the length.

Weaving 14. Bracelet with shaped fringe. Illustration 87

The fringe is woven with the bracelet. It *can* be added when the work is complete, but the band will then be much stiffer due to the extra thread which must pass through it in order to secure the fringe. The fringed part does not extend quite the whole length of the weaving – this is to make it easier to fasten the bracelet. If you wish, you can begin the fringe closer to the ends of the work.

The fringe is worked in such a way that it becomes an extension of the pattern on the woven band but does not have the background (brown) beads. This omission makes the shaped edge.

Materials:
 Size 10 brown, pink and gold lustre Rocaille beads
 Two 6mm brown wooden beads for the fasteners
 Brown Polytwist thread
 Size 10 beading needle
 Beeswax
 Brown hem tape
Key:
 b – brown
 p – pink
 g – gold

Set up the loom for nine beads: 10 threads + 2 = 12 = 9 spaces.
Pattern, weaving 14:

Rows		Fringe
1–6	9b	
7	7b 2g	+ 2g
8	6b 2g 1p	+ 1p 2g
9	5b 2g 2p	+ 2p 2g
10	4b 2g 2p 1b	1b 2p 2g
11	3b 2g 2p 2b	2b 2p 2g
12	2b 2g 2p 3b	3b 2p 2g
13	1b 2g 2p 3b 1p	1p 3b 2p 2g
14	2g 2p 3b 1p 1b	1b 1p 3b 2p 2g
15	1g 2p 3b 1p 1b 1g	1g 1b 1p 3b 2p 2g
16–23	Repeat rows 14–7	
24	6b 2g 1b	1b 2g
25	5b 2g 2b	2b 2g
26	4b 2g 2b 1g	1g 2b 2g
27	3b 2g 2b 1g 1p	1p 1g 2b 2g
28	2b 2g 2b 1g 2p	2p 1g 2b 2g
29	1b 2g 2b 1g 2p 1g	1g 2p 1g 2b 2g
30	2g 2b 1g 2p 1g 1b	1b 1g 2p 1g 2p 2g
31	1g 2b 1g 2p 1g 2b	2b 1g 2p 1g 2b 2g
32–39	Repeat rows 30–23	
40–62	Repeat rows 22–1	

The fringe and end of the bracelet are now complete. Remove the work from the loom.

Knot the warp ends securely in pairs and trim approximately 13mm ($\frac{1}{2}$in) from the knots. Turn the threads and knots to the back of the work and cover with tape. Make two loops at one end of the bracelet. The working thread is attached and brought out at the second bead. Pick up 13 size 10 brown beads and pass back into the second bead from the opposite side. Take the thread around the loop again and bring the needle out after the seventh bead. Make another loop as before and when complete fasten off the working thread by working back into the rows of weaving.

At the opposite end make a stem and bead fastener using three beads for the stems, a 6mm brown wooden bead and three size 10 brown beads for the bobble. The stems are worked over the second and eighth bead respectively. Go around each fastener twice. Fasten off the thread in the rows of weaving and trim the excess close to the work.

A fully-fringed bracelet like that in illustration 87 has the same number of beads on each fringe strand. To extend the previous pattern fringe into a full fringe simply include the brown beads of the woven band in the fringe pattern and omit the extra gold bead at the end of each centre fringe thread on the original pattern. The full

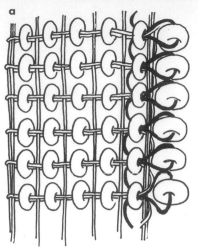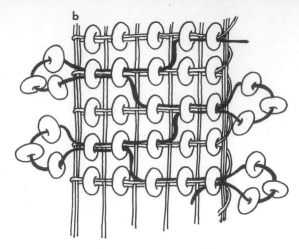

Diagram 128   Bobbles for chokers and bracelets   a one bead each row, these may also be woven in   b three beads every alternate row

fringe bracelet (no pattern) was woven with all lustre beads. If you decide to use lustre for any of the patterns, remember that you will need a pearlized bead for the fastening.

Illustrations 87 and 94 show a whole variety of edgings as well as straight-woven bands. The edgings are either loops, fringes or bobbles (see diagram 128 for bobbles and another way to make loops). These may be applied to any of the straight bands you weave, whether choker, belt or bracelet. Many of these edgings look best if the woven pattern on the band actually touches the edge of the work. In this way the bobbles, loops or dangles may be the same colour as the beads used in the pattern and, in some cases (as with the chevron bracelet on p. 168) they will extend the woven pattern into the edging. Three bead bobbles are attached to every alternate row. Single bobbles to each row (see diagram 128), or they can be spaced as the weaver wishes. Random loops and bobbles can be seen in the Bobble and Loop Edged Belt in illustration 71.

Inserting a missed row

Sometimes during your weaving, a row of pattern may be accidentally missed out. If this mistake is not obvious then it is wisest to leave it and continue the work. If it is a pattern repeating from the centre and the error is on the first half, weave the second half to match. If, however, it will spoil the overall effect there is a method of inserting the missing row which is reasonably successful. It works best if the missing row is spotted before the weaving is completed. Remove the weaving from the loom and ease it through the fingers, holding firmly onto the point just below the missing row. Run the fingers firmly along the

work and using the thumbnail or a blunt bodkin, pull the rows of beads back from the row before the missing one – this should leave a gap in the wefts. If using the nail fails to leave a space large enough for the beads, fold the weaving over a finger and with the bodkin push back the beads to make a gap. Only if the warps have not been pierced during weaving will this succeed. Be gentle when doing this and do not strain the warps too much.

Replace the weaving on the loom and insert the missed row using a new weft thread. If the wefts have been parted correctly the finished article should be as flexible as usual, if however the space was a little tight and the beads were forced into it, it may be rather stiff until it has been worn several times. It is only possible to correct a mistake in this way if there is not too much weaving beyond the point where it occurred.

Narrow weavings and braids

The very narrow weaving in illustration 88 is an adaptable and useful accessory. It can be a belt tied either once or twice around waist or hips or a headband worn Indian style around the forehead or, alternatively, like an alice band. It is also worn as a necklace looped several times around the neck and tied in an overhand knot with the fringed ends hanging at the front, and as a choker it is equally effective either wound several times around the neck and tied with the fringes at the front or the side, or sometimes wound only twice with the long dangles hanging in front. The longer the weaving the more adaptable it is.

The belt in illustration 88 is only three beads wide and approximately 146cm (4ft 8½in) long. The fringes add another 20cm (4in) or so to this overall length. So that the length should not be curtailed for lack of thread the loom was set up using six reels of black Polytwist thread. The ends had to be tied around the bar by knotting the whole of the six strands together, splitting into two groups, passing these over the bar to make a loop, and then passing the reels through the loop. When pulled tight this method of attaching the warps is the same as that used for a double thread. The threads were then secured as usual and the weaving begun. To keep the reels of thread separate and prevent them tangling they were put into matchboxes with a notch cut into one end of the inner 'drawer'. Thus the work could be wound on and the warps drawn out without trouble.

Patterning a weaving so narrow is far less difficult than it might appear, and the weaving was used as an experiment for patterns suitable for such a width. I began (and ended) with dots in a series of one, two, and so on, spaced by plain black rows of weaving, and used this at intervals in the work along with zigzags, crosses, diamonds, flowers and other designs. In fact I discovered that there are a whole host of patterns which are quite effective.

The whole length could, of course, be one pattern only and any combination of colours can be used. Plain narrow weavings are also extremely effective. The ends of the work are untaped, the warps simply being tied in pairs then with an overhand knot. The remaining length of warp is used to make a fringe in the manner shown in diagram 118 (belt fringe). A weaving so narrow is not really suitable for a braid, but one with a weft of five beads serves this purpose. The same technique for setting up the loom should be used to weave braids intended for clothing and you should also have a clear idea of the actual length

88 Narrow, three-bead wide weaving with fringed ends

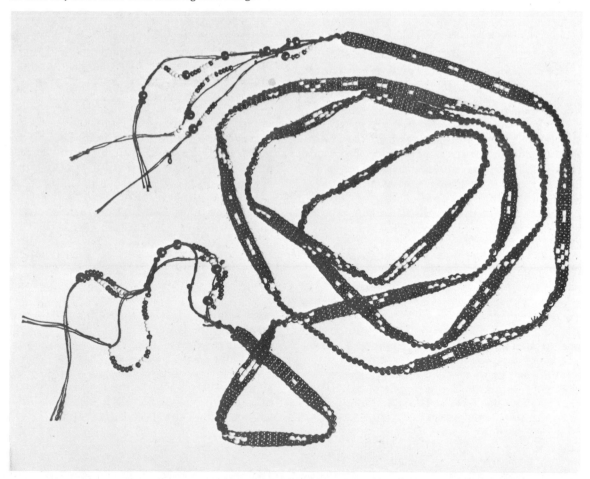

required. Beadwoven braid cannot be cut like fabric braid and the lengths for specific garments should be carefully calculated: perhaps two short pieces for the cuffs or across pockets, a long strip for the hem of a jacket and another for around the neck and down the two front edges on a collarless jacket.

If you want to braid the hem and fronts of a jacket it is possible to weave all the braid in one operation, but it should not be a continuous long strip because this is almost impossible to mitre at the corners. Careful planning must be done before attempting this braid. Measure the garment and weave the length to go around the neck and down the sides of the garment. Make a slip knot over the outside warps when the last row is complete. Do not cut working thread but make another slip knot 25mm along the warp and begin to weave again. Continue until the length for the bottom edge has been made. With practice the weaving can be started and finished each time with a diagonal end so that when the braid is stitched to the garment the corners are mitred. To attach the braid to the fabric make tiny slip stitches across outer warps and into the fabric. The lengths of warp which allow the braid to be 'turned' around a corner should be tucked out of sight beneath the braid as it is stitched to the fabric.

Other ways to use narrow weavings

A watch strap (see illustrations 89–90) can be made from a narrow weaving. The way in which a watch strap is constructed depends entirely on the watch for which it is being made. However, most watches have a bar on either side of the face to which the conventional leather strap is attached either by stitching, a metal pin or staple, or by passing the strap over one bar, under the back of the face and over the bar opposite. The following pattern is designed for a watch with this type of fixing device.

The beads do not pass across the back of the watch since they would be too bulky and probably very uncomfortable. The watch face is threaded onto the warps when the first section of the strap is complete (see illustration 89). The strap is finished off by tying the warps together and trimming them as for weaving 1. The process is completed by backing the ends with 13mm ($\frac{1}{2}$in) hem tape. This makes the ends of the strap firmer and therefore stronger. The fastening is a hook and a buttonhole loop. This is an extremely safe fastener providing the hook

is placed on the 12 o'clock end of the strap. You may, however, prefer a buckle of some kind so the finishing-off process will be somewhat different. One piece of the strap should be longer than the other to allow for it passing through the buckle and being drawn tight. The end of this piece should be shaped in the same manner as weaving 3. Of course your watch may be large and the strap therefore quite wide but the way in which it is woven and attached to the watch is the same.

Weaving 15. Watch strap (five beads wide). Illustrations 89 and 90

Materials:
   Size 10 black, gunmetal and brown Rocaille beads
   Size 9 or 10 needle
   Black Polytwist thread
   Black hem tape 13mm ($\frac{1}{2}$in)
   Beeswax
   Hook or buckle if preferred
Key:
   b – black
   br – brown
   g – gunmetal

Set up loom with 6+2 warp threads (for five beads). This pattern will fit a 6in wrist if worn tightly; on a smaller wrist it will be slightly loose.

Pattern, weaving 15:

Rows		Rows	
1	5b	15	1g 1b 1br 1b 1g
2	2b 1br 2b	16	1b 1br 1b 1br 1b
3	1b 1br 1b 1br 1b	17	1br 1b 1br 1b 1br
4	1br 1b 1g 1b 1br	18	1b 1br 1b 1br 1b
5	1b 1g 1b 1g 1b	19	1br 1b 1g 1b 1br
6	1g 1b 1br 1b 1g	20	1b 3g 1b
7	1b 1br 1g 1br 1b	21	2g 1b 2g
8	1br 3g 1br	22	1g 1b 1br 1b 1g
9	2g 1b 2g	23	1b 1br 1b 1br 1b
10	1g 3b 1g	24	1br 1b 1g 1b 1br
11	2b 1br 2b	25	1b 1g 1b 1g 1b
12	1b 1br 1b 1br 1b	26	1g 3b 1g
13	1br 1b 1g 1b 1br	27	5b
14	1b 1g 1b 1g 1b		

Stop weaving and release the warp threads at the end of the loom (leave the weaving and the beginning of the warps in place and leave the working thread and needle at the side). Fold a piece of adhesive tape over the ends of the warps to keep them parallel; pass the tape, which should stiffen the ends of the warp, through the back of the watch. Pull the threads to straighten them

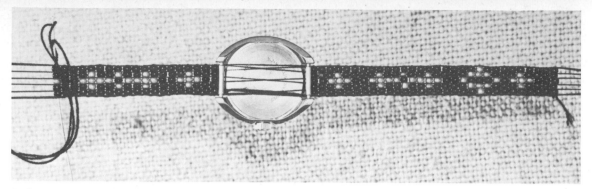

89 Reverse of watch strap showing warp threads across back of watch

90 Woven watch strap on the left almost complete, and watch with chevron pattern completed on the right

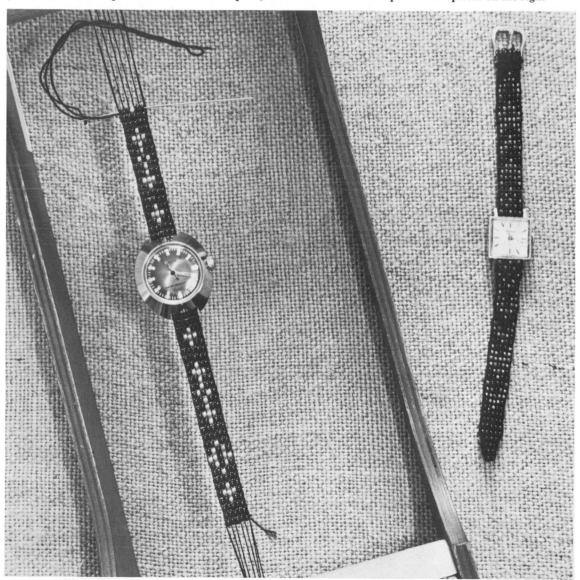

and secure them in the loom again. The tape can be removed or left until the work is complete, when it can be cut off.

Push the watch face up against the last row of weaving so that the beads sit against the face. Pass the needle and thread through the back of the watch and make a slip knot over the outside warp close to the side of the face. Weave one row of pattern (second half of strap is first half in reverse: follow pattern rows 27–1) and push it close to the watch face so that the warps which pass under the face do not show. Do this each time a row is woven for the first three or four rows of the second half of the strap.

If you are going to use a buckle to fasten the watch, weave rows of black at the end of the half in the following order. Finish pattern with 5b, weave 5b 5b 3b 3b 1b. If strap needs to be longer weave extra rows of 5b. Remove the strap and watch from the loom. Tie warps in pairs and trim back the ends of the work with tape for 13mm ($\frac{1}{2}$in). Make sure this is not too bulky. For the hook and eye fastener, make a buttonhole loop across the very end of the weaving at the 6 o'clock end and sew a hook to the other end. Cover the hook as shown in diagram 104.

A buckle is attached to the 12 o'clock end of the strap. Tie off the warps in pairs but do not trim yet. Thread the warps over the buckle bar and pull them so that the weaving covers it. Thread each warp separately onto a needle and weave the ends back into the strap making slip knots to secure them. Alternatively they may be sewn to a taped back and then covered with more tape. The shaped end has the warps woven back into the rows of weaving and is not taped. If the buckle has a prong this is secured in the beadwork when the watch is fastened. Take care that you do not push this through the warps and break them. If the end of the strap is long make a buttonhole loop across the strap behind the buckle so that the shaped end can be slotted through it. For a wider strap the pattern is extended at the sides and, if you wish, the extra width can be plain black so that the pattern forms a strip down the centre of the strap. Otherwise, use your own pattern or adapt one of the other pattern examples.

Lettering and beadweaving

Cross-stitch patterns have been suggested as source material for beadwork on the loom because of their geometric character. Samplers worked by nineteenth-century children provide excellent examples of cross stitch and usually contain good examples of letter forms which are easily translated into woven beads.

Before beginning to weave a lettered strip, the letters should be drawn onto graph or squared paper so that you have a clear idea of how they should be placed and the number of beads required for each one. Spacing is important, and if the letters are to be read it is essential that this is correct. The planning stage is not difficult: one square equals one bead (or two squares vertically if you wish to see approximately how the letters will be extended when woven). Lower and upper-case letters in several styles are possible, though script is less easily woven.

Lettering is fun to use on woven work. Initials on bracelets and chokers, perhaps even full names, personalize a beadwoven gift. Special greetings can also be woven (see illustration 91) and make an extremely effective birthday, or special occasion 'card'.

Bookmarks with letters of several kinds or with the intended owner's name are yet another way to use letter forms. An Alphabet (illustration 92) strip with letters arranged as in the illustration or down the length would make an unusual present for a young child just starting to read or learn the alphabet. Capitals and lower-case letters might be used so that they are seen in pairs, perhaps on a wider strip, placed one above the other. Single beads can be used for the width of the letters, or use double rows. Make sure that the size, width and depth of the letters is balanced and that the spacing is correct. Two plain rows of weaving is sufficient between individual letters, three or more between words, or the letters of the alphabet.

Alphabet strip (woven letters). Illustration 95

Strip is 17 beads wide: 18+2 warp threads = 17 spaces.

Spacing is two rows of black weaving.

Letters take up a space six beads wide × 11 beads deep, with three black beads above and below each letter. If letters are surrounded by the background colour they look better than if they extend to the edges. Q is the only letter which extends into the lower edge of black. M and W are nine beads wide and V is seven. These were impossible to fit into a six bead wide area.

91 Woven strip using letter forms to spell out 'Happy Birthday'

92 Alphabet strip

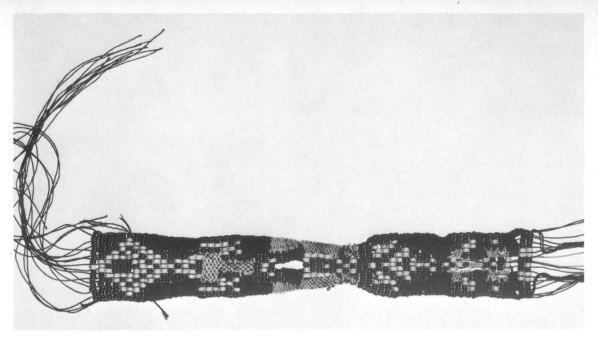

93 Test piece of augmented weaving

If the letters are woven vertically (perhaps so that the weaving can be hung on a wall) the spacing across the work – under each letter – should again be two rows of plain black weaving. The spacing at the sides will be different and you should increase the size of the letters to seven beads in order to make the work symmetrical, in which case there will be five beads in black down the sides. The wider letters (M, W and V) will, however, look odd if they extend beyond the line of the others, so it is worthwhile either finding other forms for these or adjusting all the letters and making them wider. Experiment for yourself: any kind of block lettering will adapt well so that it can be used as a beadweaving pattern, and even diagonals are simple to work using the 'stepped' method.

Combined techniques

Beadweaving and other simple weaving techniques are easily combined. This adds interest and yet another dimension to the technique. Another advantage, which applies also to the cords used for the weavings on p. 164 and 165 is that if you are short of beads, either generally or of just one particular colour, or if you simply want to economize with your stock of materials, then the use of another kind of weaving will aid this economy (see illustration 93).

The weaving with needle and thread which forms part of the example in illustration 93 can be done as the beadweaving progresses, or the sections of beadwork may be woven first and the thread weaving put in later. The threads, which should be a double or treble strand of the weft thread or a thicker crotchet cotton or similar material, should be woven as closely as possible and taken as close to the beadwork as you can manage.

The warps were pulled in on the example in places. At first this happened accidentally and then, having decided that I liked the effect, deliberately. When a full-width section of weaving is reached, oversew along the outer warps down the side of the beads and begin the needle weaving again. The movement of the needle under and over the warps is the same as that used for darning. Several different colours can be used; the example has black warps and in places red crotchet thread was used to weave over and under, thus forming a check or tweedy effect. In other places the wefts were pushed close together so that a solid red area was produced; similarly there are areas of solid black weaving which were given texture by using single strands in some places and double or more in others. This type of weaving with the beadwork makes a very strong watch strap or belt.

Several different colours would make a very effective pattern and these might also combine textures: wool, linen, thread, bouclé and shiny threads. If these are combined with wooden and glass beads the textures of the threads complement the surfaces of the beads. Try using very dull threads with lustre beads, or shiny thread with wooden beads for different effects.

Sections of beadweaving can be mounted on fabric or leather bands which again allows a small stock of beads to go further. For instance, woven squares of beadwork finished off so that the warps are hidden, sewn to a leather or canvas belt, are just as interesting as solid beadweaving. An alternative is to sew sections of beadwoven work to small pieces of leather or suede or other 'fabric' thus making a patchwork. The beadwoven parts can all be woven at the same time if the method described for continuous braids is used. Simply leave enough of the warp free between each section for the work to be tied off when the pieces are cut from the strip.

If the pieces are to be mounted onto a long piece of fabric or leather the warps can be used to sew them in place. Each is threaded, separately or in pairs, onto a needle and taken through the fabric. Pass the needle back through fabric and into the beads; make a stitch over a weft taking care not to push the rows apart; take the needle back into the rows of beads and secure the thread. The sewing should be as invisible as possible.

The same technique may be employed with small pieces of fabric. Many linking pieces can be used, pieces of fabric, leather, suede, brass, wooden or plastic rings (curtain rings, perhaps) crotchet shapes, chain links, or strung sections of warp as in weaving 6 on p. 152.

Many of the ideas for using other techniques and other materials to extend the beadwork and to add interest are untried on full-size weavings, but all of them have been worked as experimental pieces and are successful. There is never time to weave all the things one would like, and often there are too few beads. I hope however that you will be inspired to go on experimenting, that you will find ways and means of developing your beadwork beyond the examples and the suggestions here, and that you will discover for yourself better ways of doing some of the things I have suggested. There are many accessories you can make. Weaving is as versatile and decorative as you care to make it. It can be used in the home in the ways that other techniques are used, and braids for clothing are only a small part of the 'fashion' use of woven beads. Panels of beads on a yoke or a pocket, complete cuffs with buttons and buttonholes. Motifs for shoes, bags, hatbands, bag straps, sandle straps and dress straps are possible and not at all difficult to design and make. Purses, bags, or simple panels for them, take the technique and related ones full circle back to the nineteenth century, and if you would like to imitate Great Grandmama further, weave

94 Three stages of beadwork by Carol Lister: strings, arrow pattern threading, and weaving with looped edges

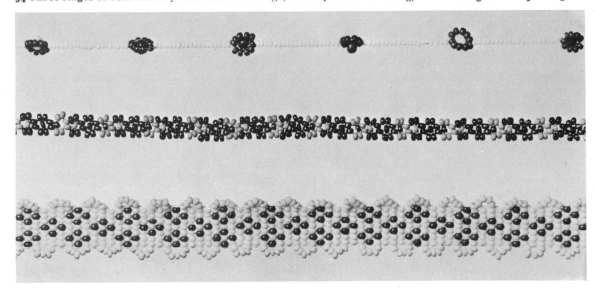

a top for your pincushion and write on in beads – BEADS.

Purses, incidentally, need a wide piece of weaving and it is often easier to work several bands (three of 3in width, for example) and sew them together along the outer warps. (Patterns can be repeated on three bands or designed so that each strip continues a large motif.) Work the flap/strap separately and sew the pieces together, or fold the work into three so that the flap and purse are one. If the work is woven full width then the tension must be checked frequently. The wide belt in illustration 75, though only 25 beads wide, was very difficult to keep taut for the first 15cm (6in) or so, and the weaving progressed very slowly indeed up to that point; after that it seemed easier to control.

When you begin to see the results of the time and effort put into learning the basic techniques of a craft you will begin to design for yourself. Developing your own ideas is intensely satisfying and makes the effort well worthwhile. The beadwork in illustration 97 shows a progression from strings to threading, to weaving with a looped edge. All the items were made by a 14-year-old schoolgirl.

Beadwork techniques have survived, in some cases over centuries of neglect. Whether you use them as a pleasant hobby, simply for fun, or become so involved that you 'live your beads', I hope that you will help to keep some of these techniques alive. Perhaps you will teach your children or your friends something of them, maybe you will wear some of the results of your labours, or give them as gifts and, in return, stimulate the recipients into asking how to make things for themselves.

Working with beads is rooted in traditional techniques. My aim is to help you to go beyond the mere reproduction of past styles and methods and hopefully to stimulate the development of this old craft into something new and alive.

bibliography

Mowatt Erikson, J., *The Universal Bead*, Norton, New York.

Seyd, M., *Introducing Beads*, Batsford, London. Watson-Guptill, New York.

Hinks, P., *Jewellery*, The Hamlyn Publishing Group, London, New York, Sydney, Toronto.

Hunt, W. B., *Indian Crafts and Lore*. The Hamlyn Publishing Group, London, New York, Sydney, Toronto.

Edwards, J., *Bead Embroidery*, Batsford, London. Taplinger, New York.

Nye, T. M., *Cross Stitch Patterns*, Batsford, London. Out of print.

Groves, S., *Old Needlework Tools and Accessories*, David and Charles Co. Ltd., Newton Abbot, Devon.

Where to see Beadwork – museums to visit

Beaver House, Great Trinity Street, London EC4 (Hudsons Bay Co. headquarters).

British Museum, London WC1.

Museum of Mankind (British Museum), Burlington Gardens, London W1.

Horniman Museum, Forest Hill, London SE23.

London Museum, Kensington Palace, London W8.

The Castle Museum, York.

The Kirkstall Abbey Museum, Leeds.

Your own local museum may well have examples of Victorian and Edwardian beadwork. And look in the attic, you never know where beads and beadwork might be lurking.

Stockists

*Hobby Horse Ltd
15–17 Langton Street
London SW10

An enormous range of beads – glass, wood, ceramic and bamboo. Most of the beads used to work the examples, and the articles in the photographs, came from here. Threads, needles, and beadlooms are also stocked.

*Ells and Farrier Ltd, 5 Princes Street
Hanover Square, London W1

Masses of beads. Also beadlooms.

*The Needlewoman Shop
146–148 Regent Street, London W16 BA

Beads, threads and beadlooms.

Fred Aldous Ltd
37 Lever Street, Manchester 1

Many kinds of beads.

All the above offer a mail order service and will supply a catalogue on request. Samples may also be available. In most cases you will have to pay for the catalogue.

Beads of various kinds are also available from:
Baku Beads
80 Portobello Road
  London W11

African Tribal Art
45 Monmouth Street
London WC2

African trade beads, eye beads and Venetian-glass beads are available at several specialist shops in London.

The Neal Street Shop
Neal Street
London WC2

Sells African tribal beadwork, some of which is of considerable age. Trade beads are also stocked.

Afro Art
9 St Martins Court
Charing Cross Road
London W2

Examples of tribal beadwork.

* loom stockists

Index

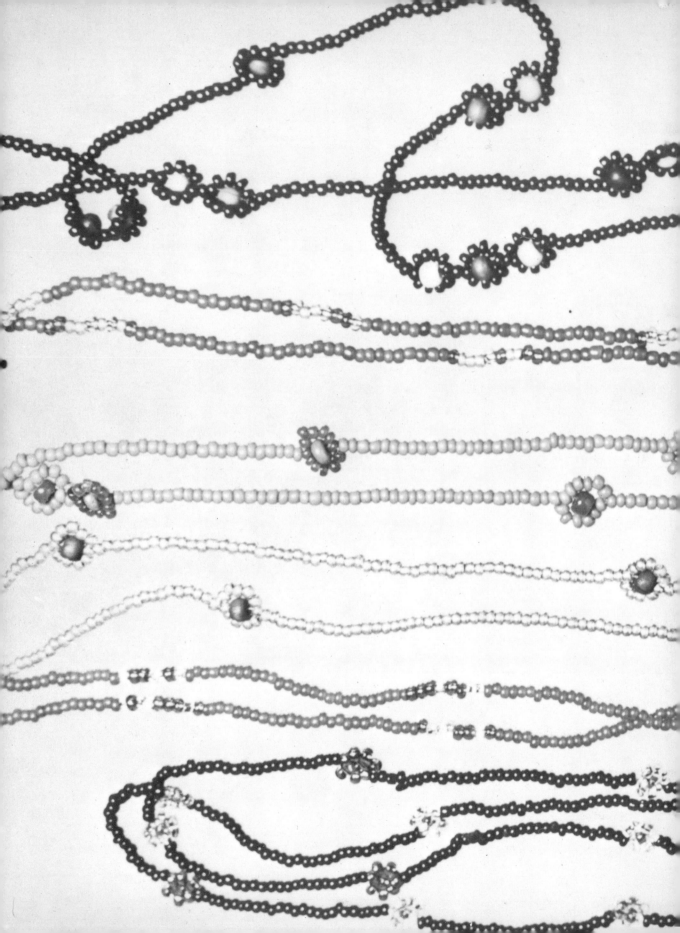